Reclaiming the Last Wild Places ≈

A New Agenda for Biodiversity

Roger L. DiSilvestro

JOHN WILEY & SONS, INC.

New York · Chichester · Brisbane · Toronto · Singapore

Copyright © 1993 by John Wiley & Sons, Inc.

Library of Congress Cataloging-in-Publication Data

DiSilvestro, Roger L.
    Reclaiming the last wild places : a new agenda for biodiversity / by Roger L. DiSilvestro.
        p.   cm.
    Includes bibliographical references (p. 253).
    ISBN 0-471-57244-6 (cloth : acid-free paper)
    1. Biological diversity conservation—United States.   2. Wildlife conservation—United States.   3. Biological diversity conservation—United States—Philosophy.   I. Title.   II. Series.
    QH76.D58   1993
    333.95'16'0973—dc20   92-46457

Printed in the United States of America

10   9   8   7   6   5   4   3   2   1

With special thoughts of those who along the way have been critical to my career and calling, even if they may not agree with all I have said: James Deane, Amos S. Eno, Dean Graham, Les Line, Chris Palmer, and Chris Wille.

≋

Does anyone want to take the world and
   do what he wants with it?
I do not see how he can succeed.
The world is a sacred vessel, which must
   not be tampered with or grabbed after.
To tamper with it is to spoil it, and to
   grasp it is to lose it.

Tao Teh Ching

The battle we have fought, and are still fighting, for
the forests is a part of the eternal conflict between
right and wrong, and we cannot expect to see the end
of it.

John Muir, 1895

Inevitably, of course, the paths of our lives lead some
of us to be more influenced by the values of developing a virtuous life and practicing stewardship, while
others of us are more influenced by the values of
prosperity and protecting the rights of private property. Consequently, in any area of the nation, conflicts
over how land should be used are almost certain to
arise.

Frederick Kirschenmann, American Journal of
Alternative Agriculture

CONTENTS

ACKNOWLEDGMENTS

Special thanks for help in the preparation of this book belong to Wendy Hudson, Sara Vickerman, and Kathy Tollerton of Defenders of Wildlife; Sherrard Foster of the National Oceanic and Atmospheric Administration; Trish Byrnes, William Reffalt, and Jay Watson of The Wilderness Society; Ginger Merchant of the National Wildlife Refuge Association; Pat Toll of Everglades National Park; Paul Pritchard, David Simon, and Bill Chandler of the National Parks and Conservation Association; and an anonymous friend in the National Forest Service. Keep your powder dry, friend.

I also owe heart-felt thanks to people with whom I have had conversations, sometimes long and occasionally very brief, that helped shape the ideas in this book. They are Gary Soucie, a former Sierra Club lobbyist and former editor for *Audubon* and *National Geographic*; Ken Strom of the National Audubon Society, from whom a few brief comments led to much thought; Chris Wille and Diane Jukofsky, a husband and wife who have launched their own endeavor at forest protection in Costa Rica; Steve Johnson, an independent environmental consultant with Native Ecosystems in Tucson, Arizona; Eugene Knoder, director of the Audubon Appleton-Whittell Research Ranch; and once again Sara Vickerman, with whom I have had years of environmental dispute and agreement. Most have tried to bridle my penchant for the occasional extreme and deserve praise for it. Anything in the ensuing pages that is completely off the wall is entirely my doing and none of theirs.

xii *Acknowledgments*

I also owe a long-distant thanks to writers Stephen Fox (*The American Conservation Movement: John Muir and His Legacy*), Roderick Nash (*Wilderness and the American Mind*), Curt Meine (*Aldo Leopold: His Life and Work*), and Susan Flader and J. Baird Callicott (*The Mother of the River of God*). I have never met or even talked with any of them, but their books provided not only helpful information but a banquet for thought.

Finally, I owe sincere thanks and appreciation to my wife for her unflagging support and encouragement, and particularly for hiding the *Washington Post* from me on several occasions so that I would not sacrifice mornings on the keyboard to deep explorations of that news journal. Her training in psychology seems to have prepared her perfectly for the ups and glooms, manias and obsessions of life with a writer.

INTRODUCTION

This is a book about boundaries.

It is about the boundaries that we mark upon the land, boundaries that determine whether wild places will be protected from human intrusion or studded with acre upon acre of houses, factories, malls, and office buildings.

It is about the boundaries of our knowledge, the shortfalls in our understanding of wild places and wild creatures that, coupled with our enthusiasm for reshaping the planet, pose a danger to life everywhere on Earth.

It is about the seemingly impregnable boundaries that we draw around ourselves, defining who and what we are politically, philosophically, and intellectually and dividing us into warring tribes.

It is about the boundaries of human compassion, about our ability to care for living things outside of ourselves and to sympathize with rivers, mountains, deserts, forests, and plains.

Boundaries are everywhere. Even nonhuman animals lay boundaries upon the land. They may be invisible to our eyes, but they are there and they are recognized by the animals that need to know and obey them. Wolves, mountain lions, bobcats, and other predators mark rocks, shocks of grass, and lumps of wood with urine and body scent to create boundaries, to show where their territories begin, to warn other members of their species that they will not tolerate intrusions without a challenge. Songbirds mark out territories, too, advertising the boundaries by singing along the edges.

Territorial boundaries are ancient; they are artifacts dating from a primordial world. They are, in essence, established for the exploitation of the Earth. Male songbirds set up territories to expropriate the best nesting sites for themselves and their mates. Wolves defend their territories to ensure that they can raise their pups in areas that offer the best den sites and perhaps the best sources of water and prey. Certain ant species in the tropical rainforests live in colonies beneath the bark of *Cecropia* trees and will rush out to attack anything that touches their tree. Evolution has shaped the ants to want the tree for their exclusive use.

Without doubt, for millions of years tribal groups of humans and even protohumans defended territorial hunting grounds, or at least the areas where they made their homes, from invasion by other tribes or groups. Certainly the earliest humans, as chimpanzees do today, claimed a territory and made war on other groups that claimed nearby lands. Throughout the history of modern society, dating back at least 5,000 years, boundaries have served as guidelines for domination, determining who, without interference from neighbors or government, could exploit which piece of land in which way. Building a fence or surveying a border in order to protect land or wilderness for its own sake was long undreamt, with the marginal exception of the exclusive hunting reserves of the nobility.

Only in the past century has humanity begun to set the protection of wildlands as a broad social goal, creating national parks, national forests, wildlife refuges, even protected wilderness areas. This is something truly new under the sun, and every protected wild place is a monument to humanity's uniqueness. The greatest qualitative difference between us and nonhuman animals is not that we can change and modify our environment. Practically every living creature does that, from the AIDS virus that destroys its own habitat, to herds of hoofed animals that trim grasslands, to chimpanzees that make spoons from leaves, to birds that build nests, to ants and termites living in teeming arthropod cities. But we are the first living things, as far as we know, to make a choice about the extent to which we will apply our abilities to influence our environment. We not only *can* do, but we can choose *not* to do. Thus, what is unique about the boundaries we place around parks and other sanctuaries is that these boundaries are created to protect a region from our own actions.

Because this book is about boundaries that protect wild places, it is also a book about progress. When Scottish inventor James Watt tightened the last bolt on his eighteenth-century steam engine, giving birth to the Industrial Revolution, society little knew the costs of clouding the air with industrial pollutants, of darkening rivers and shores with toxins, of destroying entire species and ecosystems. Today, we who have seen urban skies clouded by poisoned air, who have seen multimillion-dollar fishing industries destroyed by pollution, who have seen the ecological integrity of Ethiopia and Somalia fall victim to careless agricultural practices, know increasingly well the costs of environmental degradation. We tally those costs in human lives, in human health, and in the financial expense of defusing threats posed by pollution and the loss of critically important species. These are biological deficits with which, like the national debt, the present generation is saddling future generations for millennia to come. These are also initiatory rites of passage that have brought industrial society into maturity. They have provided us with a more accurate and realistic understanding of how the world works and of how we fit into it. Many of us now recognize that human survival is founded on the integrity of natural habitats. From healthy seas, forests, and grasslands we take everything from food to clothing to building materials. Beneath an invisible dome of ozone we hide from the sun's deadliest rays. The quality of our lives is tied to such natural events as ocean currents—the Gulf Stream and El Niño—and volcanic eruptions that cool our summers and deepen our winters. No longer can we speak of balancing human needs with environmental protection as if environmental protection were not a human need. No longer can industry cavort about the planet with an adolescent heedlessness of the effects of its actions. No longer can we think of ourselves as masters of the natural world. Rather, we are partners with it.

As a result, our understanding of our place in the world is changing, and we are slowly redefining our perception of what constitutes progress. We sense that real progress—evolutionary progress, revolutionary progress—lies not in slapping down another oil well in offshore waters or on the Arctic National Wildlife Refuge, as the last two presidential administrations have sought to do, nor in erecting another housing development, nor in opening another toxin-belching factory, nor in building more automobiles. We sense that progress today lies in recognizing that humanity's new inventions are threatening nature's oldest creations, things such as plants and animals and us, and that we must address these threats and find solutions to them. We sense that progress is constraint, that progress is placing boundaries around our ability to exploit the world, that progress is the orderly determination that some wild places will be left wild and that we will no longer overrun the planet without thought for the vast natural world upon whose integrity and well-being our health and survival depend.

Much of progress begins with the knowledge that we do not know all that we need to know about sustaining life on Earth. It begins with an understanding that we will perhaps never fully understand the planet's most profound secrets—life's great complexity and the baffling interrelationship of all living things. Knowing that we do not know, understanding that we do not understand, are the best devices we have for eliciting the caution we need in all our tamperings with the planet's clockworks. They will help us rein in our inclinations for immediate gratification.

Many of us now know that we must, willy-nilly, protect the wild places of the Earth because they are the reservoirs from which we draw all that sustains us as well as the many qualities, such as solitude and beauty, that make life finer. In this context, we can no longer accept as accurate any measures of economic, industrial, political, or social success that do not factor in such overheads as environmental damage and the loss of species or that fail to include the protection, *for our sake,* of wild places and species—what some call biodiversity, the full variety of living things. We know now that protecting biodiversity and reclaiming or restoring wild places damaged by human intrusion are not merely nice things to do or ethical practices or academic exercises, but rather important elements in protecting the quality of human life at such fundamental levels as food and water supplies.

Unfortunately, most of the methods we use for protecting biodiversity were created roughly a century ago, when destructive pressures were less pervasive. In recent decades, humanity has redoubled its assault upon the natural world, making it impossible to protect wild places by merely drawing boundaries around them and administering them as national parks, wildlife refuges, and forests. Moreover, because the old idea that natural resources exist only for the taking still prevails, our society balances on a cusp between the old ways of exploitation and the new directions in which increasing scientific knowledge is pushing us. Those who have long profited from the old ways do not give them up willingly, preferring short-term profit for themselves to long-term gains for society. The result has been an increasingly rapid decline in biodiversity, in wildness, within our own nation, a decline that bespeaks the need for a new approach to protecting biodiversity, an approach that elevates the importance of biodiversity protection to a higher social plane and that ensures that economic considerations measure costs not only in terms of dollars and cents but also in terms of the real overhead of environmental destruction.

At its heart, then, this book is about the shortcomings in the protective boundaries we have drawn upon the land; about the terrible toll that they have taken on our last wild places, from national forests and parks to wilderness areas; and about the need to establish new methods of protection that will meet the challenges of an increasingly human-dominated world. This book tells a story that begins in the distant past and is still unfolding today, a tale of rival factions seeking to choose the direction in which society and the world will travel, many roads diverging, the best traveled leading mostly to a starved and lesser world. It is a tale in which we are all embroiled.

Reclaiming the Last Wild Places

PART ONE

O Wilderness

CHAPTER 1

This Problem of Protecting Public Lands

≋

The Everglades National Park is at last a reality. It will save the lower Glades and the Cape Sable beaches. . . . It will be the only national park in which the wild-life, the crocodiles, the trees, the orchids, will be more important than the sheer geology of the country.

Marjory Stoneman Douglas, 1947

Establishing a national park, the highest form of land protection in the United States, does not, in itself, insure that the resources within the park will be preserved in perpetuity. The fact is that the future of many units of our national park system is more in the hands of state and local agencies and political leaders . . . than [in the hands of] the managers and policy makers that govern our national parks.

Robert S. Chandler, former superintendent,
Everglades National Park, 1992

≋

At the southern tip of Florida, where earth fades gradually into sea, lies a strangely primeval world. The sky seems bigger there than anywhere else east of the Mississippi, a great blue emptiness meeting a flat, featureless land at distant horizons. The land itself is empty, too, a beautiful emptiness where winds play freely over tall, trembling grass.

Grass is the dominant feature, sawgrass, fed by waters that have oozed down the Florida peninsula from as far as 200 miles away, the drippings of the Kissimmee Basin and of Lake Okeechobee, largest body of water in the United States south of the Great Lakes. The grass is waist-high and brown or green in season, an ocean of grass punctuated by wooded strands—islands of dark trees that lie against the grass like brooding shadows.

This is Everglades National Park, where the biggest and most powerful animals are alligators and crocodiles, Jurassic refugees that lurk beneath the deep grass and occasionally scuttle across roadways, automobiles bearing down upon them in a peculiar juxtaposition of ancient and modern lives.

Park visitors are witnesses to an alien, cold-blooded world. They can watch alligators cruise in black streams, snouts scarcely above water, tails moving in languid yet powerful thrusts that propel the creatures silently among thrashing schools of fish. Along the single sun-baked highway that arcs from east to west through the park, visitors may find soft-shelled turtles bigger than dinner plates scuffing the earth with hind feet, perhaps in preparation for depositing a cargo of eggs. On the seashore they may come upon a much larger sea turtle depositing its shelled progeny into a scooped-out hole in the sand. These are the ageless rituals of creatures unchanged since that distant time when their ancestors crawled across the fresh tracks of dinosaurs.

And dinosaurs remain here, too, disguised as birds. Herons, egrets, and ibis stalk boldly along streams, glinting eyes alert for fish in shallow waters. With stilt legs, snaking necks, and rapier bills they look like modernized tyrannosaurs on the prowl—as well they should, if paleontologists are correct in describing birds as living dinosaurs, as feathered reptiles. These long-legged waders are also a hallmark of this reptilian world.

Along the main highway, park administrators have placed trail heads where visitors can park their cars and wander down little-traveled dirt paths into the sun-swept 'glades to stand surrounded by natural world—a velvet sweep of grass, a distant ridge of trees, all overtopped by endless sky. Except for the scant etching of the footpath, it seems a pristine world.

Everglades National Park was authorized by Congress in 1934 and established in 1947. Although most of our national parks were created to protect geological features and other scenery, Everglades was the first set aside primarily for its wilderness and wildlife values. The legislation creating it said the park "shall be permanently reserved as a wilderness and no development of the park or plan for the entertainment of visitors should be undertaken which will interfere with the preservation, intact, of the unique flora and fauna and essential primitive natural conditions now prevailing in the area."

Everglades National Park has been expanded three times and now encompasses some 1.5 million acres of mixed habitat, including more than 100 miles of coastline. It contains seven different ecological communities: sawgrass Everglades, mangrove forest, salt marsh, cypress forest, pine forest, West Indian hardwood hammock forest, and coastal prairie. It ranks as the second largest national park in the coterminous United States and has received international recognition as a World Heritage Site, an

International Biosphere Reserve, and an internationally significant wetland under the multinational wetlands-protection treaty called the RAMSAR convention. As Robert Chandler, a former superintendent of Everglades National Park, points out, "By all accounts, this should be a remarkable conservation success story. It is not. Today, Everglades National Park is considered the most threatened or endangered national park in the United States."

Warning signs at the entrances to some footpaths attest to the park's precarious existence. In red and black capital letters on a white background the signs read: WARNING. HEALTH HAZARD. DO NOT EAT BASS CAUGHT BEYOND THIS POINT DUE TO HIGH MERCURY CONTENT. The signs communicate more than just a stark warning. They declare that the ecosystem is in serious trouble, that this park, this fragment of an ancient world, has been affected deeply by modern times—affected, that is, in the sense that someone sick with malaria has been affected by a microbe.

But Everglades National Park is no different than many of the nation's parks, wilderness areas, national forests, and wildlife refuges, for the bulk of our protected lands are tottering beneath a burden of political entanglements and environmental insults that undercut their entire purpose. A closer look at Everglades National Park shows not only what is happening in South Florida, but what is happening on protected wildlands all across the nation.

A Lost World

The Everglades is the largest freshwater marsh in the world. A century and a half ago, the Everglades started at the southern end of Lake Okeechobee and extended south 150 miles or so to the mangrove forests of Florida's south and southwest shores, where the Caribbean meets the Gulf of Mexico. From the Atlantic coast the Everglades swept west for 40 miles, fading into the drier, pine-dominated reaches of Big Cypress Swamp.

The Everglades was built of muck and water on a foundation of porous limestone. The water came from the skies in the form of May to September rainfall—as much as 63 inches a year in some parts—and from overflows farther north. During the rainy season a chain of lakes some 200 miles north would overflow into Lake Kissimmee, which would in turn overflow into the Kissimmee River Basin, swelling the narrow, contorted, 100-mile-long river into a 2-mile-wide, 50-mile-long sheet of water. The swollen river would, in turn, flood shallow Lake Okeechobee, causing it to spill over its southern bank and feed its sheet flow into the Caloosahatchee River to the west and into the Everglades to the south.

The Everglades region is shaped like a saucer. The deepest part is in the center, with the sides rising gently to higher elevations. The rim does not flood, at least not for long. The center is often flooded, and here deep peat soils have built up. The saucer tips gently toward the Gulf of Mexico, dropping about 15 feet from north to south. In the past, this ensured that the water would flow slowly across the Everglades in a vast sheet, a shallow river 40 miles wide.

This natural drainage created some 3,500 square miles of Everglades, a marsh ecosystem dominated by sawgrass, with blades as long as swords and just as pointed. Sawgrass covered the full length of the Everglades, surrounding narrow strands of trees, sweeping like a green velvet carpet from Okeechobee all the way to the mangrove forests that fringe the azure sea at land's end. After the grass died it eventually sank beneath the water, where it was reduced to peaty muck that lay as much as 10 feet deep just south of the lake.

Even after European settlers had ravaged most of the continent, the Everglades remained remarkably unscarred. As late as the mid-nineteenth century it was seemingly impenetrable to Manifest Destiny, a refuge for Indian peoples and escaped slaves beleaguered by whites pouring, like the lake waters, into south Florida from the north. Hundreds of thousands of wading birds fed and nested there, and 15-foot reptiles weighing several hundred pounds still roared in the night all across the wet country, and Indian warriors who would never, ever, sign a peace treaty with the U.S. government found there a modicum of freedom until finally they and their descendants forced the government to recognize their right to a portion of the Everglades—making them the only Native Americans who did not succumb to treaty signatures.

But by 1845 even the Everglades was about to feel the crush of development. President John Tyler signed a bill making Florida a state, and the new state legislature asked Congress "to examine and survey the Everglades with a view to their reclamation." In short, the freshly minted solons wanted to "reclaim" the Everglades from the massive shiftings of water that had created and sustained it for millions of years. Subsequently, an 1848 report prepared by a state legislator from St. Augustine suggested that draining the Everglades, according to a general consensus of military and other opinion, could be easily achieved by building a few canals that would run the marsh waters into the Atlantic. The state was further encouraged to undertake drainage when, on September 28, 1850, Congress enacted the Swamp and Overflowed Lands Act, which granted 20.3 million acres of federal wetlands to Florida, provided that any funds the state realized from sale of the lands were invested in drainage. The legislature quickly set up administrative bodies to oversee the disposal and drainage of the Everglades.

Before any work could begin, however, the Civil War stalled Everglades development, and Florida's support of the losing team in that conflict further delayed drainage. Not until the 1880s did work begin in earnest, but that effort collapsed in failure when Everglades muck proved resistant to the rudimentary engineering skills of the era.

Finally, in 1907 the state legislature created the Everglades Drainage District, an agency charged with administering a massive drainage plan. Within 20 years the agency had dredged 440 miles of canals, built 47 miles of levees and 16 locks, and erected a peat dike around Okeechobee's southern edge. Five large canals drained the lake's overflow into the Atlantic.

When the Everglades Drainage District went broke in the

late 1920s, the legislature created the Okeechobee Flood Control District to work in cooperation with the U.S. Army Corps of Engineers. By the late 1940s the district had completed most of the major drainage works in use today. In 1949, responding to local fears of flooding after a destructive hurricane in 1947, Congress created the Central and Southern Florida Project, which covered 16,000 square miles, including 1,340 square miles of conservation flood pools to protect urban areas on the eastern side of the state. Today, virtually every river and stream in southern Florida has been turned into a canal—nearly 1,400 miles' worth. Water flow from Lake Okeechobee has been mastered, and the only water that follows the ages-old pathway into the Everglades is the water that people allow. The Everglades as a natural ecosystem is defunct.

But the first half of this century was not all bad news for the Everglades. In the 1930s a plan was advanced by the Everglades Fresh Water Park Commission to create a national park that would begin in the Florida Keys and sweep north to encompass about half of the Everglades region. When Congress created the park in 1947, several large tracts sought by park advocates were left out. The park still encompassed the bulk of the lower third of the state—a sizable piece of wilderness back then—but the process of paring down the park destroyed an opportunity to save an entire ecosystem. Instead, the National Park Service was given a fragment of an ecosystem and told to keep it in a pristine state, even though the park could not escape the influence of the much-changed surrounding lands from which park waters still flowed. This led directly to many of the problems that the park still faces.

For example, 700,000 acres south of Lake Okeechobee have been converted from Everglades marsh to farmland, primarily sugarcane fields but also sod farms and vegetable farms. During the rainy season pesticides and fertilizers drain into surrounding waters from these fields. Much of the land north of the lake is now used for dairy farms. From these farms more fertilizers and excrement reach the lake. Farther south, just outside park boundaries, lie the geometric fields of vegetable farms. Water released from the various canal systems that drain these regions brings yet more agricultural and other effluents into the park, the last large stretch of native Everglades. Thus, protecting the national park, says Pat Tolle of the park's public affairs office, "is like trying to restore a natural area in a sewer."

Pat Tolle has worked in the park for 20 years. She remembers an earlier era in which agricultural interests dominated state water management, with the result that Everglades National Park's water needs were a very low management priority for officials outside of its borders. Thanks to a burgeoning environmental awareness among the general public, she says, that is changing, but still Everglades National Park remains a protected wild land "that's dying, that's in trouble."

The basis of that trouble, she adds, is "water, water, water, water, and water."

The Trouble with Water

As recently as 1947 the protection and management of wild lands was perceived by park administrators as a relatively simple matter of declaring a natural area off-limits to development and human encroachment. Says Tolle of the management philosophy of that recent era, "It's build a fence around it and protect it from outside influences. It's siege mentality."

It is impossible, of course, to isolate Everglades National Park from outside influences. The way the park is laid out, and its innate biological workings, will not permit it. The southern Everglades has always been a receptacle for water from farther north. Without this water the ecosystem could not survive. Yet after canals, levees, dikes, and other accoutrements of water management turned the Everglades water system into what some call the world's largest plumbing project, the water no longer flowed into the park in the quantities needed or at the right time of year. It became common practice among water managers north of the park to dump excess water regardless of whether the park's water capacity had already been reached, says Tolle. This created unnaturally high water levels that flooded wildlife nesting areas and made hunting more difficult for fish-eating birds.

The process threatens to continue. The state is considering a proposal to serve Miami-area water needs by locating a water-well field adjacent to the park. Regulations would put limits on how much water can be pumped, but the field is being designed to draw up to some 70 million gallons per day, which, Chandler says, "would be devastating" to the park.

Given the immense pressures placed on Everglades water ecology by Florida's growing human population—which has swelled by 30 percent during the past decade—it is little wonder that many Everglades species, from wading birds to alligators to white-tailed deer, have taken a beating. In the 1870s, before Everglades plumbing was refitted, an estimated 2.5 million wading birds fed, squawked, flapped, and nested in South Florida—primarily snowy egrets, great egrets, great blue herons, wood storks, white ibis, tricolored herons, and little blue herons. Today, about 90 percent of this number have disappeared. Solid data document the continuing decline in recent years. Between 1975 and 1989 the white ibis population shrank from nearly 12,000 to only 1,600 pairs, while the wood stork fell from 1,235 to 515 pairs, the great egret from nearly 3,000 to fewer than 1,900 pairs, the snowy egret from 4,474 to 506 pairs, and the tricolored heron from 2,900 to 650 pairs. The roseate spoonbill population has decreased 50 percent since 1980. The Everglades kite dropped from 668 birds in 1984 to 418 birds in 1991, apparently because of changes in the timing, volume, and distribution of water flow, which affected the kite's ability to obtain its primary food source, the apple snail. The decline of these species is a sign of profound disruption in the park and in the Everglades ecosystem itself. Says Chandler, "Water management is the number one problem, but not the only one."

The warning signs by the trail heads remind us that water is not all that drains into the park from clouds and surrounding terrain. Both surface waters and rainfall bring with them a motley collection of chemical pollutants. While the park encloses about 16 percent of the historic Everglades ecosystem, agriculture accounts for about 25 percent of the ecosystem's present land use, water conservation areas for about 30 percent, and other uses—primarily development, drainage, and urban water projects—for what remains.

From farms comes a variety of chemical and organic fertilizers that stimulate the algal and other vegetative growth slowly suffocating Lake Okeechobee. While fertilizing a lake, stream, or marsh may sound like a good idea, a consequent explosion in plant growth throws the aquatic ecosystem out of balance. Bursts of algal growth, called blooms, can lead to a warming of surface waters and to a loss of dissolved oxygen, particularly as the plants die and decay. These changes can destroy the aquatic ecosystem's food base.

The flow of nutrients, particularly phosphorus, from farmlands around Lake Okeechobee into the typically low-nutrient marshland has resulted in the conversion of nearly 40,000 acres of sawgrass Everglades into a marsh dominated exclusively by cattails. An ecosystem or biological community founded upon a single plant species is a monoculture, and monocultures typically do not support the diversity of life characteristic of more varied ecosystems. In the Everglades, the sudden density of cattails in many areas has driven out native wildlife.

Even though the national park is 60 miles south of agricultural areas, water-quality monitoring stations have detected phosphorus—a potent fertilizer—entering the park at nearly 10 times the natural background rate, resulting in harmful changes in the algae that form the food base for all Everglades species. Phosphate concentration in unaffected Everglades marsh is about 4 parts per billion. In the park it is 33 parts per billion. The difference is due to the extremely high levels of phosphates in the water sources that feed the Everglades: Okeechobee's water is 100 parts per billion phosphates, canals within the Everglades agricultural area are at 355 parts per billion—90 times the background—and inflows to water conservation areas north of the park are at 40 parts per billion.

Nitrates are also seeping into the park at alarmingly high levels. In unaffected, natural marshes, nitrates are found at 10 parts per billion. Compare this to affected park waters, where nitrates occur at 96 parts per billion—nearly ten times the background concentration. And no wonder: Okeechobee nitrate levels stand at 100 parts per billion and water-conservation-area inflows at 1,017 to 2,165 parts per billion. It is hard to imagine it could get much worse, but it does. The canals within the Everglades agricultural area are at 2,700 parts per billion—exactly 270 times the background level. Nitrates cause loss of native algae and undermine the biological workings of the park.

South Florida also has the highest levels of mercury pollution in the nation—some 2 million acres of freshwater systems are laced with the dangerous chemical. It is no surprise that high concentrations of mercury are also found in park wildlife, including the endangered Florida panther, a subspecies of mountain lion that probably numbers no more than 50 individuals, all in South Florida. In 1991 a male panther that died from no apparent cause was found to have in his liver 110 parts per million of mercury—roughly 75 times the 1.5 parts per million that the federal government believes safe for humans. The mercury was a likely contributor and perhaps the cause of the cat's death. He probably got the mercury from eating raccoons, which picked up mercury from contaminated fish and other aquatic organisms.

The male panther was not an isolated case. In June 1991 a female that died in the park had 35 parts per million of mercury in her liver and 15 parts per million in her blood. Mercury also was suspected in the death of a second female in July 1991. These were the last female panthers in Everglades National Park. Today only five panthers are known to remain in the park, and blood samples from these animals show elevated mercury readings.

Alligators and turtles also show high mercury levels. Alligators in the Everglades conservation areas bear such high levels of mercury—2.7 to 3.1 parts per million, roughly twice the amount considered safe for human consumption—that in recent years planned hunts were cancelled. Mercury levels in soft-shelled turtles have been recorded at .30 to 1.53 parts per million. High levels of mercury also were found in white ibis and other wading birds in studies conducted in 1973 and 1986.

If wildlife is this affected, can people be far from harm? Certainly not. Early in 1989 the Florida Department of Environmental Regulation discovered that in water conservation areas north of the park—860,160 acres of freshwater supplies for several southern Florida counties and cities and the source of about 50 percent of the water for the eastern portion of Everglades National Park—mercury levels in fish hovered around the 1.5 parts per million considered dangerous to human health. As a result, park officials, with assistance from the U.S. Fish and Wildlife Service and the Florida Department of Health and Rehabilitative Services, took samples from six freshwater locations in the park. They discovered alarmingly high concentrations of mercury in the fish they tested. Park administrators immediately designated affected bodies of water as either no-consumption or limited-consumption fishing zones.

A state task force has been unable to locate a point source for the mercury, although, suggests Chandler, "agricultural and water management practices are clearly involved." Likely sources include mercury that occurs naturally in Florida soil and is freed incidental to agricultural activities; the yearly burning of sugarcane prior to harvests, which may release into the air mercury trapped in cane tissues; and mercury blown out of incinerator smokestacks, which falls to earth and accumulates in soils and surface waters. Every year, some 22,000 pounds of mercury spew from Florida garbage incinerators and power plants— enough on an average day to contaminate Niagara Falls six times over.

The state is currently undertaking studies to locate the source of the mercury and to assess the possible health hazards that the mercury poses to people. Meanwhile, agricultural interests have used their considerable political clout to preserve federal rules that exempt them from having to decontaminate runoff from their land.

The boundaries that Congress drew when creating the park also have contributed to current problems because Congress left out vital pieces of the ecosystem. Perhaps the most important missing piece is East Shark River Slough.

In the past, when water flowed from the Lake Okeechobee basin in a southwesterly direction through the Everglades into Florida Bay and the Gulf of Mexico, most of the water moved through the Shark River Slough just north of the park. When the park was established, only half of the slough was included in it. The eastern portion—some 153,000 acres lying between the original park boundary and the urban/rural limits of Dade County—was left out. This area represents most of what remains of the eastern portion of the original Everglades marshland ecosystem in Dade County.

The undeveloped portions of the East Everglades still provide crucial feeding and nesting habitat to many wildlife species that commute between the East Everglades and Everglades National Park, making the East 'Glades a *de facto* adjunct to the park. It is a valuable piece of wild country in its own right, supporting 359 recorded species of fish, reptiles, mammals, birds, and amphibians. Endangered species include the Florida panther, Cape Sable sparrow, bald eagle, wood stork, and snail kite. The area also harbors a variety of threatened species.

The East Everglades includes the headwaters of the Northeast Shark River Slough and Taylor Slough, the primary water sources of the park. During the rainy season, from April to October, water levels rise to the edge of the slough and during drier months recede to the center, an ebb and flow crucial to the survival of much of the area's wildlife. Water management by the U.S. Army Corps of Engineers and the South Florida Water Management District have redirected the natural flow of water so that the western half of the slough, which has traditionally carried 40 percent of the water, now receives 90 percent. The flow through the eastern half has been reduced to only 10 percent.

East Shark Slough is beset with familiar problems stemming from this rerouting of natural water flow. For example, fish populations in the East Everglades are 80 percent smaller than those of unaltered marshes. The declining fish populations cause corresponding declines in fish-eating alligators and wading birds. The area once provided 35 percent of the feeding habitat available to Everglades National Park's wood storks, but is no longer suitable for these birds during the crucial nesting period. Wood storks have suffered routine nesting failures in the East Everglades since the early 1960s. As elsewhere in the Everglades, the decline is caused mainly by loss of feeding habitat. The shrinkage of habitat in the East Everglades thus has directly affected the park.

The many tamperings with water flow north of the park have affected even the park's southernmost edge. About half the park is coastal marine and estuarine habitat dominated by mangrove forests and riddled with hundreds of miles of tidal creeks that interconnect a maze of ponds, lagoons, and backwater bays. The park's 300,000 acres of tropical mangrove habitat—among the most extensive mangrove ecosystems in the world—as well as adjacent coastal bays are vital to many economically important marine species that spend their juvenile lives there. According to Chandler, these nursery areas support a lobster, crab, and shrimp fishery that generates more than $50 million yearly. Commercial fishermen say the industry is worth even more: $250 million a year.

The region's health and productivity are directly dependent upon the flow of freshwater from upland areas, which has been reduced by as much as 90 percent. When water does arrive, it comes in large, or pulse, discharges of floodwaters from more northerly canals. Flow reduction and pulse discharge have altered salinity levels over a wide area of Florida Bay and have contributed to an extensive die-off of seagrass beds within the bay during the the past five years. Since 1987 an estimated 10,000 acres of dense seagrass bottom in western Florida Bay have been denuded, and an additional 55,000 acres have suffered somewhat less severe damage. Marine biologists Michael

Robblee and W. Jill Di Domenico reported in *Park Science* magazine late in 1991 that "Loss of seagrass habitat on this scale is unprecedented in tropical seagrass systems and potentially threatens the bay's water quality, its sport fishery, and its nursery." This threat is serious because seagrass serves as the food base for the entire estuary ecosystem and provides shelter for various species. Some studies suggest that upland water levels also may alter salinity within the estuary, a factor that could have serious consequences for species that tolerate only very narrow fluctuations of salinity.

Florida's burgeoning human population has affected the park estuary, too. Development in the Keys since the 1950s has brought several hundred thousand residents and tourists into that extremely narrow chain of islands immediately bordering park waters. Septic tank effluents, air pollution, petroleum pollutants that wash off pavement during rainfall, and intensive mosquito spraying from airplanes are all potential contributors to estuary degradation. Recent studies have documented increased concentrations of fertilizer chemicals around the Keys as well as increased algal growth in nearby marine waters. Boating activity is ever increasing within the park itself, penetrating all habitats. Nearly 45,000 recreational fishing trips are made into the park yearly, and more than 7,000 fish are taken each week. Since 1980 fishing has been increasing at a rate of about 11 percent yearly. However, commercial fishing was eliminated in 1985 because of declines in fish populations, and recreational fishing has been cut back by reductions in the number of fish anglers may catch and by tighter restrictions on seasons and the size of legal fish.

The park is thus victim to changes in water flow, increasing pollution, lack of protection for critical portions of the ecosystem, and overpopulation and overuse by humans. But that is not all. Even plants seem to be in league against the park.

Exotic plants have been spreading across Florida for some 40 years virtually out of control, except, observes Chandler, where they have been replaced by houses. Of the 400 exotic plant species in South Florida, the park has 220. One of these is the

Australian *Melaleuca* or punk tree, which since the 1950s has infested more than 2.5 million acres in South Florida and has converted some 100,000 acres into punk tree forests.

Another exotic plant that has been running rampant across South Florida is the Brazilian pepper tree, which grows rapidly as a shrub and crowds out native vegetation. The park's first known Brazilian pepper tree was found in 1961. Today, the species infests more than 20,000 acres and is rapidly invading critical coastal feeding areas for wading birds. It has destroyed sea turtle nesting areas and has changed the nitrogen content of soil in some areas, affecting what can grow there.

The rampant intrusion of exotic plant species, as much as the pollution warning signs, tells us that even this park—internationally valued, set aside for its wildlife and wilderness value, the second largest national park in the lower 48 states—is in trouble, perhaps even dying. To make matters worse, Everglades National Park is not atypical. The problems it faces trouble protected lands throughout the nation.

The Bigger Picture

Everglades National Park is one piece of a continent-wide constellation of protected public lands. As are all national parks, it is administered by the National Park Service. The park service and three other federal agencies—the Bureau of Land Management, the Forest Service, and the Fish and Wildlife Service—are expressly assigned the task of protecting some 625 million acres of public lands at an annual cost of about $6 billion. These lands include national forests, designated wilderness areas, and national wildlife refuges. A fifth agency, the National Oceanic and Atmospheric Administration in the Department of Commerce, is charged with creating and protecting marine sanctuaries.* In

---

*While the states also protect parcels of land, they will not be covered in this book. With rare exceptions, these lands are too small to ensure the protection of biodiversity. In addition, the sheer variety of state administration makes it impossible to cover the states comprehensively in a book of this size.

addition to the federal agencies, the management and protection of these lands are monitored by a myriad of nongovernmental conservation organizations—the National Wildlife Federation's *Conservation Directory 1991* listed 467 international, national, and regional conservation groups. These groups have millions of members and spend millions of dollars yearly to help ensure that public lands and wildlife are protected as U.S. laws and regulations mandate.

Nevertheless, the lands we protect are neither vast nor sheltered from human activity. A scant 9 percent of the nation is protected by law from human development, and even that tiny amount is not completely protected. Wildlife refuges, national forests, and even wilderness areas are subject to oil and gas development, mining, grazing, logging, and a host of other activities. Developers and industrialists begrudge even the small amount of wildland that we do modestly protect and mount annual assaults against the protection of these lands. For example, Florida's agricultural industry and water-management agencies, along with the U.S. Army Corps of Engineers, did not share willingly a single drop of the water needed to put Everglades National Park into better balance. The logging industry, thanks to its clout in Congress, has been liquidating the last of the ancient trees on national forests and other public lands in the Northwest and in Southeast Alaska. The oil and gas industry has scattered thousands of drilling rigs over national forests and wildlife refuges and has even sought to open to oil drilling the coastal plain of the Arctic National Wildlife Refuge, the last stretch of Alaskan arctic coast that has not been developed. As discussed in the chapters that follow, on a national scale commercial interests set much—indeed too much—of the agenda for federal attempts to protect wild places and wild creatures.

The consequence? Our parks, refuges, and other protected lands are becoming increasingly isolated and vulnerable in a world of rampant development, turned into broken shards of relative wilderness scattered across a landscape of cities, suburbs, and agricultural lands. As wild lands become fragmented, the creatures and plants that live within them are jeopardized by shrinking habitat and by increasing contact with human development and its byproducts. Florida's dwindling water birds are not, unfortunately, a unique group. Ten percent of all mammal species in the United States are in danger of extinction. Some 500 species of all types—plants, birds, mammals, insects, clams, the whole gamut of living things—are so severely jeopardized that they have won places on the federal endangered species list. Another 4,000 species have been nominated for listing, and the listing process is so backlogged that many of them will become extinct before they are listed.

Many of our national wildlife refuges are threatened with pollution, oil and gas development, mineral extraction—they are even used by the Air Force for bombing practice. Some are so badly polluted that refuge managers are forced to protect waterfowl by chasing them away from refuges created for them in the first place. A 1986 study by William Newmark, published in *Nature* in 1987, showed that an alarming number of wildlife species have been lost in what we presume are some of our finest national parks. Yosemite, Rocky Mountain, Zion, Bryce Canyon, and Lassen Volcano national parks have all lost at least 25 percent of their original species, while Glacier and Yellowstone have lost 7 and 4 percent respectively. A recent study showed that more than 70 percent of public grasslands administered by the Bureau of Land Management—thousands of acres leased to ranchers at a fraction of the cost of leasing private land—are in only fair to poor condition because of overuse by livestock. Virtually the last of the nation's virgin forests—lying on public lands in Montana, Idaho, northern California, Oregon, Washington, and Alaska—have been reduced by government-sanctioned logging to only a tiny percentage of their original acreages. In Washington State, 90 percent of the forests already have been cut. In Oregon, cut acreage equals about 95 percent of the pristine forest. And cutting continues.

Is this what we get for the $6 billion in taxes we place each year into the hands of federal land-management agencies for the protection of wild places and the plants and animals that live on them? Is this what we get for the millions more that we donate to conservation groups? What is happening? What is wrong? How is this happening? Why?

To begin the search for answers to these questions, we need to examine our reasons for protecting wildlands and then look at the history of our efforts to protect wild places and wild living things.

CHAPTER 2

Biodiversity: Saving Wildness

The value of biodiversity is the value of everything there is. It is the summed value of all the GNPs of all countries from now until the end of the world. We know that, because our very lives and our economies are dependent upon biodiversity. If biodiversity is reduced sufficiently, and we do not know the disaster point, there will no longer be any conscious beings. With them will go all value—economic and otherwise.

Bryan Norton, Professor of Philosophy,
University of South Florida

Assigning value to that which we do not own and whose purpose we can not understand except in the most superficial ways is the ultimate in presumptuous folly.

David Ehrenfeld, Professor of Biology,
Rutgers University

~~~

The entire cause of the conservation movement has been, in recent years, boiled down to a single word. Unfortunately, that word is *biodiversity,* which does not have the ring of a clarion call to arms. Unlike such phrases as *endangered species* and *save the whale,* or the all-encompassing *save the Earth,* biodiversity smacks of the scientific and the esoteric. It is not a term with which to move the masses and win ardent public support. And yet it is, in fact, synonymous with saving the Earth, or at least with saving enough of it to ensure that our economic and social lives can continue without threat of catastrophic disruption.

Biodiversity is shorthand for biological diversity, which in turn describes a fairly complex set of conditions.

On one level, biodiversity refers to the variety of life forms found in a given area or ecosystem or on the planet as a whole. We can refer to the biodiversity of the rainforest or of the desert or of the entire globe.

No one knows exactly how diverse life is on the planet. Biologists have named about 1.5 million species (a species may be roughly defined as a group of genetically related organisms that can produce fertile offspring). This is only a fraction of the planet's total array of life forms, which has been estimated at anywhere from 5 million to 30 million species, estimates that show we lack the foggiest notion of how diverse life really is.

The concept of biodiversity incorporates more than mere numbers. It also alludes to the interrelationships of species. It is probably safe to say that all species interact with others on some level. This is certainly true of the species that we see all around us. Birds and insects interact with trees and shrubs. Squirrels interact with birds, cats, dogs, and people. Wolves interact with moose and caribou. Species interactions can be as simple as a grizzly preying upon a ground squirrel, but they can also be subtle and complex. They are often vital. Some plants can reproduce only if pollinated by a particular species of insect. For example, most tropical orchid species can be fertilized only by a single species of bee. Each orchid species has its own pollinating bee species. Should an insect species involved in such a relationship vanish, so will the associated plant. When the plant disappears, so do other species dependent on it. The importance of biodiversity is thus underscored by the vital interrelationships that exist among species.

On the second level, biodiversity refers to the genetic diversity each species represents. Consider the house mouse, as Harvard biologist E. O. Wilson does in the opening chapter of *Biodiversity.* The cell nucleus of a house mouse contains about 100,000 genes, each organized from four strings of genetically encoded chemicals called DNA. DNA molecules are microscopic, but if the cellular DNA were uncoiled it would measure more than 3 feet. Enlarged to the diameter of kite string, the DNA molecule would run about 650 miles long, with about 20 "letters" of genetic code per inch. If the letters of the molecule were enlarged to the size of the typeface on this page, they would fill nearly all 15 editions of the *Encyclopedia Britannica* published since 1768.

The vast amount of information contained within an individual mammal constitutes a small amount of the genetic diversity represented by an entire species. Each individual, except in species that reproduce without exchanging genetic information through cross-breeding, is genetically different from all other individuals. The more individuals a species contains, the greater the genetic diversity of that species. When something reduces a species' numbers, such as poaching or habitat destruction, vast amounts of genetic diversity are lost even if the species continues to survive.

Globally, we are losing biodiversity at a terrific rate. Wilson estimates that in tropical rainforests alone we are losing about 17,500 species yearly—roughly 1,000 to 10,000 times the rate at which marine species vanished at the end of the Paleozoic and Mesozoic eras, which until now marked the quickest rate of extinction in the past 65 million years. Present losses are caused primarily by human activities and are much more thorough than those brought on by nature. In the Paleozoic and Mesozoic eras, most plant species survived; today, both animals *and* plants are rapidly vanishing.

But what has this to do with us?

Why Worry about Biodiversity?

"Why" is a question ever on the minds of conservationists, and the irreducible answer is *people*. The central concern of most conservationists is the physical, spiritual, and emotional well-being of humankind. All these things are subsumed in wildness, in nature, which is what we preserve when we protect biodiversity. "In wildness is the preservation of the world," wrote Henry David Thoreau—to which might be added Loren Eiseley's observation: "Nature is the receptacle which contains man and into which he finally sinks to rest. It implies all, absolutely all, that man knows or can know." When we chip away at the biodiversity of planet and homeland, we chip away at our potential for knowing more about, and surviving better in, the world.

The protection of biodiversity gives us our city parks, our zoos, our wildlife refuges. It gives us Yellowstone and Yosemite national parks. It gives us national seashore recreation areas where we can walk among sand dunes and listen to the rumble of the surf.

The protection of biodiversity lies at the heart of many emotional, intellectual, and spiritual pleasures. Protection of biodiversity, of wildness, offers us a diversity of opportunities for experience, which in turn offers a solution to at least one discouraging aspect of modern life: the extent to which we have all become spectators. Most of us spend more time watching other

people engaging in various activities than we do actively participating ourselves. Urban life especially is built around watching
rather than doing. Urban dwellers pride themselves on the variety of things they can watch: theater, films, ballet, symphony
orchestras, museums, zoos, sports, television, television, television. How often does conversation with friends, family, and as-
sociates gravitate toward events that one or all have merely
witnessed?

If wild places offer us anything they offer us this: participation. Even a nature trail in a city park is participatory. Your body
must work to get there and work to be there. If the place is big
enough to get lost in and perhaps be attacked in—if only by ticks
and black flies—so much the better. You have broken into the
realm of participation, you have escaped a world in which there
is a great deal of cause and no real effect. You are compelled to
plan or contemplate or decide what you yourself must do, rather
than merely watch others make decisions.

But wild places offer us more than participatory recreation.
They offer us connections as well.

Among the crumbling arches of the Roman Colosseum, or
the marbled ruins of the Forum, or the tawny stonework of the
pyramids of Egypt, we can sense connections to an ancient past,
to the shadows of vanished hopes and dreams. These monuments tie us to the lost societies from which we sprang, to the
homelands of our individual ancestors—Italians to the Romans,
British to the Celts, French to the Gauls, Germans to the Vikings,
African Americans to the Ashanti, Chinese to the dynastic no-
bles, Japanese to the Samurai.

But wildness takes us to something far older and deeper,
returns all of us, regardless of race or nationality, to one and the
same place: the birthing ground of humanity, where all our ancestors, regardless of present race, color, or creed, spent much of
their time chipping tools from stone, hunting animals, gathering
plants, and huddling around open fires. Wildness brings us all
back home and reveals the world that shaped, created, and nurtured us. As long as wild places exist, we can go home again. We

can meet unvarnished the fears and trials faced by our earliest human ancestors and measure the broad limits of our species' ability to survive. We can learn how resilient and tough and independent we really are.

But in wildness we learn about more than ourselves. Said John Muir, one of the premier defenders of natural places at the turn of the century, "The clearest way to the Universe is through a forest wilderness." For those eternally locked in human society, whose primary concerns are money and status, this may not seem much of an offering. But to those blessed with a desire to understand life itself, it is invaluable. Social critic Christopher Lasch, in *The Culture of Narcissism,* pointed out that few people today, caught in the web of earnings and status, escape a feeling of meaninglessness, a malaise of life. They lack a *purpose* in life. As novelist Russell Hoban put it, the central question of life is not *what does it all mean,* but *who are we doing it for?*

The answer lies well outside ourselves, for life, that is to say, *Life,* is not synonymous with humanity. Our species is only a small part of life, a type of life. Trying to understand the purpose of our strivings and joys by studying humanity, by focusing on humanity, is like trying to define a giant sequoia by looking at a single plant cell. Humanity as we know it has tramped over the surface of the globe for about a million years. Life, however, has been here for 3.5 *billion* years. We have much to learn from examining life in all its variety and interaction, from looking outward rather than inward. We must plunge into the pool of life—into tropical rainforests, deserts, mountains, oceans, and streams. To live happily, we need to discover our links to the larger world, to wildness, and we need to escape the ego-focused doctrines that salve our desire for personal importance while undercutting the ecosystems that give us life.

When we seek to protect wildness, we seek to protect eternity, to protect that which came before us and produced us, that which nurtures and preserves us, that which will provide for all future generations. We may destroy the natural world, but we cannot escape it, for ultimately we are one with wildness. As

Muir put it, spend time in the wild and eventually "you lose consciousness of your separate existence: you blend with the landscape, and become part and parcel of nature."

We cannot, in the end, be separated from the natural world. We absorb directly our physical environment. Our lungs take in air, and if that air is riddled with pollutants, then those pollutants are incorporated into our muscles, our blood, and our bones. Thousands of years from now, if scientists still exist, they will be able to distinguish our bones from those of sixteenth-century people by the amount of industrial pollutants incorporated into our bodies' most durable organs. We drink water, and our digestive tract absorbs whatever minerals and pollutants it contains. We eat animals, and our bodies absorb and hold the steroids we have pumped into livestock and the pollutants we have pumped into wild systems. Pesticides sprayed on southern cotton fields have migrated north on the wind to settle in rainfall upon the Great Lakes, where microscopic creatures have absorbed them, and the pesticides have worked their way up the food chain into lake trout that are also depositories for a variety of other Great Lakes pollutants, including cancer-causing toxins. From the trout the toxins have worked their way into eagles and otters and us.

When conservationists suggest that the planet's biodiversity is decreasing, they are talking about a potential catastrophe for humankind. At worst, rapid loss of species could undercut our own biological supports, stranding us in a denuded world for which we are not adapted and in which we cannot survive. At best, we will almost certainly lose species that could be of critical importance to our well-being and to the improvement of our daily lives.

And now we are down to the hardcore pragmatic reasons for protecting biodiversity. Even people who have little regard for the spiritual and emotional benefits of biodiversity protection will likely be interested in the fundamental things that wild species bring to our daily lives, such as food, medicine, and even jobs.

"Wild species are in fact both one of the Earth's most important resources and the least utilized," wrote Wilson. "We have come to depend completely on less than 1% of living species for our existence, the remainder waiting untested and fallow. In the course of history . . . we have utilized about 7,000 kinds of plants for food; predominant among these are wheat, rye, maize, and about a dozen other highly domesticated species. Yet there are at least 75,000 edible plants in existence, and many of these are superior to the crop plants in widest use."

You need look no further than the pharmaceutical industry to see another way in which the survival of the natural environment is critical to human society. For the past quarter-century, 25 percent of the prescriptions sold in the United States have contained plant extractions as active ingredients. Some 119 medicinal chemicals used worldwide are extracted from plants. These plants number fewer than 90 species, but the planet produces about 250,000 species of plants. The bulk of these have never been tested for their potential value as medicinal substances, and some valuable plant species are disappearing. For example, in the Pacific Northwest, the yew tree was until recently cut down and burned as a trash species. In the 1980s scientists discovered that yew bark contains a chemical effective against some types of cancer. Unfortunately, large quantities of bark are needed to produce useful amounts of the chemical, and too few yew trees of adequate size remain to make the natural source promising. Similarly, in the heavily logged Philippine rainforest some 1,500 plant species are used in traditional medicine. Many of these may offer little more than a placebo effect, but if even a fraction of them are medically useful their extinction would be a major loss to human society.

Wild plants are also valuable because they can help ensure the health or enhance the utility of crop plants. Wild relatives of domestic crop plants sometimes contain genes that give them resistance to threatening diseases. An African species of wild coffee contains a gene that makes it resistant to rust, a disease that in recent years jeopardized the world's coffee crop. Crossbreeding domestic coffees with the wild variety halted the epidemic. A wild grass discovered about 10 years ago in Mexico proved to be a relative of domestic corn. Corn is an expensive crop because it must be grown from seed each year. The Mexican wild grass regrows without reseeding. If its genes for reproductive strategy can be bred into domestic corn, the once-obscure wild grass's potential value—translated into income and jobs—will top $7 billion yearly.

It is impossible to calculate the dollar value of every species because complex and indispensable relationships between species compound the value of any given type of plant or animal. A species that seems to have no intrinsic worth might be critical to the survival of another, more clearly valuable species. For example, the Brazil nut is a valuable export crop, bringing in about $1 billion annually to Brazil. But it has never been successfully cultivated—it exists only in the wild. No one knows why it cannot be cultivated, but probably the Brazil nut is in some way dependent on the hidden activities of certain other species, such as insects or rodents. Thus the billion-dollar Brazil-nut industry might depend ultimately on the fate of some unknown moth.

Even a species of obvious value to humans may have greater value to its ecosystem. The African elephant, for example, is critically related to a wide number of other species. During droughts, elephants dig waterholes in river beds, providing moisture for uncounted other species. The seeds of some trees, such as the acacia, germinate best when they have passed through an elephant's digestive tract. Elephants knock down mature trees, helping to keep grasslands open—a critical factor for many grazing species, such as antelopes. The elephant's value is thus more than the price of its tusks or the money it brings from tourism. It is the value of nearly all the large animals that share the elephant's habitat.

The mutual dependence of species makes the protection of biodiversity critical. As we remove species from any ecosystem, we begin to upset the balance of all species. Remove enough species, or a keystone species such as the elephant, and the whole system veers toward collapse.

Underlying the survival of all species is habitat itself. Without proper habitat—whether it be virgin forest, open grassland, the bottom of the sea, or the human intestine—no species can survive. Habitat protection, which includes the protection of everything from wilderness areas to city parks, is the foundation of all efforts to protect species, to preserve biodiversity. This is why it is so vital to save such vanishing habitats as the temperate rainforests of the Pacific Northwest and the tall-grass prairies of the Midwest. They represent the last of a certain type of ecosystem. When they are gone, we risk losing all that these ecosystems offer us. This is equally true of wetlands and coastal zones. The loss of these habitats results in a net loss of species, a diminishing of biodiversity and all that it promises us in foods, medicines, and other products.

Many of those who stand to profit from environmental destruction would argue that biodiversity is of no consequence. Extinction, they say, is a natural process that began long before the arrival of humankind. Like glaciers and comets, humanity is merely another cause of extinction, neither more nor less natural as an agent of species loss.

This argument overlooks the scientific point that we are causing extinctions at thousands of times the rate of anything in the past and that we are destroying the entire spectrum of species—everything from plants to insects to mammals. When the ecological bottom drops out and ecosystems begin to collapse, a domino effect comes into play so that even species that are not directly touched by human activities could vanish. If we destroy enough species and disrupt enough ecosystems, we will almost certainly destroy the way of life to which we have become accustomed.

It will happen by slow degrees. We already find ourselves unable to eat fish from certain bodies of water, or to breathe comfortably the air in some urban communities, or to swim along some ocean beaches—and we adjust our lives accordingly. We will continue to adjust and adjust as more and more warning signs are erected along rivers, lakes, and seas—*do not fish here, do*

not swim here. And though as a species we quite likely will survive, right down to the most extreme scenario short of global
conflagration, nevertheless if we persist in our actions we will
bring down the ecological superstructure on which is mounted
our social, political, and economic life, and we will find ourselves living a less desirable, much degraded existence.

Fortunately, we need not function with the mindless inex-
orability of a glacier. If we so choose, we can be barriers to death,
destruction, and extinction. We can empathize with wild places
and creatures for their sake as well as our own. Australian genet-
icist O. H. Frankel, quoted in the Worldwatch Institute's booklet
"On the Brink of Extinction: Conserving the Diversity of Life,"
observed, "We are *not* the equivalent of an ice age or a rise in sea
level: we are capable of prediction and control. We have acquired
evolutionary responsibility."

Because we have a choice, we can pause in our actions and
ask ourselves what we are sacrificing biodiversity for. William
Faulkner, in *The Bear*, put it neatly when he had Ike McCaslin
say over the dead body of a buck he has shot, "I slew you; my
bearing must not shame your quitting life. My conduct forever
onward must become your death."

Is our conduct worthy of the untolled species and vast ecosystems we have wiped out? We sacrificed the dusky seaside
sparrow—a bird abundant along the eastern Florida coast a
mere 20 years ago—to suburban houses and insect spray. A land
developer in Oregon wants to sacrifice the Oregon silverspot
butterfly for the construction of a golf course. Southern California real-estate developers want to sacrifice the Stephen's kangaroo rat for housing tracts—the same sort of tracts that threaten
California cougar populations. Loggers want to sacrifice the last
expanses of ancient forests in the Pacific Northwest for perhaps
five more years of work, after which they will be both treeless
and jobless. These actions reveal a horrifying depravity in the
human spirit.

But that depravity did not arise wholecloth in our time. To
find its origin, and the challenge that human society poses to

biodiversity and to its own survival, we need to catapult back about 15,000 years and trace the roots of biodiversity protection. The world then was in many ways a much more complex place, biologically at any rate, because more species were thriving. Many large mammals now extinct were still living and breeding. Complex forests grew where now we see human-caused deserts, as in the Middle East and parts of India. Vast herds of bison, antelope, wisent, mammoths, and woolly rhinos roamed the land, and countless ducks, geese, wild pigeons, and other birds crowded the skies. No park boundaries had yet been drawn on the land, nor were they needed.

CHAPTER 3

The Invention and Overthrow of Wilderness

꙳

America is a land of wonders, in which everything is in constant motion and every change seems an improvement. . . . No natural boundary seems to be set to the efforts of man; and in his eyes what is not yet done is only what he has not yet attempted to do.

Alexis De Tocqueville,
Democracy in America

Oh for a lodge in some vast wilderness,
Some boundless contiguity of shade,
Where rumor of oppression and deceit,
Of unsuccessful or successful war,
Might never reach me more.

William Cowper

≋

Some 10,000 or 15,000 years ago there was no wilderness. There was only the Earth, and it, as the ancients put it, abided forever. The relationship between humanity and the rest of nature was seamless. All peoples lived in and of the natural world. They depended upon wild plants and animals for food; upon rainfall, streams, and ponds for water; upon rock and bone and hide for tools and clothing. These distant ancestors of ours were not particularly fruitful and did not multiply with surpassing speed. Drought, disease, starvation, fangs, claws, bad weather, and all the other slings and arrows of the hunting and gathering world kept their numbers low. It was the dominant way of life for millions of years.

Then, at various sites around the globe—in the Middle East and in Southeast Asia, for example—some innovative peoples began to cultivate the plants they had been gathering from the wild. Agriculture was born.

In a short time, wilderness was born, too, for wilderness is a relative term. Our forebears could not have conceived of wilderness until they had placed boundaries around their farm fields and seen the contrast between those fields and the natural world. Eating the fruits of the first crops gave humankind new knowledge—the power to create life from seeds—and separated humanity forever from the wilderness. When the earliest farmers looked upon their crops, and then beyond to the natural world, they saw wilderness for the first time, and saw too the nakedness with which humankind had always faced the world, the defenselessness of peoples struggling to find water during times of drought, to slay for meat creatures armed with fangs, claws, tusks, and bulky muscle. They cloaked their nakedness in protective layers of crops and livestock.

Everything we now are or pretend to be is linked directly and irrevocably to that time when men and women began to scratch at the soil and bury fertile seeds. Cultivation of plants and the domestication of animals intensified humanity's sense of tribal territoriality. People had to settle and live near their fields, and fields had to be defended from interlopers. Villages grew, then towns, then cities. Surpluses in food permitted the development of professional specialties—farmers, soldiers, rulers, priests. Populations grew as natural bounds on birth and mortality were breached by an upstart species. Human history became the history of the fall of nature as grasslands were plowed and forests felled to make way for crops and livestock. A great tradition was established: the founding of fortunes on the destruction of the natural environment. Humanity did not leave the wilderness, the metaphorical Garden of Eden. Humanity stayed in one place, wiping out the wilderness and destroying the garden. Nature, not humankind, had fallen from grace. The agricultural and urban systems combined in an effort to carve up and reshape the world, putting up fences and walls. In the process, they created the vast gulf that lies between the developed and the natural worlds—the schism between civilization and wilderness. Ever since, we have lived in a dual world, civilization on the one hand and wilderness on the other.

For wilderness, its new status as a distinct entity within human consciousness was a mark of doom. In the Old World, wilderness fell victim to an array of disreputable associations. If the religiously zealous wanted to prove their fealty to God and all that was good, great, and sinless, they would torture and mortify themselves by retreating, as the Essenes did in Christ's era, to the inhospitable world of the wilderness. There they could escape the temptations of the flesh and lead perfectly moral if miserable lives. Wilderness was also a place of punishment for the man "whose heart departeth from the Lord," wrote Jeremiah, "for he . . . shall inhabit the parched places in the wilderness, in a salt land and not inhabited." John the Baptist's preachings were said to be the cry of a voice in the wilderness. When Jesus went into the wilderness, who should visit him but the devil, with his litany of temptations. During the time of Greek and Roman dominance, as well as in the medieval era, forests and wilderness were feared as places fraught with danger. There wild men would attack you with uprooted trees, there Pan waited to perform his mischievous deeds.

These were the understandings of wilderness that early settlers brought with them to the New World. Little wonder that Cotton Mather, a Puritan New England minister born late in the seventeenth century, treated wilderness as a metaphor for damnation, terrorizing his parishioners with tales of North America wilds inhabited by dragons, devils, and "fiery flying serpents." He and later settlers believed that the wilderness posed a threat to personal moral integrity. Life in the wilderness would corrode the veneer of civilization, revealing the hard core of savagery that lay repressed in every human heart, a pathway to sin and hellfire.

Of course, the early settlers did not need such moral and religious considerations in order to share a hatred for wilderness. These people came to the New World for a New Life, but found the untamed forests and mountains damned hard to live in. The settlers could not readily embrace a wild land that so stalwartly opposed their attempts to improve it with plow, axe, and flame. John Eliot, a seventeenth-century settler, wrote that in the wilderness "nothing appeareth but hard labour," to which Mather added in 1693 that wilderness was a sort of purgatory "thro' which we are passing to the Promised Land."

It was that Promised Land that made the struggle so worthwhile, for everyone was also well aware that despite its shortcomings the wilderness could leave you rolling in money. There was gold in them there hills, as well as furs, timber, meat, and land for development—a veritable treasure trove.

Commerce drove the discovery of the New World. It was all business from the very beginning. English kings and queens laid claim to the tall, straight trees of eastern forests, perfect for masts on war ships; Spanish Conquistadors enslaved indigenous peoples and robbed them of gold; and European companies set out to trade in New World furs, nearly wiping out the beaver, river otter, and sea otter and indeed flaying for profit the last sea mink ever found. Boundaries were laid all over the continent to serve as guidelines for domination, determining who, without interference from neighbors or government, could exploit which piece of land in which way.

With belief in a confluence of purposes so fortuitous that the skeptical might think it contrived, the settlers were confident that the replacement of untamed nature with all the productive works of humankind was not only *their* goal but also God's. The fact that the white settlers found, upon their arrival in the New World, people of a different color already living off the land was irrelevant. Hugh Henry Brackenridge, an early American literary illuminary, in 1782 argued in the *Freeman's Journal or North American Intelligencer* against recognizing Native American territorial claims. Indians, he wrote, "have the shapes of men and may be of the human species, but certainly in their present state they approach nearer the character of Devils. . . ." He added, "What do these ringed, streaked, spotted and speckled cattle make of the soil? Do they till it? Revelation said to man, 'Thou shalt till the ground.' This alone is human life. It is favorable to population, to science, to the information of a human mind in the worship of God. . . . To live by tilling is *more humano*, by hunting is *more bestiarum*. I would as soon admit a right in the buffalo to grant lands, as in . . . any of the ragged wretches that are called chiefs and sachems."

The linking of godliness with wilderness destruction was still in vogue as late as 1873, when Colorado governor William Gilpin declared that "Progress is God," and "the occupation of wild territory . . . proceeds with all the solemnity of a providential ordinance." John Louis O'Sullivan put it succinctly—and perhaps most memorably—when in the July/August 1845 issue of the *United States Magazine and Democratic Review* he penned the phrase that produced a pioneer battle cry: "Our manifest destiny is to overspread the continent allotted by Providence for the free development of our yearly multiplying millions."

Manifest Destiny—it had a beautiful ring to it, swollen as it was with the intimation that God had chosen that generation of pioneers to rid the continent of native peoples too lazy to replace bison with cattle or to plant good Christian crops such as corn, tobacco, potatoes, and tomatoes—all of which the settlers had inherited from the natives in the first place.

Nevertheless, toward the end of the nineteenth century the nation's prevailing sentiment about wild places was shifting. As the wilderness vanished it became a rare commodity. More and more people wanted to see it, to experience the last of it. Theodore Roosevelt rushed about the prairies in the mid-1880s in search of any remnant buffalo he could find, so desperate was he to shoot one before all were gone. Many late nineteenth-century people took aim at that last buffalo. For most this took the form of visiting scenic remnants of the nation's wildness, such as Yosemite Valley in California. Scenery soon became big business. Consequently, at the very moment in history when the yen for profit was on the verge of wiping out the nation's last wild places, wild places became profitable. Not surprisingly, commercial interests, including such Victorian corporate behemoths as the railroad companies, came rushing to the rescue.

We can virtually pinpoint the day that the real push to save wild places began. The date was September 19, 1870, the day on which a plan was conceived to create the world's first national park.

And thereon hangs a tale.

No Grander Scene to Human Eyes

September 19, 1870. Early morning.

Roughly a dozen men are camped on the banks of Wyoming's Firehole River, surrounded by pines and the sound of flowing water. After waking early, they prepare breakfast.

It is a day of signs and portents. As they are eating, they hear a rumbling and then, from a mound of earth nearby, steam and water explode into the sky. Breakfast is interrupted as the men watch, astonished. They laugh at the discovery that they had camped all night beside a geyser, unaware. Hardy explorers with a yen for making maps and quantifying natural wonders, they engage in some triangulating and geometrizing and conclude that the spray reached 219 feet into the air. The mound of earth over the geyser reminds them of an old-fashioned straw beehive with the top cut off, so they name it Beehive Geyser.

At 9:30 they break camp, a few of the party staying behind for a while to see if another geyser will blow. When none do, the lingerers catch up with the rest of the troupe.

These are the men of the Washburn Expedition. They are led by Henry D. Washburn, a consumptive Civil War veteran and former congressman. The group includes eight other civilian explorers, a cavalry lieutenant, a sergeant, four privates, two cooks, two packers, and 35 pack horses and mules loaded with food and supplies. The military contingent is from Fort Ellis, in Montana. They were assigned to the expedition by arrangement with General Phil Sheridan. The lieutenant carries orders which indicate that he is to escort the nine civilians into an unmapped wilderness we know today as Yellowstone National Park.

The Yellowstone region, a high plateau surrounding the Yellowstone River, was in 1870 a fabled land, poorly known even to local native peoples. The Crow and Blackfeet claimed territories that bordered the region, but they rarely entered it. The only people who lived in Yellowstone itself were the Tukuarika Shoshones, a peaceful folk who found in the mountain fastnesses a refuge from Crow and Blackfoot warriors.

Native Americans besides the Shoshones sometimes traveled through the region over distinct trails overlain today by tourist routes. But apparently the Native Peoples did not follow those trails with any frequency—Indian guides who knew the surrounding country well became lost in the park, and the Nez Perce needed a white man to lead them through in 1877.

Whites had been visiting the region since the early nineteenth century, but their reports were mostly anecdotal and unofficial. Someone with the initials JOR drifted through in 1819 and on August 19 of that year carved his initials and the date on a tree a quarter-mile above the upper falls of the Yellowstone River. This enigmatic sign was discovered in 1880 by the park superintendent, who believed it authentic. Thus, JOR, whoever he was, left the earliest known record of a visit by a European to Yellowstone.

In 1829 a group of trappers from the Rocky Mountain Fur Company passed near Yellowstone and was dispersed by a band of Blackfeet. One of the trappers, Joseph Meek, lost his horse and most of his equipment and spent several days wandering lost and alone. On the fifth day, he found a vast basin of boiling springs where steam and gases issued from small craters—he had stumbled upon the park's now-familiar hot-springs district. John Colter, a trapper and adventurer who had explored the lands of the Louisiana Purchase with Lewis and Clark, had wandered through the same region around 1808 or 1809, but his descriptions of the geysers and steaming springs won him little more than ridicule. The region of which he spoke was belittled as Colter's Hell.

Rumors of this fabled place persisted, however, as other trappers drifted in and out of the Yellowstone region. Warren Angus Ferris, a clerk for the American Fur Company, decided to investigate the rumors for himself. With some Indians as companions, he traveled throughout the Yellowstone area in the early 1830s and actually dipped his hand into a geyser in May 1834. In the 1840s an article he wrote, based on a journal he kept while traveling in the Yellowstone country, was widely published, but not soon enough to lend credibility to earlier reports of the region made by Jim Bridger. Bridger—explorer, trapper, and infamous purveyor of frontier whoppers—was generally disbelieved by those to whom he related tales of trips through Yellowstone beginning in the 1830s, tales replete with geysers that sprayed hundreds of feet into the air and with quaking lands that masked hot springs. People might have been more inclined to believe him if he had not thrown in stories about magnifying-glass mountains through which you could see elk 25 miles away.

Despite these contacts, or perhaps because of them, the Yellowstone area was still *terra incognita* in 1870. The Washburn Expedition intended to correct this situation. A brief examination of the men who comprised the expedition reveals the source of their ambition.

Washburn had been brevetted a major general for his Civil War efforts and had served two terms in Congress, but was working as Montana's surveyor general at the time of the expedition. Though he was suffering from the consumption he had contracted during trench warfare at Vicksburg—it would kill him the following January—he was bent on initiating the formal discovery of the Yellowstone region. He was joined in this quest by eight other local notables, including Cornelius Hedges, a Yale alumnus, lawyer, and journalist; 54-year-old Truman C. Everts, the oldest participant, whose job as Montana's federal assessor had been taken away by appointees of the new Grant administration; Benjamin Stickney, a miner and freighter who owned a stationery shop in Helena, Montana; and 28-year-old Nathaniel P. Langford, formerly the collector of internal revenue for Montana. These men as well as the others were politicos and merchants. They had land development on their minds, and perhaps none more than did Nat Langford.

Langford was not only the expedition's scribe—he would later publish his diary of the trip—but also the very man who had provided the impetus for the expedition. In 1869 Andrew Johnson's administration had appointed him governor of Montana Territory, but he had lost the office before he could even assume it when Johnson was impeached. Through family contacts, he had joined in promoting financier Jay Cooke's plan to build a transcontinental railroad line through Montana and other northern states. In this capacity he obtained permission from Major General Winfield S. Hancock, of the Army's Department of Dakota, to organize an expedition into the Yellowstone region, where lakes, mountains, and waterfalls might offer some terrific scenery.

Scenery was of paramount interest to the railroads. During the previous decade mountains and waterfalls had turned a small state park in California's Yosemite Valley into a major tourist mecca, complete with hotels and inns. Thousands of tourists were making it their destination. It was a wise railroad man who looked for scenic places to which a passenger train could be run.

Langford and the other eight civilians were wise enough, so when they left Fort Ellis on August 22 they were in quest of new tourist attractions and investment properties. Their avowed targets were Yellowstone Lake and the waterfalls of the Yellowstone River, both known mainly from stories told by mountain men, prospectors, and lost settlers. The possibility of finding geysers and hot springs went unmentioned. Belief in those rumored wonders suggested that you were easily hoodwinked, so no one would confess to the slightest hope of finding them.

By September 19 their capacity for belief had been considerably stretched. Langford had written in his diary that they had "within a distance of fifty miles seen what we believed to be the greatest wonders on the continent. We were convinced that there was not on the globe another region where within the same limits Nature had crowded so much of grandeur and majesty with so much novelty and wonder." They had measured the falls of the Yellowstone and stood before them enraptured: "A thousand arrows of foam, apparently *aimed at us*, leaped from the verge, and passed rapidly down the sheet," wrote Langford. "But as the view grew upon us, and we comprehended the power, majesty and beauty of the scene, we became insensible to danger and gave ourselves up to the full enjoyment of it. . . . The Almighty has vouchsafed no grander scene to human eyes."

They had also found Yellowstone Lake, which Langford wrote, "as seen from our camp to-night, seems to me to be the most beautiful body of water in the world. In front of our camp it has a wide sandy beach like that of the ocean, which extends for miles and as far as the eye can reach. . . ."

They had spent a day or two in the geyser basin, coming upon it from woods so dense that they could see barely a hundred feet around them. When they had stepped abruptly out of the woods and into the open basin, they had been greeted by a vertical column of water and steam blasting 150 feet into the air. With the water glittering in the sunlight and the steam wafting across the valley on the wind, they had gaped at it in awe—their first geyser. Later that day, after observing the regularity with which it erupted, they had named it Old Faithful. It was only one of many geysers—the entire basin was punctuated with plumes of water and steaming springs. They had found one of old Jim Bridger's wonders and realized, to their surprise, that for once he was true to his word.

They had also had one of their men swallowed up by the vastness of the land itself. While wandering through the thick forest that surrounded Yellowstone Lake—the trees so close together that the expedition had woven through them a braided trail, each member finding the route that worked best for his horse—Truman C. Everts, the oldest member, had got lost. The party had spent a few days in futile search and had left some food for him by the lake in case he should happen to come along.

By the morning of September 19—despite geysers at breakfast—they had wearied of their travels. They thought of little except Everts' fate and getting home. Their eagerness to return to town was dictated in part by rumbling stomachs; they had been traveling for 33 days, but had packed enough food for only 30.

More signs and portents. After the men left the geyser basin, they came upon the largest hot spring they had seen. Mineral deposits from the boiling water surrounded the spring for 200 yards, leaving the spring itself above the valley floor. As the explorers looked on, a flock of ducks came in for a landing but veered off a few inches above the water. One luckless duck could not make the sudden shift, crashed into the water, squawked once or twice, and died in the scalding spring, today known as Hell's Half Acre.

They traveled that day about 18 miles and camped at the

junction of the Firehole and Gibbon rivers. Everts was still missing, and although they hoped that he had somehow made it to civilization on his own, they knew he was probably dead.

The conversation that night, around a fire on the rocky bank of the Firehole, turned from Everts' grim fate to what could be done with the Yellowstone country. The consensus seemed to be that the geysers, hot springs, lake, and towering waterfalls should be turned into lucrative tourist attractions. This was exactly what had happened at Niagara Falls, so why not at Yellowstone? One member of the party suggested that they should claim quarter-sections of land at the most prominent points of interest. Another refined the idea, suggesting that they obtain title to two or three quarter sections opposite the lower falls of the Yellowstone and extending down river above the canyon. A more pragmatic explorer countered that it would be better to claim a quarter section of the upper geyser basin, since tourists could reach it more easily. Another, apparently anxious about coming up short, suggested that any claims they made should be put into a common pool from which all would share the profits.

At about this point Cornelius Hedges spoke up as a lone dissenter. He said he didn't like any of these plans, that no private party should own any part of Yellowstone. Instead, the whole region should be set aside as a great national park. And each one of them, he said, should work to see that this was done.

Hedges' idea was not original. Thomas F. Meagher, while acting governor of Montana, had suggested in 1865 that the Yellowstone region be set aside for public use. Hedges quite likely knew of this. David Folsom, who had explored the Yellowstone region with two other men during a 36-day expedition in 1869, had written about his travels in an article published in the July 1870 issue of *Western Monthly*. In his manuscript he too had suggested that the region be made a park, but this text was cut out of the published version. However, Folsom reiterated the idea to General Washburn before the 1870 expedition set off.

Folsom seemed to have a gift for dropping his notions upon deaf ears. Hedges, however, was apparently born under a luckier star. With one exception, the entire party immediately agreed that he had come up with a capital plan. The proposal was mulled over throughout the evening with increasing enthusiasm. Wrote Langford in his diary entry for September 20, "I lay awake half of last night thinking about it;—and if my wakefulness deprived my bed-fellow (Hedges) of any sleep, he has only himself and his disturbing National Park proposition to answer for it."

The next day they continued their discussion as they rode along. Langford concluded that they could succeed with the plan only "by untiring work and concerted action in a warfare against the incredulity and unbelief of our National legislators."

As soon as the party reached Helena a few days later they set to work on two things.

First, they dispatched a search party for the long-lost Everts. Eventually he would be found near death after "Thirty-seven Days of Peril," as he would title a *Scribner's Magazine* article about his exploits. The perils apparently did him little ill—he lived another 31 years, dying in Hyattsville, Maryland, at the age of 85 after fathering a child at 76.

Second, they started the park campaign. The first public reference to the project appeared in the *Helena Herald* on November 9, 1870, in a letter from Hedges. Langford, in the ensuing months, spread the word through a series of lectures.

Meanwhile, things were moving apace on other fronts. In the autumn of 1870 two printers from Deer Lodge, Montana, went into the Firehole basin and cut a large selection of saplings with which they planned, the following summer, to build a fence around the principal geysers and lay claim to them. Visions of tourist dollars were dancing in their heads. They mentioned the scheme to fellow Montanan William Clagett, who told them they should abandon it in favor of turning the region into a park.

Clagett's conversation with the printers could not have occurred at a better time, from the park's perspective, if the Fates themselves had ordained it. Clagett was elected to Congress the following August, and shortly thereafter met with Langford and Hedges to discuss the park idea. Fully cognizant of the threats to the park, they agreed that they needed to create it quickly, before developers established a stranglehold on the area.

By then, another crucial event had taken place. In the summer of 1871 the federal government had sent two more expeditions into the Yellowstone region, this time to map and photograph the area. One expedition was led by captains John Barlow and D. P. Heap of the Army Corps of Engineers, the other by Dr. F. V. Hayden of the U.S. Geological Survey of the Territories. The expeditions produced two valuable assets: photographs that proved the existence of the fabulous wonders previous explorers had described, and maps that would help establish the boundaries for a potential park.

In December 1871 Langford went to Washington, D.C., and joined forces with Clagett. He obtained from Hayden the information needed to outline the park boundaries, and Clagett wrote a bill to create the park and introduced it in the House on December 18, 1871. Kansas senator Samuel C. Pomeroy, chairman of the senate committee on public lands, asked if he could introduce the bill in the Senate.

While the proposal was being considered in Congress, photographs and samples from the Hayden expedition were exhibited in Washington (most of the Barlow expedition's photographs were lost in the Chicago fire and consequently had no role in legislative developments). According to Hiram Martin Chittenden, in his turn-of-the-century book *The Yellowstone National Park,* the photos and samples probably were seen by every member of Congress and "did a work which no other agency could do, and doubtless convinced every one who saw them that the region where such wonders existed should be carefully preserved to the people forever."

Langford himself was also reaching elected officials. He wrote propark articles that appeared in the May and June issues of *Scribner's Magazine.* Four hundred copies of the magazines were placed on the desks of congressional members on the days when the park law was being brought to vote. In addition, throughout the winter of 1871 Langford, Clagett, and Hayden buttonholed virtually every member of Congress to expound their message.

It all paid off. On January 30, 1872, the Senate passed the Yellowstone act. The House did the same on February 27. Ironically, Clagett missed the vote because, as he later wrote Langford, "I happened to be at the other end of the Capitol."

The bill that went to President Ulysses S. Grant ordered that the Yellowstone area be "dedicated and set apart as a public park or pleasuring ground for the benefit and enjoyment of the people. . . ." The secretary of the Interior was assigned the task of creating rules and regulations "for the preservation from injury or spoilation of all timber, mineral deposits, natural curiosities or wonders within said park, and their retention in their natural condition." The secretary also was allowed to issue building permits to provide accommodations for tourists, with money from concession fees earmarked for park management and the construction of roads and bridlepaths. Last of all, the secretary was ordered to protect fish and game from wanton destruction. Grant signed the bill into law on March 1, 1872, creating not only the nation's but the world's first national park. Langford was named its first superintendent, an unsalaried position that he held for five years while also working as the federal bank examiner for the territories and Pacific Coast states.

Not everyone wanted to see a park created. On March 6, 1872, the Helena *Rocky Mountain Gazette* expressed regret over the park. As late as 1883 Kansas senator John Ingalls was saying, "The best thing the Government could do with the Yellowstone National Park is to survey it and sell it as other public lands are sold." Nevertheless, creation of the park was a momentous feat. As Chittenden wrote, "Never before was a region of such vast extent as the Yellowstone Park set apart for the use of all the people without distinction of rank or wealth."

The occasion also marked the beginning of a new era in the federal government's relationship to land. Although a few sites had been federally protected prior to Yellowstone—hot springs in Arkansas had received federal protection as a public bathing ground as early as 1832, and in 1864 the federal government had given Yosemite Valley to California for a state park—nothing on the scale of Yellowstone had ever been placed under the federal wing. Previously, the government had acted as a distributor of land, handing it out to veterans, homesteaders, railroad companies, and other concerns for development. Yellowstone National Park was an innovation, and it set the course for federal protection of wildlands.

The irony of this is that the park would not have been protected if the minions of the railroad industry had not been looking for a good tourist attraction.

The idea of protecting wild places had been in the air for nearly half a century. Writers and painters had been extolling the virtues of wilderness and the American West for years, but who listens to writers and painters? The first mention of a national park came in George Catlin's writings about American Indians, which appeared in print in the 1830s. Catlin was a Philadelphia portraitist who was so taken with a visiting contingent of Indian chiefs in full regalia that he subsequently spent seven or eight years in the West, over the protests of wife and family, painting portraits of individual Native Americans as well as scenes of their daily life. In 1833, writing about the glories of bison and the Plains Indians, he added,

> And what a splendid contemplation too, when one . . . imagines them as they *might* in future be seen, (by some great and protecting policy of government) preserved in their pristine beauty and wildness, in a *magnificent park,* where the world could see for ages to come, the native Indian in his classic attire, galloping his wild horse, with sinewy bow, and shield and lance, amid the fleeting herds of elks and buffaloes. What a beautiful and thrilling specimen for America to preserve and hold up to the view of her refined citizens and the world, in future ages! A *nation's Park,* containing man and beast, in all the wild freshness of their nature's beauty!

In suggesting the formal protection of wilderness, Catlin was nearly half a century ahead of his time. "I would ask no other monument to my memory, nor any other enrolment of my name amongst the famous dead, than the reputation of having been the founder of such an institution," Catlin wrote in 1833. Nonetheless, by the time of the Washburn Expedition not a single *nation's park* existed in the United States—or in the world, for that matter.

It was not for lack of appeals in the press. Throughout the nineteenth century, wilderness acquired a growing allure in the mass media. As early as 1833 an anonymous writer for *American Monthly Magazine* lauded wilderness as a gentle retreat from "the busy haunts of sordid, money-making business." In mid-century, Joel T. Headley, a New York *Tribune* reporter, wrote in *The Adirondack: or Life in the Woods*, "I love the freedom of the wilderness and the absence of conventional forms there. . . . I love it, and I know it is better for me than the thronged city, aye, better for soul and body both." Washington Irving, best known for his stories about Ichabod Crane and Rip Van Winkle, wrote about the glories of riding across the western plains on horseback in hot pursuit of bison, and novelist James Fenimore Cooper made his woodsmen hero Natty Bumpo a personification of wilderness virtues. Under such influences, people toward the end of the nineteenth century began to value wilderness in and of itself, even came to believe that they needed it, now that it was almost gone. Wilderness served "as a great breathing-place for the national lungs," as Missouri congressional representative George Vest once said.

But despite this growing diversity of interest, land protection did not commence until commerce came into the issue. Shortly after Yellowstone was created, protection of publically owned forest lands began. Presidents Grover Cleveland and Benjamin Harrison in the seven years following passage of the Forest Reserve Act of 1891 set aside 33 million acres of forest reserves. In 1905 the Forest Service was created under President Theodore Roosevelt, who added 132 million acres more to the National Forest System. These presidents did this because it was becoming clear, at the turn of the century, that loggers would soon clearcut every tree they could find, from saplings to centuries-old giants.

Left to the avarice of the lumber industry, the nation would be thrust into a lumber famine.

Few things show the dominance of commercial interests in the early protection of wild places as clearly as the first national forests. In the 1880s and 1890s the drive to protect the vanishing forests was spearheaded by John Muir, who founded the Sierra Club in 1892. When the first national forests were created, Muir thought they were being saved for their own sake. He was soon disavowed of this illusion when Gifford Pinchot, a wealthy Pennsylvanian trained by European foresters, used his influence to ensure that the national forests would be managed as sources of timber, not as natural wonders. Forests, in Pinchot's eyes, were living lumberyards. When Muir realized what Pinchot had in mind, he fought for the protection of the national forests as places where trees and all the wildlife they support would be safe from loggers, but he lost the battle. Pinchot, under Theodore Roosevelt, became head of the Forest Service and set the precedent that the service still follows in its management of the national forests—the chief emphasis is on the production of timber, on the sale of trees to private lumber companies.

Early land protection thus grew out of commercial interests. National forests were created to provide logs to lumber companies. National parks such as Yellowstone and Glacier were created under lobbying pressure from the railroad industries and were designed to protect scenery for the tourist trade. In later years, the Bureau of Land Management, which today administers more land than any other federal agency, was created to monitor grazing and mining on public grasslands, mostly in the West.

The early and persistent link between land protection and commercial interests has clouded the purpose of federal land management since the first days of federal protection. Congress has given federal land agencies confusing and contradictory orders for wildland management. Virtually every federal land manager in the nation is unsure about whether he or she is supposed to focus on the protection of economic interests such as logging, mining, and grazing or on other public interests such as wildlife, recreational opportunities, and water quality. A quick look at the four federal agencies most directly involved in the protection and management of wildlands shows what, why, and how we are failing in our protection of wildness and biodiversity.

PART TWO

What's So Public about
Public Lands?
Protecting Wild Places
in the United States

CHAPTER 4

Why Federal Protection?

꙰

On the evidence of several generations of exploita-
tive freedom no one could guarantee the future its
share of the American earth except the American
government.

Wallace Stegner

Government cannnot own and operate small parcels
of land, and it cannot own and operate good land
at all.

Aldo Leopold

≈≈

Aldo Leopold—the father of wildlife management, a man in-strumental to the creation of the national wildlife refuge system and the founding of The Wilderness Society—wrote his indict-ment of the federal government as a land manager in a 1939 essay entitled "The Farmer as Conservationist." Leopold was a great believer in the importance of private land as the linch-pin of wilderness protection. He did not trust the government—with its sophomoric partisanships, its vagrant patronage system, and its pusilanimous obeisence to special interests—to protect much of anything beyond economic concerns, making public lands too insecure for the protection of wildlife and other natural resources.

Ironically, Leopold, who was right about so many conser-vation issues, failed to observe that wildlife habitat is seldom protected on private lands. It is no coincidence that the most extensive wilderness areas remaining today are on public lands. Private landowners and their heirs are generally interested only in what their lands can produce. Little wonder that in the Pacific Northwest the last of the ancient forests lie on public lands, while privately owned forests have been cut down. Little wonder that the surviving great wetlands, such as Okeefenokee in Georgia and the southern Everglades in Florida and the Great Dismal Swamp in Virginia, survive on public lands. Little wonder that, were it not for federal protection, Yellowstone National Park would be crossed by railroads and its geysers made subservient to dubious hydrothermal projects.

Federal agencies may do a less-than-ideal job of protecting wildlands, but the results they produce are far better than the vast majority of management efforts on private lands. The most important factor behind the survival of large wild tracts on public lands is the diversity of ideas and opinions that influence federal land-management policies. The government must take into consideration a broad array of constituencies when making decisions about public-land use. The private landowner, however, can ignore all dissent in initiating actions. If the private owner of thousands of acres of centuries-old redwoods wishes to cut them down in one swath—as is happening now in northern California—those who favor the existence of redwoods can do little to stop it. In matters concerning public lands, however, the voices of citizen conservationists can be more clearly heard, even if they frequently must shout over the din of commercial developers. When held to the fire of public opinion, developers and administrators alike may kick and scream, Congress may groan, presidents may wail, and all or any of them may in the end win the day for development, but at the very least citizen conservationists have some hope of shaping the management of public lands. Consequently, it is clear today that protection of wild values is tied to public lands.

Of course, Leopold was writing at a time when the nation lacked many of the strong environmental laws that it enjoys today. We can fire regulatory rockets in behalf of wildlands protection, while Leopold and his contemporaries were armed with bureaucratic BB guns. Leopold could never have predicted in detail the array of environmental laws that strengthen land protection today. But still, on another level, Leopold overlooked a powerful argument in favor of public lands: They exist *for the public*. Everyone can use them, giving all citizens a vested interest in their management. For example, a landowner today may see the protection of wildlife habitat as the highest use of her private forest. She may even allow outdoor enthusiasts to visit her land. But tomorrow, her son the logger may take over, closing gates and cutting trees. In contrast, the government, its policies stabilized by laws and regulations, offers at least some consistent management policy. When James Watt was Interior secretary during the early Reagan years he attempted to change federal land management to its foundations, selling off coal deposits at basement prices, opening offshore waters to oil and gas development, and blocking the acquisition of new park lands. He failed, his hands tied by laws and regulations, his plans shattered against the brick wall of history—although his abrasive personality probably contributed to his failure. Within certain limits, federal management can vary, but by and large the various land agencies have to meet the fairly consistent goals set by Congress, both a curse and a blessing, as discussed below.

One of the most consistent polices has been the preservation of open access to public lands, a sharing among the public of the pleasures of wild places. The administration of public lands by the federal government helps to ensure not only that the few remaining wild places do not fall victim to unbridled development, but also that they do not become the domain of only the rich, that gorgeous vistas do not vanish behind gated walls.

Henry David Thoreau, the New England philosopher and protoconservationist, inadvertently made this point in the mid-nineteenth century. Writing of the region around his home in Concord, Massachusetts, he observed,

> At present, in this vicinity, the best part of the land is not private property; the landscape is not owned, and the walker enjoys comparative freedom. But possibly the day will come when it will be partitioned off into so-called pleasure-grounds, in which a few will take a narrow and exclusive pleasure only—when fences shall be multiplied, and man-traps and other engines invented to confine men to the *public* road, and walking over the surface of God's earth shall be construed to mean trespassing on some gentleman's grounds.

Roughly a century later, Harold Ickes, secretary of the Interior under Franklin Roosevelt, made much the same point about placing stretches of seashore under federal administration:

When we look up and down the ocean fronts of America, we find that everywhere they are passing behind the fences of private ownership. The people can no longer get to the ocean. When we have reached the point that a nation of 125 million people cannot set foot upon the thousands of miles of beaches that border the Atlantic and Pacific Oceans, except by permission of those who monopolize the ocean front, then I say it is the prerogative and the duty of the Federal and State Governments to step in and acquire, not a swimming beach here and there, but solid blocks of ocean front hundreds of miles in length. Call this ocean front a national park, or a national seashore, or a state park or anything you please—I say that the people have a right to a fair share of it.

The very idea of sharing the public lands pervades all of federal land administration, making them a treasure trove for the nation. Public lands can even be divided into two broad categories that reflect the desire to share them fairly. One category is the multiple-use lands, such as national forests and the public rangelands administered by the Bureau of Land Management. These are required by federal law to provide a wide variety of uses, from logging and mining to camping and hunting. This poses an administrative nightmare for those who have to create management plans for a variety of sometimes antithetical purposes. Leopold, in his 1934 essay "Conservation Economics," had this to say on the subject: "The theory is that one and the same oak will grow sawlogs, bind soil against erosion, retard floods, drop acorns to game, furnish shelter for song birds, and cast shade for picnics; that one and the same acre can and should serve forestry, watersheds, wild life, and recreation simultaneously." As Leopold makes clear, many of these uses conflict with one another or with the preservation of biodiversity, making multiple use a hard nut for administrators to crack. Needless to say, the most controversial issues in federal land management focus on the multiple-use lands, such as the fights over logging in the Pacific Northwest and over grazing in the Southwest.

The other broad category is dominant-use lands, such as national parks and national wildlife refuges. The laws creating individual parks and refuges usually spell out their primary or dominant use. A refuge may be created primarily to protect waterfowl, a park to provide recreation for visitors. But "dominant use" does not mean "exclusive use," and so these lands in reality are subject to many uses. Each use is supposed to pass a "compatibility test," which is to say it is not supposed to be an obstacle to achieving the dominant use. Unfortunately, compatibility is often defined loosely, making dominant use a watered-down form of multiple use. National parks, for example, do not allow logging or grazing of livestock, but virtually all permit the development of an array of visitor facilities, from concession stands to gift shops to elaborate lodges that provide parking for hundreds of motor vehicles and rooms for thousands of visitors. These can be as harmful as mining or oil and gas development. For example, in Yellowstone, lodges have been built next to streams heavily used by grizzly bears in search of fish for food, forcing bears and people into contact, which usually spells death for the bears. Wildlife refuges are used for everything from hunting to oil and gas development to dumping of toxic waste water, but the main or dominant use is still ostensibly the protection of wildlife habitat.

Within these two broad categories the federal government administers five different types of protected lands critical to wildlife and to the preservation of biodiversity: national forests, national wildlife refuges, national parks, national marine sanctuaries, and the public domain. These lands encompass a vast array of ecosystems, from mountains to deserts, from oceans to streams. Together with some state lands managed primarily for human recreation—California has established the only state program specifically for the protection of true wilderness—these lands are all that we have for the protection of biodiversity, of wilderness, of the large predators and other creatures that do poorly in proximity to human society. With the exception of designated wilderness areas and national marine sanctuaries, which are new developments, all were established in a bygone era when the concept of land protection itself was new and when no "experts" in the field existed, at least not in any modern, meaningful sense of the term. Even with the best of intentions, early conservationists possessed too rudimentary a knowledge of the natural world to understand precisely what needed to be protected and how to go about it. This led to serious mistakes both in the *what* and the *how* that the protoconservationists finally settled upon. In addition, because land protection in the past was intimately tied to commerical interests, no land was protected with the intention of keeping it untrammeled by humanity and permanently wild. The parks were expected to earn their budgets by catering to visitors. National forests were even more overtly commercial, as were the rangelands administered by the Bureau of Land Management. They were leased to lumber companies, ranchers, miners, and other developers.

This past casts a long, dark shadow within which federal land agencies today blunder blindly about. Consequently, although the pressures put upon wildlands by development have intensified, the methods for protecting wildlands have not changed. Our land-protection agencies remain mired in the nineteenth century, wedded to traditions established long before terms such as *ecosystem* or *biodiversity* had even been coined, before even remote understanding of their implications was possible.

The histories of the agencies show what these traditions are and why they are slow to change. The declining state of our public lands shows what adherence to outmoded concepts has wrought.

CHAPTER 5

The Forest for the Trees: National Forests

If a man walk in the woods for love of them half of each day, he is in danger of being regarded as a loafer; but if he spends his whole day as a speculator, shearing off those woods and making earth bald before her time, he is esteemed an industrious and enterprising citizen. As if a town had no interest in its forests but to cut them down.

Henry David Thoreau

I am convinced that most Americans of the new generation have no idea what a decent forest looks like. The only way to tell them is to show them. To preserve a remnant of decent forest for public education is surely a proper function of government, regardless of one's views on the moot question of large-scale timber production.

Aldo Leopold, 1942

≋

The harmful effects that commercial dominance has had on the public's wild lands are scarcely anywhere more visible than on our national forests. During most of their history, the nation's forests have been protected not for the sake of forests but for the sake of trees—and yet, not really for the sake of trees, but for the sake of lumber. Congress and various presidents created our national forests primarily to serve as sources of wood. Over the years and decades, this has focused a great deal of controversy on the national forests because they have always been coveted by two opposing camps: the preservationists, who believed that forests should be saved unspoiled, and the conservationists, who believed that forests should be put to use as a sustained source of lumber. The latter have had their way since the 1890s, which is ironic given that the first forest preserves were very definitely *preserves* in the strongest sense of the word. To see how this came about, we have to go back to the late nineteenth century, when virtually uncontrolled logging and a rash of forest fires inspired fears of a timber famine.

This was at the end of a long era during which the federal government had given away massive amounts of public land, the sheer contemplation of which must make land developers today sick with envy. In all, the government disposed of 62 percent of its 1.8 billion acres of public domain.

It did this in a variety of ways. An 1840s swamp act authorized the government to give millions of acres of wetlands to the states, provided that the states used funds raised from the sale of these wetlands to finance drainage schemes. Millions upon millions of acres of prairie grassland were given away by a series of homestead acts designed to populate the West. Vast rights-of-way across the West were given to railroad companies. Retrospectively, we can see that the government was giving away broad reaches of wildlife habitat in blissful ignorance of how this affected uncounted ecosystems. Few people indeed would have viewed these areas as anything but wastelands. There were few complaints when the tall-grass prairies disappeared beneath the plow, when the Everglades and other wetlands were slowly mopped up.

Forests were another matter. The rapid decline of the forests had been recorded by keen observers as early as mid-century. In his journal entry for October 10, 1857, Henry David Thoreau wrote, "The smokes from a dozen clearings far and wide, from a portion of the earth thirty miles or more in diameter, reveal the employment of many husbandmen at this season. Thus I see the woods burned up from year to year. The telltale smokes reveal it. The smokes will become rarer and thinner year by year, till I shall detect only a mere feathery film and there is no more brush to be burned." In *The Maine Woods,* Thoreau observed, "The very willow-rows lopped every three years for fuel or power, and every sizable pine or oak, or other forest tree, cut down within the memory of man! As if individual speculators were to be allowed to export the clouds out of the sky, or the stars out of the firmament, one by one. We shall be reduced to gnaw the very crust of the earth for nutriment."

During and after the Civil War, concern about forest survival grew as the nation witnessed the decline of woodlands as a result of the war. Forests were converted into fuel, fortifications, railroad ties, and weapons—a single gun factory required 28,000 walnut trees for rifle stocks. The military burned forests to get them out of the way of maneuvering troops and blew them away incidental to battle. The war also destroyed towns that had to be rebuilt with great quantities of fresh lumber.

No surprise that after the war, fear of a timber famine struck the nation. In the East, for example, a scarcity of fuel wood impressed upon residents the value of the forests they and their ancestors had squandered. The first green movement was born as the nation embarked upon an orgy of tree planting. Railroads planted trees along rights of way and agricultural societies urged farmers to leave some woodlots standing. The seedling mania led to efforts to plant trees even where they did not belong. Congress passed the Timber Culture Act to encourage the sowing of trees on the prairies, and Arbor Day was established by Nebraskans living on the Great Plains.

In 1873 the membership of the American Association for the Advancement of Science heard Franklin Hough speak on the subject of forestry. Although Hough backed tree-planting schemes, he also believed that surviving forests should be better protected. He suggested that the government teach forestry methods to farmers, revise tax laws to discourage clear-cutting, and establish forest reserves. As a result, Hough found himself chairing a special association committee appointed to advise Congress on forest management. Congress subsequently provided $2,000 for the study of forests and timber production, and the secretary of the Interior created a forestry agency as an information service.

And an information service it remained all the way through the 1880s because western timber interests were determined to prevent the creation of a government agency that might put controls on logging. The timber industry was adept at achieving this goal. It had successfully staved off federal efforts at timber protection since 1831, when Congress made it a felony to cut and remove timber from public land. In following decades, the industry threatened and cowed federal agents appointed to protect forests and manipulated homestead laws to legalize timber that was cut illegally. The Department of the Interior and the General Land Office, which alternately adopted responsibility for forest protection, exacerbated the situation by permitting their agents to sell confiscated, illegally cut timber to timber companies. This approach prevailed throughout the 1880s, and timber fell throughout the nation virtually without control. Destruction was so rampant that finally even the most pragmatic politicians had reason for concern. If constraints were not put on the logging industry, the nation would soon be robbed of its only source of native timber.

One of those who came to the rescue was Secretary of the Interior John W. Noble, who persuaded a House and Senate conference committee late one evening to add an amendment to the General Revision Act of 1891, designed to redress various problems posed by earlier land legislation. This broke a rule against the addition of new language in a conference report, an infraction that did not seem to trouble the committee, dominated as it was by several midwestern conservationists. The amendment, called Section 24 was drafted by William Hallett Phillips, a wealthy Washington lawyer. It authorized the president to make forest reserves from "any part of the public lands wholly or in part covered with timber or undergrowth whether of commercial value or not. . . ." In addition, the law provided the reserves with iron-clad protection: They were established as inviolate sanctuaries in which a ban was imposed on logging, mining, trespassing, and hunting.

This was a rider that could not have offended more constituencies had it been designed to do so. Anyone who wanted to build roads or pitch camp or cut trees or hunt deer or mine for gold on forested public lands would have opposed it. Noble and Phillips succeeded in attaching this rider to the bill only by keeping a very low profile and drawing little attention to the new language. The bill moved like a whirlwind through the Senate— time was running out, so debate was limited and the bill was not even printed. Much the same happened in the House. Later renamed the Forest Reserve Act, the bill was enacted with little or no public participation. Some observers sensed that even the majority of those in Congress who had voted on the amendment had no idea what they had done. "Probably no one who read over the bill before it became law understood what the section meant," observed George Bird Grinnell, another leading conservationist of the day and founder a few years before of the National Audubon Society.

What it meant was that the president could unilaterally create forest reserves without public or congressional input. This was strong medicine for a severe environmental illness and one not likely to stand for long, given that it bestowed a great deal of power on the president—something Congress usually disdains to do—and was destined to raise the ire of politically powerful western land interests. But initially no one seemed to recognize the immense discretionary power Congress had dropped into the president's lap—no one, perhaps, except Noble and his colleagues, who moved quickly to implement the law. Noble advised President Benjamin Harrison on the need for forest reserves, and Harrison responded by creating some 13 million acres of them.

However, the Forest Reserve Act was silent on a crucial point: It gave no direction for *how* the reserves were to be managed. As a consequence, livestock were still grazed on the reserves, which struck some conservationists as an offense, including Charles Sprague Sargent, a wealthy Bostonian and director of the Arnold Arboretum at Harvard, and John Muir.

Muir, whose writings had been published in *The Atlantic, Century,* and other popular magazines, was a leader in the forest-protection movement. A Scotsman who had been brought to America as a child, he was raised on a Wisconsin farm by a father whose severe approach to child rearing was sharpened by his addiction to hellfire-and-damnation Christianity. As an adult, Muir escaped to greater freedom and happiness in the mountains and forests of California, where he lived for a time in the area that today is the heart of Yosemite National Park. He also wandered widely in the Sierras, living out-of-doors for months on end and becoming an ardent proponent of forest protection. He believed forests should be permitted to exist for their own sake and for the refuge they offer to people in need of an escape from humanity. He loved trees. "I never saw a discontented tree," he wrote. "They grip the ground as though they liked it, and though fast rooted they travel about as far as we do." In his yearning to protect forests and mountains he helped found the Sierra Club, serving as its first president until his death in 1914. He seems himself to have become embued with some of the qualities of forest trees. Photographs invariably show him gaunt and weathered, his hair tangled and his beard hanging like a matted spray of Spanish moss. His eyes are riveting, pale gray, clear as glass. People who knew him reported that his eyes had always a faraway look.

Muir went with Sargent to Washington, D.C., and lobbied Noble's successor, Hoke Smith, for the removal of sheep from forest reserves. Muir was an inveterate sheep hater because he had seen the severe damage done to Yosemite when more sheep were put into the area than the area could support. He called sheep "hooved locusts." And he won his case with Hoke Smith, who banned sheep from the reserves.

Virtually every such measure designed to protect forest reserves infuriated some politically powerful entity. The logging industry was a natural enemy of the reserves, but even Congress was disgruntled with the 1891 law, because it had put so much power into the hands of the president. At the same time, forest preservationists themselves were not happy. Muir and Sargent, for example, wanted the rules for administering the reserves to be clarified. Thus, virtually everyone with an interest in forests had a reason for wanting the 1891 law revised.

Consequently, in 1894 Sargent and some of his allies succeeded in winning the sponsorship of the National Academy of Sciences for a forest commission that would survey western lands and make recommendations for the management of the reserves. Congress provided the $25,000 needed for expenses, and Sargent set out with five other men to tour the West.

The youngest commissioner was 30-year-old Gifford Pinchot, whose ideas about forestry had been shaped by his studies in Europe, where the original forests had long since been replaced with neat rows of commercial trees, the ground below kept clear of pesky undergrowth. A photograph taken of him in his middle years shows piercing eyes that look straight into the camera and a heavy handlebar moustache that masks what seems a faint smile. He was a protégé of Charles Sprague Sargent, who had helped launch his career. It was a successful launch: In the 1890s Pinchot's voice became increasingly prominent in matters regarding forest reserves.

While traveling with the commission, Pinchot renewed an earlier acquaintance with John Muir, who tagged along as an unofficial observer. The two hit it off well, spending nights talking beside the campfires and under starlight even though Pinchot lacked Muir's enthusiasm for camping out. Pinchot soon showed that he also lacked Muir's enthusiasm for forest preservation, a fact that would cause Sargent to lament later that "it is badly on my conscience that I started his career."

The falling out began with a dispute over who should administer the forest reserves. Muir and Sargent wanted the military to take over on the presumption that this would shelter the forests from political chicanery. The military had been administering the national parks for several years, and Muir thought they were doing a good job. "In pleasing contrast to the noisy, ever-changing management or mismanagement of blustering, blundering, plundering, moneymaking vote sellers," he wrote, "the soldiers do their duty so quietly that the traveler is scarcely aware of their presence. Blessings on Uncle Sam's soldiers. They have done their job well, and every pine tree is waving its arms for joy."

Pinchot, on the other hand, wanted the reserves to be managed by "a forest service, a commission of scientifically trained men," the sort who had maintained Europe's manicured log farms. Moreover, Pinchot wanted the forests cut for wood, although in a manner that would ensure a sustainable supply of timber. This did not mean that forests would be preserved in any meaningful sense of the word. Old forests, in which centuries-old trees no longer produced much new woody growth in any given year, would be cut down and replaced with younger, faster growing trees that could be cropped in years ahead. In effect, the forests would be replaced with tree farms. Pinchot defined his approach as providing the greatest good for the greatest number of people, an approach, however, that Muir and Sargent believed would negate natural values, such as wildlife and wilderness, in favor of lumber.

When the commission published its report, counseling Congress on the management of forest reserves, the Muir/Sargent faction had won: The report called for the removal of sheep and for protection by the military. But the victory, if sweet, was short, and Pinchot soon had his day. It dawned in 1897, when President Grover Cleveland, about to leave office, approved the forest commission's request for nearly 22 million acres of new western reserves. All hell broke loose in the West, where the lumber and livestock industries tightened their grip on their elected officials. They were, as Sargent warned Muir, "out for blood."

Muir tried to hold off the blood letting by writing an article for *Harper's Weekly* in which he made a case for strong forest protection and attempted to undermine both Pinchot's intentions and the popular argument that struggling miners and settlers would be put out of business if locked out of the reserves. "Much is said on questions of this kind about 'the greatest good for the greatest number,'" he wrote, "but the greatest number is too often found to be number one. It is never the greatest number in the common meaning of the term that make the greatest noise and stir on questions mixed with money. . . . Complaints are made in the name of poor settlers and miners, while the wealthy corporations are kept carefully hidden in the background."

All to no avail. Congress had caught the West's anger over forest reserves. In June 1897 Congress passed the Forest Service Organic Administration Act, which declared that the forest reserves existed to serve three purposes: forest protection, the protection of rivers and streams (watershed protection), and establishment of a perpetual source of timber. Never mind that the first two purposes are often excluded by the last one, for the hand of Gifford Pinchot was writ large here. The law also opened the reserves to mining and grazing and suspended all but two of Cleveland's reserves for nine months pending further study.

And to whom did the new McKinley administration assign the task of studying the Cleveland reserves? Gifford Pinchot. As Stephen Fox points out in his excellent book, *The American Conservation Movement: John Muir and His Legacy,* from which much of the material on Muir in this book is drawn,

> Instead of fighting the political reaction [to forest protection] the administration was feeding it by entrusting the reserves to an agent with a known bias toward human use. His old colleagues felt betrayed. "One feeble part of the Forest Commission," wrote Muir to Sargent, "has thus been given the work that had already most ably been done by the whole, without even mentioning what had been done. For a parallel to this in downright darkness and idiotic stupidity the records of civilization may be searched in vain."

Pinchot saw to it that sheep were soon grazing on western reserves and later reported to Congress on the need for managed logging. This was the beginning of the ascendancy of Pinchot's star, and it set the stage for federal forest management down to the present. In 1898 President William McKinley named Pinchot the head of the Agriculture Department's Division of Forestry. The Land Claims Office in the Interior Department continued to control large amounts of forest acreage, and Pinchot lobbied for the transfer of these forests to his division. Looking back on this era during the closing years of his life, Pinchot wrote, "Obviously to bring Uncle Sam's forests and foresters together was nothing more than common sense. Brought together they were going to be, if I had any luck, and when they were I proposed to be the forester in charge."

Pinchot had more than luck on his side. Because he wanted to open the forests to logging, and the land office did not, he won the support of the western timber industry. In 1905, during the second term of Pinchot's friend Theodore Roosevelt, the Forest Reserve Transfer Act moved administration of the reserves from the General Land Office to the Division of Forestry. Pinchot subsequently restructured the division into the Forest Service, serving as its first director. Two years later the forest reserves were rechristened as national forests and, under Pinchot's leadership, were dedicated to the protection of trees—not as wildlife habitat or even as recreation grounds for people, but as sources of lumber. Timber production has ever since dominated Forest Service management of the national forests. And Congress, recognizing a potential pork-barrel project when it sees one, has often at the behest of various state delegations demanded that the Forest Service meet arbitrary levels of annual timber production sometimes so large as to jeopardize forest survival. The Forest Service, ever game for cutting trees and compelled by the congressional hands on its purse strings, has always complied.

Pinchot also set about shaping the psyche of the Forest Service. In 1900 he founded the Yale School of Forestry, which more or less became his private recruiting station. For decades it produced foresters inculcated with the Pinchot-approved idea that ancient, virgin forests were wastelands crowded with trees that were past their prime and begging for replacement with stands of young trees, preferably planted as seedlings selected by foresters for rapid growth.

With little understanding of the complexity of forest biology, early foresters divided trees into useful species and weed or trash species. This concept, which at heart suggested that only tree species suitable for conversion into lumber were worth growing, gripped the Forest Service for at least two generations and guided national-forest management. It is a legacy from Gifford Pinchot that even now dominates the thinking of old-school foresters.

Pinchot had to fight hard to win a place even for his relatively conservative conservation measures. He was opposed throughout his career as Forest Service director by his former allies, the western timber interests who preferred wholesale clearcutting. Some of them, such as Weyerhaeuser, are still among the leading voices in western logging politics. As Pinchot put it uncompromisingly in his posthumously published autobiography, *Breaking New Ground,* "In practice, thanks to lax, stupid, and wrongheaded administration by the Interior Department, the land laws were easily twisted to the advantage of the big fellows, and Western opinion was satisfied to have it so."

These "big fellows" had prospered on the open market, when the government virtually gave away public timber. But the National Conservation Commission, headed by Pinchot, released a three-volume report in 1908 showing how federal policy had gutted the forests and robbed the public. The timber industry, fed by a cheap and seemingly limitless public supply, was wasting vast quantities of timber. A fourth of all standing timber was lost as stumps, trimmings, and broken trunks. Supposedly inferior species were dumped unused. Young trees were destroyed. Mills wasted a third of all wood sawed and a fourth of all wood from final products. Roughly 65 percent of each individual tree was wasted between cutting and final product. In the Great Lakes region, for example, one timber company produced only 160,000 board feet of lumber (a board foot is one foot square and one inch thick) out of trees that should have yielded a million board feet. Every year, loggers cut down an area the size of Maryland—roughly three and a half times more than new growth could replace.

When this information became public, Pinchot started to win the measures he needed to better protect the forests as sources of lumber. Meanwhile, land speculators—even as they attempted to erode public support for national forest regulation by asking "Shall the people or the bureaus rule?"—were making money hand over fist as it became clear that the open market was about to close. A spruce and hemlock tract in West Virginia that was purchased for $12,000 in 1901 sold for $500,000 in 1906. Timber in the South that sold for $4.75 an acre in 1897 commanded $50 an acre 10 years later. Between 1891 and 1909 the price of timber land in the Pacific Northwest rocketed from $2.50 an acre to $115 an acre.

Pinchot fell on bad days in 1910, when William Howard Taft was in the midst of his single-term presidency. Taft had failed to catch the drift of the new conservation movement and had appointed an arch anticonservationist, R. A. Ballinger, as secretary of the Interior. Ballinger supported an effort by J. P. Morgan to grab coal and timber lands in Alaska, Pinchot fought them, and

Taft fired him. Theodore Roosevelt, incensed at this abuse of his close friend, responded by running against Taft in 1912 as an independent candidate, splitting the Republican vote and helping Woodrow Wilson win the election.

This was an explosive event in Pinchot's career, but it was not really the end. He went on to become governor of Pennsylvania and continued to influence federal conservation policies. His prescription for logging as a means for providing the greatest good to the greatest number continued to work relatively well until after World War II. Logging on the national forests was managed under the highest standards of the day, and the wasteful practices of the previous generation were on the wane.

After the war the nation was struck by a housing boom, and demand for lumber went into orbit. The Forest Service responded by intensifying the logging of the national forests, virtually turning them over to private logging companies for minimal prices. This era—perhaps—is only now coming to an end, as we begin to hear the first rumblings of a new movement within the Forest Service, one that seeks to protect ecosystem values and to restore the service's reputation for sound management that was blackened during the excessive decades following World War II. Nevertheless, Forest Service management plans are still dominated by logging, posing a threat to the last large stands of virgin forests outside national parks.

The National Forests Today:
The Greatest Good for the Best Connected

The Forest Service is one of the largest businesses in the United States. Claiming nearly $50 billion in such assets as recreation, timber, and grazing lands, the service, were it an industrial corporation, would rank among *Fortune* magazine's top five, along with companies such as General Motors and IBM. It employs nearly 35,000 people with a yearly budget of about $2.5 billion. It possesses the largest road system in the world, some 350,000 miles with more on the way every year.

Forest Service commercial activities often conflict with the protection of wildlife and national forests. One of the leading activities is energy and mineral development. The 191-million-acre National Forest System includes 45 million acres with potential for oil and gas development. National forests in Montana, Utah, and Wyoming hold an estimated 50 billion tons of coal beneath 6.5 million acres. Some 17 million acres in the Great Basin and Pacific Coast states bear promise for geothermal development. National forests are also sources of such strategically important minerals as chromium, nickel, tungsten, and molybdenum and overlie significant deposits of gold, silver, copper, and phosphate. Private developers have leased roughly 35 million acres of national forest in quest of such minerals.

Under federal law, all mineral extraction operations in the national forests are administered by the Bureau of Land Management in the Department of the Interior. The Forest Service provides guidance to the bureau to reduce damages to surface resources such as streams and forests. In some cases, the Forest Service can block a bureau decision. Under the terms of the 1872 Mining Law, developers can lay claim to federal mineral resources by locating and developing an extraction site and paying a fee of $2.50 to $5 per acre. This is far below fees charged for leases on private land. Independent forestry economist Randall O'Toole has said that Forest Service receipts from mineral extraction could double, to about $600 million, if leases were sold at fair market value. Obstacles to raising lease fees will be discussed in the next chapter.

Mineral, geothermal, and oil and gas development pose some threats to wildlife that live in the national forests. Land clearing, road building, and extraction facilities can drive wildlife out of prime habitat. Oil and gas exploration involves the use of explosives, and some research indicates that explosions can drive away grizzly bears, listed as threatened under the federal Endangered Species Act. Road building opens remote areas to a full range of human intrusion that can lead to declines in wildlife populations. Mining and oil development can pollute rivers and lakes. In essence, mineral development brings the technological world into a large proportion of the few wild places left for wild species.

Nevertheless, because these operations do not involve the destruction of vast acreages they have had relatively restricted impact on wildlife. For example, although a mining plan for a national forest in Montana in the early 1980s risked driving out a local grizzly population, forcing it from limited habitat, the operation did not threaten an entire forest or species.

The two biggest commercial activities in the national forests—livestock grazing and logging—do.

In terms of acres involved, grazing is the second-highest commodity use of the national forests. More than half of the National Forest System, some 104 million acres, is tied up in grazing allotments. This acreage represents only 6 percent of rangelands nationwide—an insignificant amount in terms of the entire livestock industry, but a significant proportion of national forest lands.

Every year, nearly 15,000 livestock raisers set at large on 10,300 national-forest grazing allotments some 2.5 million cattle, sheep, and horses. Most of the grazing allotments are in the West, where private grazing on public lands is a long tradition.

Allotments are leased to individual livestock raisers for 10 years at a time. On private lands, stock raisers pay roughly $8 to $12, sometimes more and occasionally less, per animal unit month (AUM), a unit of measure equal to the amount of grazing a horse, a cow, or five sheep will do over the course of a month. The price per AUM on the national forests averages $1.35. For the past decade, grazing use has stood solid at about 9 million AUMs yearly, putting grazing receipts several million dollars below the roughly $35 million the Forest Service spends yearly on range management and improvement.

Grazing puts the Forest Service into direct conflict with its mandate to protect rivers, streams, and wildlife. Livestock competes with wild species, such as deer and elk, for vital food resources. Wild species are fighting a losing battle in the grazing war because, during hard winter months, wildlife may be left with limited food supplies while livestock receives supplementary commercial feeds. Livestock also tends to be less selective about what they eat than are wild hoofed animals, chewing to the ground an array of plant species that could support a variety of wild herbivores.

Research has shown that elk are reluctant to share pastures with cattle and can be forced off prime grazing range by the presence of livestock. Sheep and cattle can also conflict with grizzly bears in national forests in Wyoming, Montana, Idaho, and Washington State. These forests—which hold a total population of about 1,000 grizzly bears, about 1 percent of the population that thrived all across the West before European settlement—represent the last strongholds of the grizzly bear in the lower 48 states. Putting livestock into them was for many years a death sentence for any hungry grizzly that tried out this new food source. Marauding bears were shot as soon as possible. In recent years, the Forest Service has adopted the policy of moving livestock out of an area in which a grizzly has been spotted, giving the bear priority use of its natural habitat. But grazing in grizzly range still opens the possibility that public-lands ranchers will simply shoot, rather than report, a grizzly found near livestock, an old western tradition called "shoot, shovel, and shut up."

Livestock raisers exacerbate grazing problems by overcrowding the range. In *Reforming the Forest Service,* Randall O'Toole points out that in the late 1980s, grazing on nine of the 11 national forests in New Mexico and Arizona exceeded the feeding capacity of the land by an average of 25 percent. On one national forest, grazing exceeded capacity by 65 percent. But livestock damages more than range. Rivers and streams also are damaged because cattle usually congregate around water sources, trampling grassy stream banks into a muddy soup and clouding the streams with silt. The clouding of the water alters its temperature, its ability to hold dissolved oxygen, and its clarity, making it deadly to many aquatic species. However, because congressional appropriations for rangeland improvements for each national forest are based on the forest's level of grazing, forest supervisors are reluctant to reduce grazing levels.

As a result, only 24 percent of national-forest rangelands are classified as being in good condition, which does not mean much. A rangeland will be classified as good as long as it is producing no less than 60 percent of its ecological potential.

Any difficulties that grazing poses to the national forests could be resolved by sound management, such as putting tight limits on the amount of livestock a rancher can release on an allotment and charging a fair-market fee per AUM. A much stickier and more Gordian conundrum lies behind the Forest Service's biggest business: the sale of timber from the national forests.

National Forests and Ancient Trees

Timber production has been the primary purpose of the National Forest System virtually since its inception. The service was established to bring an end to the ravaging of forest lands by the timber industry and to initiate managed logging. Until World War II, the Forest Service did a relatively good job of controlling the cutting of the national forests, surveying tracts of forest, dividing it up into sale units, and offering these to timber companies for cutting.

In the prewar era, cuts were generally accomplished through selective logging, in which selected trees on any given sales tract were either cut or spared. This helped preserve the integrity of the forest as an ecosystem and limited the loss of wildlife habitat. In their accounts of that period, former foresters look back with nostalgia and pride. They look at the present with disappointment and dismay.

The big change came after the war. As returning GIs stimulated a boom in real estate, the need for lumber in new housing intensified pressures to remove trees from the national forests. Clearcutting, in which loggers cut down every tree on a sales tract, came in vogue. It was fast and cheap, and if any Forest Service staffers complained that it ravaged the land and wrecked streams and fisheries, they could always be reassigned or fired. By 1970 clearcutting accounted for more than 60 percent of all logging operations on the national forests. It also accounted for a wide array of problems, destroying wildlife habitat and affecting the quality of human life. For example, cities downstream from national forests that had been clearcut discovered that erosion of the denuded lands added more silt to streams, which in turn caused urban reservoirs to clog. Staff at water treatment plants found the removal of silt from drinking-water supplies difficult. Wallace Stegner, in a 1989 article in *Sierra* magazine, summed up the shift in Forest Service management: "Once the most respected of federal bureaus, [the Forest Service] has for 30 years been diligently trying to destroy its image as a protector of a vital resource. In the view of many environmentalists, including me, it has become the stooge of the timber industry and an enemy of conservation. . . . It overroads and overcuts, often at a financial loss, at a time when the world should be planting ten trees for every one it cuts down, and perhaps should be cutting no trees at all."

Opposition to clearcutting by local conservation activists and forest advocates led in the 1970s to enactment of federal laws that limited the use of clearcutting to relatively small tracts of less than 100 acres. Congressional intentions were good, but by and large this has led to an era in which national forests are being destroyed piecemeal rather than wholesale. This is particularly evident in the ancient forests of the Pacific Northwest, the last large stands of virgin forest in the nation outside southeast Alaska.

The ancient forests of the Pacific Northwest, including those in Southeast Alaska, are as unlike forests in other parts of the nation as a diamond is unlike a lump of coal. If you enter an ancient forest for the first time with expectations based on experiences in eastern forests, you will be awestruck. Rain-dripping ferns crowd the forest floor, glittering with fragments of sunlight that sift through the high canopy. Bright green mosses lie over rock and fallen tree, soft as velvet to the touch.

Every footfall is hushed by the mosses and the dense undergrowth, and you move soundlessly through the forest, like a phantom merging with shadow and silence. The trees on all sides are so high that you must put your head back and back to find their leaf-hidden crowns. Spread your arms wide apart and still you cannot span their living trunks. Roots greater in girth than a large man twist 20 or 30 feet across moss-covered rocks and among the glistening ferns before sinking again into the damp soil. Fallen trees, moldering trunks so large that you cannot see over them, serve as nutrient-laden platforms for younger trees that grow directly upon them, life upon former life. The younger trees cast roots around the dead trunks in a strange vegetable embrace, a botanical feeding frenzy in which the young roots absorb nutrients from fallen forebears that may have weathered the winds of a thousand winters before dying.

The forest is silent and still but for the rush of a stream tumbling over smooth rock and boulder and around downed trees, the clear water ice blue with the reflected hue of the sky. All else is silence, pungent silence, silence tangible and poised as if part of some great waiting. This undoubtedly was the type of forest Henry David Thoreau had in mind when he wrote in *The Maine Woods*,

> I have been into the lumber-yard, and the carpenter's shop, and the tannery, and the lampblack factory, and the turpentine clearing; but when at length I saw the tops of the pines waving and reflecting the light at a distance high over all the rest of the forest, I realized that the former were not the highest use of the pine. It is not their bones or hide or tallow that I love most. It is the living spirit of the tree, not its spirit of turpentine, with which I can sympathize and which heals my cuts. It is as immortal as I am, and perchance will go to as high a heaven, there to tower above me still.

Even down here on planet Earth the trees have an ethereal grandeur, for when you stand among them you sense that they do what the human body and mind were never meant to do— survive the ages. For them, the Crusades, the Magna Carta, the witchcraft trials of old Salem, the founding of our nation, the Industrial Revolution, and the moon landing are all incidents of a single lifetime. Pre-Columbian natives, Lewis and Clark, and modern hikers may all have sought shelter beneath the same living tree. Even in death they outlast us—a 1,000-year-old tree will take nearly half a millennium to rot away after it dies.

The best of the original forest lay in the lower elevations. In the coastal strip and at the foot of the mountains, trees half a millennium old may stand 300 feet tall, while a tree the same age on higher, colder, rockier mountain elevations may be less than 100 feet tall. Most of the lower-elevation forest has been cut because it stood on private land or in national forests. The fully protected forest tracts lie mainly in high elevations. For example, if you look at a map of Washington State's Olympic Peninsula, you will notice that Olympic National Park lies roughly in the center. Around it are national forests. If you visit the park, you will notice that almost every road or path that leads into it goes uphill. The park contains some of the highest elevations on the peninsula. It shelters some lower forest and a lot of high mountains, rock, and glaciers.

Some 90 percent of the original forests of the Pacific Northwest have been cut. In Oregon, only about 5 percent of the ancient forests have survived. When the forest goes, we lose more than trees. Some 200 vertebrate species live in the forests of the Pacific Northwest, and a quarter of them are most abundant in the ancient forests. Among them are the northern spotted owl, the pine marten, northern goshawk, red-backed vole, marbled murrelet, and pileated woodpecker, the largest surviving woodpecker species on the continent. Among these species, 33 are on the federal Endangered Species List, including the northern spotted owl, American peregrine falcon, and bald eagle.

The tremendous diversity of the ancient forest—with its varied canopy, dense stands of trees, open glades, and intermittently dammed streams—is a biological cornucopia. The ancient forest nurtures a vast array of species, many of which, we have recently learned, cannot survive without it.

For example, biologists discovered only in the past five or six years that three amphibian species—the tailed frog and the

Olympic and Del Norte salamanders—are dependent upon ancient forests. So is a shorebird called the marbled murrelet, whose need for nesting sites in ancient forests was revealed only in the late 1980s. Other species recently discovered to do best in ancient forests include the red-backed vole, red tree vole, hermit warbler, and golden-crowned kinglet.

The ancient forest is important to human interests, too. Logging in the Six Rivers and Shasta-Trinity national forests of northern California led to erosion along streams, so clouding the water that chinook salmon populations declined by 88 percent and steelhead by 60 percent, destroying valuable fishing businesses. Careless logging also threatens urban water supplies, such as the $24 million worth of domestic water that comes from Mt. Hood National Forest each year.

Recognition of the biological importance of ancient forests is new. Only 25 years ago ecology students were taught that old-growth forests were ecologically bereft, with little plant growth on the ground to provide food for wildlife. Better to cut them down, the traditional wisdom went, and let in the sun so that undergrowth could sprout food for deer and other herbivores.

Biologists based this interpretation upon studies of mature second-growth forests. These are the forests that grow after a virgin or ancient forest is cut down. Initially, undergrowth flourishes. Then, after roughly a century, the crowns of the tallest trees spread out until their branches touch, forming a closed canopy that blocks all sunlight. The earth over their roots becomes barren of shrubs and other undergrowth. At this stage, traditional wisdom demanded that the trees be cut again to let in the sun. Forests are generally scheduled to be cut every 80 to 120 years. The interval between cuts is called a rotation. A forest allowed to regrow for 80 years before being cut again is on an 80-year rotation.

The old-growth forests that conservationists talk about are another matter entirely. They are forests that have never been cut. Though their oldest trees may be 1,000 years old the canopy is not closed, but uneven or broken. Some trees thrust above it, and holes created when old giants fall perforate the forest ceiling. This lets in sunlight, stimulating undergrowth. Thus old-growth forest is a diverse ecosystem where open glades are scattered among deep forest into which sunlight filters through the broken canopy.

Three other characteristics distinguish this type of forest. The tops of many of the oldest trees are broken and hollow, offering nesting sites for birds and tree-climbing mammals. Dead trees called snags—traditionally removed from second-growth tracts—stand throughout the forest, hollowed out and rotting but still an important part of the biological community because they offer homes to a range of species from bears to eagles to salamanders. And fallen trees lie scattered over the forest floor, serving as nurse logs to young trees and often blocking the flow of streams, slowing the rush of the water and creating miniature ponds in which fish, insects, amphibians, and other animals find food and shelter, particularly when young.

Despite the new information that biologists have gathered about ancient forests, logging persists in the Pacific Northwest at the rate of about 170 acres per day, some 62,000 acres per year. Satellite studies by scientists from the National Aeronautics and Space Administration's Goddard Space Flight Center in Greenbelt, Maryland, show that these forests are in worse shape than the tropical rainforests of Brazil. In Brazil, the forest is like a vast blanket that has been clipped at the edges. It is a smaller blanket than it once was, but still a blanket. In Washington, Oregon, northern California, and parts of southeast Alaska, private lands are largely cut over and the Forest Service has for years permitted a myriad scattering of clearcuts 40 to 60 acres in size, so that the original forests are like a blanket that has had holes cut all over it until it is little more than a perforated shred of useless fabric. Many of the virgin patches that remain are too small to support wildlife dependent on ancient forests.

How this happened is not hard to imagine, given the vagaries of the logging industry in the past and the lack of data to support concerns about how forest destruction affects wildlife. But why the logging persists even though it is a threat to a wide range of species—most infamously the northern spotted owl—is another matter.

Forget the Northern Spotted Owl

The long and tragic saga of the northern spotted owl has been thoroughly aired in the press for some years now, but still merits discussion here because it foreshadows the likely fate of any wildlife species that conflicts with powerful business interests. The roles played here by industry, Congress, government agencies, private conservation groups, and the presidential administration are typical of their roles in many environmental controversies and reveal why we are losing our last ancient forests and, for that matter, biodiversity across much of the nation.

The northern spotted owl lives primarily in the coastal mountains and the Cascade Range of Washington and Oregon south to northern California, where early in the 1980s it numbered about 2,700 pairs. Logging of ancient forests underlies the bird's decline in recent years, with the population falling at about 0.8 percent yearly in Oregon and 0.45 percent in Washington. Biologists discovered during the past decade or so that although the owl will occasionally use cutover and second-growth forest, it is primarily a denizen of ancient stands, apparently because only there does it find abundant supplies of its primary food as well as nesting and perching sites where it can be safe from the great horned owl, which often preys upon its young.

The northern spotted owl's dependence on ancient forests has put it into direct and heated conflict with human economics. About 20 percent of Washington State's economy and fully half of Oregon's are related directly or indirectly to timber production. A report prepared in the late 1980s by the Oregon governor's Forest Planning Team indicates that in southwestern Oregon, fully 70 percent of the economy depends on the timber industry and that at least 20 percent of revenue in nine western Oregon counties comes from logging. The bulk ofthe timber reaching mills today comes from the public lands, and about 80 percent of the trees cut there—both on national forests and on public domain administered by the Bureau of Land Management—are from ancient forests, the owl's essential habitat.

After biologists in the early 1980s discovered the owl's dependence on ancient forests, management plans for its survival immediately ran afoul of Congress and the Reagan and Bush administrations as well as the Forest Service and the Bureau of Land Management, both of which administer the bulk of the public lands in the Pacific Northwest. In the mid-1980s a federally appointed panel of biologists concluded that the northern spotted owl could not survive in Oregon unless the two federal agencies agreed to protect a total of 400 owl pairs, setting aside 1,000 acres of virgin forest for each pair.

These figures were the bare minimum the panel believed necessary. Nevertheless, the Bureau of Land Management agreed to protect only 300 acres per pair, and the Forest Service agreed to protect only 263 pairs, although the panel asked it to manage for 290 pairs. When later research revealed that the amount of habitat an owl pair requires varies from place to place, reaching a maximum of 4,500 acres per pair, the federal agencies set the maximum for protection at less than 3,000 acres.

Such management failures stimulated private conservation groups to become increasingly involved in the ancient-forest issue. The private groups looked at logging in the Pacific Northwest and concluded that it had to change. During the 1980s loggers were removing about 4.4 billion board feet of lumber yearly from public lands, accounting for fully half of all trees cut in the Pacific Northwest and threatening to wipe out the last ancient forest within a decade or two. However, little or no legal means existed for protecting the vanishing ecosystem, since federal law is not geared to protecting ecosystems or biodiversity. So the private groups turned to the northern spotted owl and the Endangered Species Act, which makes illegal the destruction of habitat vital to listed species.

The owl was clearly a species heading toward extinction, so in 1988 an Oregon chapter of the National Audubon Society requested that the Fish and Wildlife Service list the bird under the Endangered Species Act in the hope that protection of the owl would bring protection to the ancient forests. Such indirect approaches will remain the primary means for ecosystem protection as long as U.S. conservation programs continue to focus on single species rather than on ecosystems.

At that point the feathers hit the fan. Loggers and residents of logging towns came out in opposition to the owl listing, and they were nothing if not strident. In the late 1980s some Pacific Northwest newspapers published spotted owl recipes. In one small logging town on the Olympic Peninsula visitors were greeted at the border with a peculiar display—a mock gravesite marked by artificial flowers and a 10-foot-tall wooden cross upon which were perched owl decoys along with an epitaph reading "The Dreams of Our Children." In one small-town annual parade, a state agency involved in logging entered a float upon which a "hunter" shot at children who dressed like owls and threw feathers into the air. Bumperstickers urging "Save a logger, kill the spotted owl" were common adornments on pickup trucks. Even today in the small logging towns of the Pacific Northwest loggers swagger about in suspenders embroidered with "Spotted Owl Hunter."

Bowing to local resistance and to powerful congressional interests that wanted logging to continue, the Fish and Wildlife Service stalled the listing of the owl. Logging went on apace until several conservation groups sued the Forest Service for ignoring the plight of the owl, and eventually timber sales were reduced to 2.8 billion board feet yearly. Initially, logging continued at owl-threatening levels as the timber industry completed cuts on national forest tracts sold before the reductions.

In March 1989 the Seattle Audubon Society brought a lawsuit against the Forest Service and the Bureau of Land Management, charging them with mismanagement of public lands. Later that year, U.S. District Judge William L. Dwyer issued a preliminary injunction temporarily halting Forest Service timber sales. The timber industry, meanwhile, worked behind the scenes. Its minions in Congress attached a rider to the 1989 Interior Department appropriations bill requiring the Forest Service to set yearly timber sales at 3.85 billion board feet and to exempt the sales from certain types of lawsuits that conservationists might bring. In effect, Congress gave loggers the right to destroy a vanishing ecosystem on public lands and blocked the public from using certain legal avenues to stop it or at least to question the wisdom of doing it. Congress also directed the Forest Service to formulate a spotted owl management plan by September 1990.

But Interior secretary Manuel Lujan, Jr., and Agriculture secretary Clayton Yeutter came up with a different idea, calling for a plan that would "balance our responsibility in preserving the owl and forests while protecting the economic lives of American men and women who live and work" in the Pacific Northwest. A few months later they offered a three-page proposal that urged Congress to insulate logging from environmental laws and to set a cut of 3.5 billion board feet.

While this was going on, the question of the owl's endangered status languished on Fish and Wildlife Service desks. Finally, as the result of another conservationist lawsuit, a federal judge ordered the Fish and Wildlife Service to take action on the listing proposal. Reluctant as the service was to cooperate, it now had no choice. In July 1990 the owl finally was listed as threatened, an official designation meaning that the bird is not yet in danger of extinction but is likely to become so if conditions do not change. This is not as strong a protective category as endangered, which means the species is jeopardized with extinction. In another victory for the owl, the Ninth Circuit Court of Appeals threw out the congressional logging-exemption language two months after the bird was listed.

Then, in February 1991, U.S. District Judge Thomas Zilly, in yet another court case, ruled that the Fish and Wildlife Service could not stop at merely listing the owl but must also delineate the bird's critical habitat, an official designation indicating regions that must be protected. The service responded by proposing as owl habitat some 11.6 million acres lying across northern California, Oregon, and Washington, a figure the service later reduced to 8.2 million acres. Federal agencies in charge of logging on the public lands are legally required to protect this acreage.

These actions were familiar to District Judge Dwyer, who was in the process of ruling on the Seattle Audubon lawsuit. He accused the federal agencies involved of a "remarkable series of violations of the environmental laws" and in May 1991 blocked 80 percent of timber sales offered by the Forest Service, ruling that the service had violated federal law and had failed to address owl protection adequately in its sales plans. He ordered the service to develop new guidelines for owl protection and to finish an environmental impact statement that addressed all possible effects of logging before it began offering more tracts for sale. Logging on Bureau of Land Management forests is also very nearly at a standstill because the judge ruled that the bureau had violated federal law by failing to conduct proper studies of the biological effects of its timber sales. Sales in the Pacific Northwest now stand at about a billion board feet yearly.

Despite court actions and a burgeoning amount of scientific data supporting the biological contentions of forest advocates, the Bush administration sought throughout 1991 and 1992 to circumvent the Endangered Species Act and reopen logging operations. Late in 1991 Interior secretary Lujan convened a special panel, popularly called the God Squad, to determine if the plight of the owl should be ignored in some logging schemes. The panel was convened at the request of Bureau of Land Management director Cy Jamison for a ruling on bureau logging plans on about 4,500 acres of public-domain forest in Oregon.

Creation of God Squads is permitted under recent amendments to the Endangered Species Act as a means for providing flexibility in the law's protective measures. During the entire history of the act—some 20 years of protecting roughly 500 species, with a potential impact on literally tens of thousands of development projects—the God Squad has been convened only twice before. In all other cases in which disputes arose, the issue was solved without such dire recourse. On average, only 25 of the 10,000 permit consultations in which the Fish and Wildlife Service participates each year result in jeopardy decisions, and most are easily resolved by modifications in the proposed project.

Senior officials in the Department of the Interior attempted to manipulate the God Squad's decision. They prevented the Fish and Wildlife Service from presenting evidence which showed that the Bureau of Land Management had failed to consult with it on proposed timber sales and had failed to consider alternatives to the sales, both of which are prerequisites for convening the God Squad. The service's outside counsel in the God Squad deliberations subsequently resigned in a dispute with Interior officials who believed that airing the Fish and Wildlife Service's evidence would harm the Bush administration's position in a pending court case.

The panel ruled in May 1992 that the Bureau of Land Management could continue to sell timber on 1,700 acres encompassing 13 sales tracts. However, the committee upheld the logging ban on 31 other tracts and directed the bureau to abstain from offering any new timber sales until it developed an owl-management plan. This decision is still disputed. Environmentalists soon challenged it in court, and in early 1993 a federal judge ordered a special hearing to investigate whether senior White House officials illegally influenced the panel.

Immediately after the God Squad revealed its decision, Lujan—a marionette of the Bush administration who, despite his position as chief administrator of the Fish and Wildlife Service, called for repeal of Endangered Species Act protections—offered the public not one but two federal owl recovery plans. One was the official plan formulated by the Fish and Wildlife Service and calling for protection of 5.4 million acres, a bit more than half the amount the service designated as critical habitat in its revised figure for 1991 and only a pale ghost of the 11.6 million originally outlined. Lujan's alternative called for protecting only 2.8 million acres, a figure so low that the Bush administration acknowledged that it would lead to the owl's extinction within a century, to say nothing of the 32 other endangered species that share the ancient forest with the owl. However, the Endangered Species Act blocked implementation of the Lujan plan.

Other players continued to step onto the stage. In mid-1992 Congress was considering two ancient-forest bills. One would establish a 6.8-million-acre owl reserve, the other would protect about 9 million acres. At about the same time, the Forest Service was drawing flak from its own staff. A group of present and former service employees told a news conference in March 1992 that the nation's ancient forests were being devastated by current logging policy. They said that when they tried to expose service abuses, such as logging plans in nesting areas of federally listed bald eagles and spotted owls, they were harassed by superiors whose "reprisals were vicious, vindictive, and immediate" according to Francis Mangels, a biologist with the Shasta-Trinity National Forest in northern California.

In summer 1992 President George Bush, during a visit to Washington State, offered a pronouncement on the spotted owl controversy. He stood at a podium outdoors, surrounded by an admiring crowd from the logging community. On a table beside him tottered two tall stacks of documents which he indicated were reports on the spotted owl and its habitat. Most of these reports concluded that cutting of the ancient forest had to stop if the owl were to survive. On the other hand, Bush had concluded that the *studies* had to stop. It was time, he said, to put human needs before the owl and get back to logging the ancient forests. This is peculiarly ironic because the owl's survival is threatened precisely because we have *always* put human desires, whims, and interests—to say nothing of needs—ahead of the owl. Had we been attending to the owl's needs all along, the bird would not be in trouble. The president seemed to suggest that the northern spotted owl is some kind of biological backslider, determined to sink into extinction despite all the care we have lavished on it. Nevertheless, to be certain that he got what he wanted, the president held up a hostage: the Endangered Species Act itself.

The act comes up for reauthorization every few years, a process during which Congress can delete certain protections, exempt certain listed species from protection, or even throw the entire act out the window. At the time of the president's remarks, made during the presidential campaign, the act was slated for reauthorization. Bush told the cheering crowd he would veto any form of the act that Congress put on his desk that failed to include approval of logging despite damage to the owl.

The Bush administration's extinction plan for the northern spotted owl was merely a diversion. By focusing attention on the owl, the Bush administration was attempting to make reductions in logging seem ridiculous. But the owl was not then and is not now the real issue. We can forget the spotted owl. The real issue is the ancient forest and all that it entails, and nothing about that issue is ridiculous.

The Bush administration justified its actions in the name of jobs. If logging were stopped, according to the administration's trickle-down theories of wildlife conservation, thousands of jobs would be lost, although how many no one has yet said with any authority. Perhaps 15,000. Perhaps 61,000. If anything in the Pacific Northwest is endangered, the administration said, it is jobs.

In the field of endangered species management, months, and more often years, of study go into determining if a species is endangered. In the Pacific Northwest, before we begin designating endangered jobs, we should similarly study those jobs to determine if they really are endangered and, if so, why.

Logging and lumber-mill jobs have indeed been vanishing in recent years in the Pacific Northwest. In the early 1980s automation reduced by 35 percent the number of mill workers needed to produce a million board feet of timber. On average, a mill that in

1978 turned out 2,000 board feet of plywood veneer per employee was now turning out 10,000 board feet and using 13 percent fewer employees to do it. During the first six years of the 1980s wood-processing jobs in Washington and Oregon dropped from 133,400 to barely 100,000, while production went from 11.2 billion board feet to 12.3 billion board feet. Within the next 50 years, new technology may chop away another 26,500 jobs. Also, mills that presently can process only the large trees that come from ancient forests could be retooled to accept the smaller second-growth trees now growing on private and state lands. This would open up jobs, and federal lands would not even have to be part of the program. Shifting the emphasis of mill work away from the preparation of logs for shipment and toward the production of finished lumber or furniture would, according to one study, open up 13,400 jobs in Washington and Oregon.

If we protected what remains of the ancient forest, we would be adding not only to the biological diversity of the Pacific Northwest, but also to its economic diversity. The ancient forests are a prime drawing card for a major industry, tourism. Tourists do not visit Washington or Oregon to look at clearcuts or to camp beneath tree stumps. They come for the ancient forests, and those who come add more than $6 billion yearly to the economies of Washington and Oregon. Recreational use of national forests in these states and California account for almost 100 million visitor days a year. Tourism is an industry that will survive as long as the ancient forests do. In the long run, the greatest good for the greatest number lies in protecting ancient forests for all generations present and future, not in squandering the last of them in our time. While the cutting of the remaining ancient forests may have seemed to George Bush a solution to his reelection woes, it is not a solution to the economic ills of the average logging family. If we continue to liquidate the ancient forests, then the loggers will soon vanish anyway because they, like the spotted owl, will lose the habitat that supports them. Once the last of the ancient trees are cut, the mills and loggers dependent on them will become extinct. In their wake will lie a state studded with the ruins of clearcuts.

Beyond the Pacific Northwest

The concerns focused on the ancient forests of the Pacific Northwest are complex, but they are not unique. In the Tongass National Forest, just up the coast from Washington State in Southeast Alaska, lies another ancient-forest controversy. This is the largest surviving stretch of ancient forest in the United States. The Tongass covers some 17 million acres, but about 11 million acres are unforested rock and ice or are too poorly forested for logging. Of the remaining 6 million acres, the Forest Service has designated 4.6 million as good commercial forest. About 1.6 million acres are protected. Another 1.75 million have been slated for logging, with the rest to follow sometime in the future. In late 1991 the Forest Service proposed to raise the annual timber cut from the 1980s yearly average of 295 million board feet to a whopping 418 million board feet.

About 100,000 acres of the Tongass are considered among the finest ancient forests on the continent. The Forest Service refers to them as high-volume timber and plans to cut 91,000 of those acres. In all, the Forest Service plans to clear cut 91 percent of the high-volume timber and 77 percent of all good commercial timber lands even though the cutting will cause serious declines in local wildlife. For example, the best scientific evidence suggests that logging will reduce deer populations by 75 percent. Some 10,000 bald eagles of breeding age live in the Tongass, and logging will destroy 90 percent of their nesting and perching sites. Birds that nest in tree cavities—about 20 percent of all bird species in the forest, from owls to woodpeckers—will decline if loggers fail to leave snags. Salmon will probably decline, as will the pine marten. Southeast Alaska is home to the greatest concentration of grizzly bears in the United States, and the bears usually make their winter dens in the ancient forest. Wolves in the region may decline, too, as deer dwindle. Logging plans for the area around the Lisianski River on Chichagof Island could destroy the pristine values of the stream, which provides important habitat for deer, bears, and waterfowl and offers local people nearly $500,000 worth of salmon yearly.

Similar examples abound throughout the nation. As reported by the Sierra Club in autumn 1992, logging is slated in the Shoshone National Forest, outside Yellowstone National Park, in a region heavily used by grizzly bears, which are federally listed as threatened. Shoshone administrators are also planning to allow drilling for oil within grizzly habitat. One of the forest's staff biologists resigned in 1991 because he believed his superiors were ignoring the grizzly's needs. In the South, pine forests essential to the survival of the red-cockaded woodpecker, an endangered species, are still falling to loggers. The woodpeckers nest in large family groups, drilling cavities in pines at least 60 years old. Younger trees are worthless to the woodpeckers. The tree of preference is the long-leaf pine, which must be almost a century old before the birds can use it. As old pines are logged off southern lands, the red-cockaded woodpecker has declined. Across the South, from the Atlantic to eastern Oklahoma, only 10,000 survive. They are following in the footsteps of the ivory-billed woodpecker and thick-billed parrot, species that vanished from the United States when their forest habitat was destroyed.

Accounting for Lost Forests

The service's administration of logging on the national forest system produces in excess of 9 billion board feet of timber yearly. The return to the taxpayer? According to the Forest Service, about $650 million yearly. According to a 1991 assessment of Forest Service income made at the request of Representative Mike Synar, an Oklahoma Democrat who chairs the House Government Operations Subcommittee on the Environment, a loss of nearly $200 million dollars yearly. Why the difference? The congressional assessors contend that the service's figure includes millions of dollars that pass out of Forest Service coffers and into other hands. Among these are the 25 percent of receipts paid out to logging counties in lieu of funds the counties presumably lose because public lands are not taxable, the $80 million of overhead for federal maintenance of logging roads, the $24 million needed for boundary surveys, and the $60 million that went into insect and disease control (an expense inflated by logging because logged forests tend to be more susceptible to insects) as well as fire protection, building maintenance, and other administrative expenses. It also included $575 million budgeted for reforestation, road building, and other expenses, some of which the Forest Service amortizes across unrealistically long time spans.

For example, roads are amortized over as much as 240 years, even though the average logging road is only good for about a tenth of that time. Road building is a vexing issue even beyond mere finances. It not only drains immense amounts of federal funding—roughly $300 million yearly—but also poses a serious threat to wildlife by providing easy access into remote areas for loggers, hunters, oil and gas developers, miners, hikers, backpackers, off-road-vehicle enthusiasts, and others whose presence can force wildlife out of large segments of habitat. The problem grows by leaps and bounds every year. The Forest Service logging-road system is already eight times the size of the interstate highway system, and the service adds an average of 4,500 miles of road to it every year.

When all expenses are factored in, we discover that in 1990 only 15 national forests made money. Thus, what the American public receives in return for threats to listed species, the loss of entire ecosystems, degradation of streams, erosion of soil, devastation of tourist sites, and a reduction in biodiversity is a bleeding of tax dollars. Logging companies must come out of all this quite nicely, however, since they are the strongest supporters of this seemingly indefensible status quo.

Several factors compel the Forest Service to continue logging the public lands despite all the costs. Perhaps foremost among them is tradition. The Forest Service was founded as a logging agency. Any shift away from logging is, for old-style foresters, a betrayal of history. Moreover, the jobs of some 15,000 Forest Service staff depend upon logging.

Short-term economic considerations are also a factor. Forest Service administrators favor logging whenever their accountants indicate that the present value of national forest trees as lumber exceeds for the foreseeable future all other possible values, such as recreation or the preservation of endangered species.

In addition, service officials recognize that cutting forests in short rotations supports lumber mills that depend on public trees, while cut reductions cause the mills and surrounding communities serious economic setbacks.

Moreover, traditional foresters are obsessed with growing wood, not trees, and they want to do it at maximum rates. Since young trees produce the most wood in any given period of time, keeping forests young is the quickest way to maximize timber production.

The New Forest Service

The Forest Service is taking some new approaches to the logging issue. In Washington and Oregon, for example, the service has sought to diversify local economies by helping develop recreational opportunities in the region's national forests. But old patterns of forest use still affect this program. Russell Sadler, an author and commentator from Eugene, Oregon, remarked at a foresters conference in late 1991 that economic diversification "is jeopardized by new forest-management plans that still make timber supply the dominant, if reduced, use of the forest, often at the expense of the one alternative these communities have to begin their diversification, tourism in its varied forms."

More promising, perhaps, is a new ecosystem-management scheme outlined by Forest Service chief F. Dale Robertson in a memo he sent on June 4, 1992, to all regional foresters and station directors in which he declared, "we have been courting the ecosystem approach [to forest management] for 3 years and we like the relationship and results. Today, I am announcing the marriage and that the Forest Service is committed to using an ecological approach in the future management of the National Forests and Grasslands."

Ecosystem is a term of rather loose meaning that biologists use somewhat randomly, as has been done on occasion in this book. An ecosystem is any complete biological community and encompasses such factors as distinct associations of plant and animal species, type of terrain, amount of rainfall, and so on. The tropical rainforest, the temperate rainforest of Oregon, and the pine barrens of New Jersey are ecosystems. A pond is an ecosystem. If the pond is a prairie pothole, it lies in a prairie ecosystem. The human mouth is an ecosystem for some microbes.

Ecosystem management implies a concern for all living things, their interrelationships, and their habitat, with no attempt to isolate or emphasize one species over another. The Forest Service could not claim to manage forests as ecosystems while cutting them down or engaging in practices that wipe out species, reducing biodiversity. The promise that the service is planning to undertake an ecosystem approach to land management is thus heartening. Until you read the fine print.

A memo to field staff from Forest Service headquarters, titled "Questions and Answers on New Ecosystem Management Policy," admonishes staff to keep in mind that

> Ecosystem management is the means to an end, not an end in itself. Ecosystem management is the means we use to meet the goals specified in our programs and plans. . . . The place that the production of timber takes is and will be determined through the forest planning process given in the National Forest Management Act and its regulations. . . . We can produce timber on many acres at the same time we are producing the other benefits. And since the trees grow back, the Forest as a whole can always look the same. . . . Some uses such as wilderness and other special disignation *[sic]* do not allow for timber harvest but on most land, multiple benefits can be had simultaneously.

Just like always, it seems.

More ominous is Robertson's "Attachment 2" to his June 4 memo. It is titled "Reduce Clearcutting on the National Forests," which has a promising ring to it.

According to Attachment 2, clearcutting will be "limited to areas where it is essential to meet forest plan objectives and involve one or more of the following circumstances." Then follows a list of seven circumstances, such as research needs, or rehabilitation of newly planted stands that have grown poorly, or control of insect infestations. The circumstance at the top of the list is "to establish, enhance, or maintain habitat for threatened, endangered, or sensitive species." You can just about picture it. Several Forest Service bureaucrats meet with some timber-company representatives, note that they really would like to reduce clearcuts but, by God, they just have to plan a few anyway "to establish, enhance, or maintain habitat for threatened, endangered, or sensitive species." Preposterous as this sounds, the Forest Service already engages in this sort of subterfuge. Insect control is already used to rationalize clearcuts. For example, economist Randall O'Toole, in his statistic-laden book *Reforming the Forest Service,* cites cases in which the Forest Service justifies clearcutting for the control of mistletoe and spruce budworm even though both pose little threat to forest survival or can be controlled with cheaper and less damaging methods. Spruce budworm can help remove weak trees from forests and can even improve the growth of ponderosa pine on the eastern slopes of the Cascade Mountains by eliminating less valuable competitors.

Circumstance number 5 is particularly disconcerting: "To provide for the establishment and growth of desired trees or other vegetative species that are shade intolerant." Presumably, cutting down ancient forests to allow for the establishment of fast-growing pine farms would meet this condition.

Many signs suggest that the Forest Service is tenaciously, if deceptively, pursuing business as usual. This offers little or no promise for better management of the national forests and better protection of ancient forests and biodiversity. To achieve these goals, we need to adopt an entirely new approach to Forest Service administration, casting out traditional forest management, which is laying waste to forests nationwide and threatening to reduce biodiversity with little concern for future generations.

The use of national forests for timber production represents a failing form of socialism that takes a resource of value to all Americans and reduces it to a commodity for the profit of a tiny handful of timber-company executives and the roughly 100,000 people, including some 15,000 forestry professionals in the Forest Service, that according to the service are supported nationwide by national-forest timber. As R. W. Behan of the Northern Arizona University School of Forestry puts it, "Most of the multiple uses are *private* uses of public lands, and I believe the time has come to consider, after all, a profound shift. We need to begin emphasizing the *public* uses of the public land, and to begin winding down the private uses." For now, says Behan, "Through almost unrestricted access—encouraged and provided by the multiple-use/sustained-yield philosophy—we are using the public lands largely, primarily, for the pursuit, acquisition, and enhancement of private wealth."

Loggers and timber-industry executives can continue to pursue, acquire, and enhance private wealth on private forest lands. Public lands, the only lands on which forest protection can be made a primary goal, should be taken out of the logging business.

This means reorganizing the Forest Service, replacing old-style, timber-oriented foresters with a new breed of foresters who believe that forest ecosystems need to be managed and protected for their wild values, for the sake of biodiversity. These people are exemplified by 30 Forest Service entry-level staff from the Pacific Northwest, most of them wildlife biologists, who signed a letter to Dale Robertson declaring that

> We feel hard commodity targets [timber-production goals] are incompatible with integrated ecosystem management. Commodity outputs from the National Forests must be determined after the health and viability of the ecosystem are best protected. . . . We believe that one of the best first steps to preserve options for future generations is to eliminate commodity targets. We want to be part

of the Forest Service family which successfully adapts to today's challenges.

Eliminating timber sales is not as drastic a step as it might seem. More than 70 percent of U.S. timber lands are privately owned. Only 15 percent of U.S. timber comes from the national forests. Cutting off the supply, which could be done gradually over a period of years to ease potential disruptions, would have minimal effect.

Getting the government out of timber sales will stem the loss of 200 million federal dollars yearly. While not a bad beginning, the real order of business for this sweeping change is restoration of the forests while turning a profit. The key to achieving this is recreation.

Since World War II, national forests have been used increasingly for recreational purposes. The types of wild places offered to the American public by the national forests are themselves a commodity in decline. Keeping the national forests both wild and available to recreational users—as opposed to loggers and other developers—is clearly the greatest good for the greatest number. It is also the most remunerative approach to national-forest management.

O'Toole makes this point in *Reforming the Forest Service* when he emphasizes how logging counterproductively competes with more profitable recreational activities. Recreation on forests near Yellowstone National Park, he writes, produces four times the income brought in by logging and grazing and provides 16 times as many jobs as timber production. Yet timber and grazing budgets on these forests are consistently four times greater than funds for recreation.

The Forest Service can collect recreational fees only for activities that require development of some sort, such as restrooms and campgrounds. O'Toole has calculated that if recreational fees could be broadened to include even a mere third of the recreational values claimed by the Forest Service, receipts would exceed logging and grazing income throughout most of the national forest system. "Nationally, recreation and wildlife receipts [could] total over $900 million per year, as opposed to the $30 million now being collected," he writes.

In the matter of increased funds from recreation, O'Toole is backed by the Forest Service itself. A recent agency survey revealed that national-forest users would be willing to pay fees for many activities now permitted for free, including a fee of up to $30 a day for big-game hunting. Figures in the Forest Service's 1990 planning report indicated that if it were allowed to charge such fees, the service could generate in excess of $5 billion yearly. This would allow the service to fund its entire budget without additional funds, and entirely in the absence of logging. If private lands cannot support the work force now employed by the wood-products industry, then some of this money could be put into a program for retraining the work force and locating new jobs.

To shift from logging to recreation, generating a net profit rather than loss for the Forest Service, would require a revamping of the laws that govern national forest management, and this requires congressional action. That, in turn, calls for a massive lobbying effort on the part of forest partisans—a very long-term, hard-fought effort, because the logging industry, with all its clout, will attempt to block the way. The only stronger force is an aroused public.

Reorienting the management emphasis of the Forest Service may be only a beginning. We need to consider even broader measures if the nation is to reclaim its vanishing wild places. Before we do that, several chapters in the future, we will give the Forest Service a much deserved rest and look at another multiple-use agency, the Bureau of Land Management. This chapter already has discussed the bureau's role in forest issues. The next chapter looks at how bureau management is affecting western rangelands, where ranchers and miners, like the logging industry, are paying bargain-basement fees for the right to treat public lands as if they owned them.

CHAPTER 6

Home, Home on the Range: Public Lands in the West

꙳

In the National forests a genuine and frequently successful effort has been made to prevent overgrazing
by careful regulation, but on the public range outside
of the forests no control of any kind is exercised. First
come, first served. This lack of regulation causes each
stockman to try to get as much stock as possible on
the range at the earliest possible moment, resulting in
continuous and disastrous overgrazing.

Aldo Leopold, 1924

Current livestock grazing activity on Bureau of Land
Management allotments in hot desert areas risks
long-term environmental damage while not generating grazing fee revenues sufficient to provide for adequate management. The General Accounting Office
found evidence of damage occurring on BLM lands as
well as evidence of livestock grazing's adverse impacts
on several wildlife species. Some damaged lands may
take decades to recover if they recover at all.

U.S. General Accounting Office report, "BLM's Hot
Desert Grazing Program Merits Reconsideration,"
November 1991

≋

Among the red-rock mesas and sun-cracked treeless plains of the Far West, among the ancient firs and misty ice fields of the Far North, lies the last of the public domain, administered by the Bureau of Land Management. These lands include almost every major ecosystem found beyond the Mississippi River, from the hot deserts of the Southwest to the lush rainforests of the Pacific Northwest to the glaciers of Alaska. The importance of these lands to wildlife was outlined in the *Audubon Wildlife Report 1987:*

> The public lands protect essential and rare fish and wildlife habitats. Eighty-five percent of desert bighorn sheep in the United States reside on the public lands. The 25-million-acre California Desert Conservation Area is home to more than 700 species of flowering plants, including 217 species found nowhere else in the world. The Snake River Birds of Prey Natural Area in Idaho harbors the densest nesting population of birds of prey in the world. BLM lands support 122 federally listed endangered and threatened species of plants and animals, as well as hundreds of species under consideration for future listing. The bureau also manages vital remnants of riparian [river] and aquatic ecosystems on which a majority of wildlife species depend.

These lands are important not only because of the wide range of wildlife habitat they encompass—other protected lands also include a variety of ecosystems—but because of their tremendous acreage. The Bureau of Land Management administers more land than any other federal agency. National parks include some 75 million acres, national wildlife refuges more than 90 million, and national forests 191 million, but the public domain encloses some 270 million acres—about 12 percent of the entire United States and roughly 60 percent of all lands under federal jurisdiction. In addition, the bureau is in charge of mineral resources lying under another 300 million acres administered by other federal or state agencies or in private ownership.

To understand the origins of this robust but little-noted agency, we once again must return to the nineteenth-century and its disposal of the public domain. The public domain dates to October 10, 1780, when the Continental Congress made membership in the new federal union contingent upon donation to the federal goverment of western lands claimed by various colonies. These western lands had been bestowed upon some colonies by royal charter. For example, Massachusetts once claimed lands now lying in Michigan and Wisconsin, and Virginia extended to the Mississippi River. Other colonies, notably Maryland, had no western lands and believed that colonies owning them had an unfair advantage. The Maryland delegation to the Continental Congress suggested that since all the colonies had fought in common, these unsettled lands should be held in common. Congressional agreement with this plea subsequently made the federal government the largest single land-holding body in the new nation, with some 230 million acres at its disposal.

Thomas Jefferson's closure of the Louisiana Purchase in 1803 doubled this amount, stretching the nation from sea to sea and putting under federal administration most of the present United States, with the exception of the Southwest and the 13 original colonies. According to federal law, the government was supposed to dispose of all public domain "for the common benefit of the United States." The 1785 Northwest Ordinance set the rules for dividing up and selling the land, and in 1812 Congress created the General Land Office within the Treasury Department to handle the sale.

In the East, the public domain was quickly disposed of because the land was well watered. Settlers were eager to clear off the forest and replace it with crops. The West was a different matter. The Great Plains was called the Great American Desert. The Southwest, once it was relinquished by Mexico, was even drier. Daniel Webster summed up the prevailing attitude about the West in 1861 when he said, "What do we want of that vast and worthless area, that region of savages and wild beasts, of wind, of dust, of cactus, and prairie dogs? To what use could we ever hope to put those great deserts and those endless mountain ranges, impenetrable and covered to their base in eternal snow?"

The western regions still remain sparsely populated, although not for lack of effort on the part of the federal government. Various homestead acts gave parcels of land to settlers in efforts to encourage development of the West. But these give-aways never provided homesteaders with more than a few hundred acres. This was too little land for successful ranching or farming. Such small parcels, unless on rivers, lacked the water needed for survival. This led to a peculiar dicing up of the West. When a rancher set out to homestead, he would lay claim to his acreage along a river, where he could control the water supply. Since the homestead acts rarely allowed for claims in excess of 200 acres—too small for a profitable herd—the rancher would graze his livestock on the surrounding public domain, which no one wanted because it was too arid.

What happened next is neatly summarized in the *Audubon Wildlife Report 1985:* "Belonging to no one, the public lands belonged to everyone, and each rancher tried to get as much production out of them as possible. After the Civil War and the expansion of the railroads into the West, livestock use of the western lands suddenly burgeoned, and by the 1870s reports of extensive overgrazing began to emerge." Indeed, lands once covered in grass belly deep to a horse were suddenly barren. Streams began to dry up as the natural water flow of arid regions was disrupted by overgrazing. "By the early 1900s," continues the *Wildlife Report*, "even many stockmen, who generally object to government interference, began to call for some kind of federal intervention in range management in order to reduce conflicts over the use of the range."

Not everyone involved in the western-land issue agreed that

government action was necessary. Homesteaders and states' rights advocates fought off federal intervention. Their resolve was hardened in 1906 when the Forest Service, in a move that must have put a smile on John Muir's hirsute visage, not only reduced its grazing levels but raised its grazing fees. A large segment of the western populace was not about to let the goverment establish similar restrictions on the public domain. And so grazing reforms had to wait some 30 years before they could be initiated in even rudimentary form.

This began in the 1930s when a congressionally authorized grazing experiment in Montana, in which a local stockman's association grazed cattle under Interior Department direction, showed that grass production doubled within three years after well-regulated grazing was initiated. This promise of better grazing through proper management drew the attention of grazing-reform advocates in Congress. And then a more negative message soon riveted congressional focus. In 1934 drought struck the West, heralding the Dust Bowl and sending clouds of topsoil from the plains all the way to the Capitol Building in Washington, D.C.

Although most of the dust could be blamed on farming schemes that plowed millions of acres of arid land, Congress—working as ever in mysterious ways—decided it was time to do something about the grazing issue. The leader in this movement was Edward I. Taylor, a representative from Colorado who had long and uncompromisingly opposed federal control. As he observed the ravaged western range, however, his views slowly began to change. He concluded finally that the widespread ecological degradation rampant throughout the West was too great a problem for individual citizens or even the states to solve. As he would write later

> On the Western Slope of Colorado and in nearby states I saw waste, competition, overuse, and abuse of valuable range lands and watersheds eating into the very heart of the Western economy. Farmers and ranchers everywhere in the range country were suffering. The basic economy of entire communities was threatened. There

was terrific strife and bloodshed between the cattle and sheep men over the use of the range. Valuable irrigation projects stood in danger of ultimate deterioration. . . . The livestock industry, through circumstances beyond its control, was heading for self-strangulation.

And so in early 1934 the Coloradan introduced the Taylor Grazing Act, and on June 28, 1934, Congress enacted it "to stop the injury of the public grazing lands by preventing overgrazing and soil deterioration; to provide for their orderly use, improvement, and development; to stabilize the livestock industry on the public range."

Under the terms of the new law, the secretary of the Interior could create grazing districts that ranchers could use only after purchasing federal grazing permits. Although preference in issuing the permits was given to nearby ranchers, settlers, or owners of water rights, even they had to follow federal guidelines on when and how much livestock could be grazed. Fees from the permits were to be used in part for range improvements.

This seemed to offer some promise for range recovery, especially in regions of the Southwest where grasslands had been reduced literally to deserts. But then, ironically, Congress put a rancher in charge of the new Division of Grazing. His name was Farrington Carpenter, and he created district advisory boards that would oversee management of the public grazing lands. Congress ratified these boards in 1939 amendments to the Taylor Grazing Act, along with a requirement that board membership include—who would you imagine?—one wildlife representative and five to 12 ranchers.

Where this would lead is fairly obvious. Although the Division of Grazing, renamed the Grazing Service, was headed from 1939 to 1946 by former Forest Service land managers who wanted to cut back on grazing, little or no progress was made. The livestock industry and its grazing advisory boards fought vigorously and successfully against the administrators. The House Appropriations Committee was also hammering the administrators for failing to collect enough grazing fees to cover their costs and for knuckling under to the livestock industry to the extent of letting cattle and sheep ranchers set fees. Caught between two implacable forces, the administrators soon had their budget cut by nearly 70 percent. When the Grazing Service sought to increase fees, livestock-industry allies in Congress, notably Senator Patrick McCarran of Nevada, blocked them. Finally, the Grazing Service had to seek funds from the only likely source—the grazing advisory boards. Here stood a set of conditions unlikely to promote progress on the issue of over-grazing.

Matters deteriorated further in 1946 when the Truman administration introduced a bill in Congress for reorganization of federal agencies. McCarran used the bill as an excuse for merging the Grazing Service with the General Land Office, creating a new agency called the Bureau of Land Management. McCarran rightly guessed that grazing administration in the underfunded agency would simply become neglected. From this victory, Mc-Carran and his livestock-industry allies went on in 1947 to introduce in Congress legislation designed to turn over the 142 million acres affected by the Taylor Grazing Act to the 13 western states, which would then sell the land to the ranchers at bargain-basement prices—roughly the nine cents an acre suggested by the livestock industry. When conservationists got wind of this they took the issue to the press, and public outcry quashed the plan. However, the same impulse survives today in the advocates of the so called Wise Use Movement which seeks to put the public domain under private control for unbridled exploitation. This was also the mentality behind Interior secretary James Watt's attempts during the early Reagan years to sell off cheaply vast amounts of resources on the public domain.

During its first 15 years, the Bureau of Land Management hired increasing numbers of range-management professionals, but progress in range reclamation remained slow as ranchers, who had heavy political clout, resisted change. Nevertheless, change was on the way. In 1969 Congress enacted the National Environmental Policy Act, described by wildlife law-specialist

Michael Bean in *The Evolution of National Wildlife Law* as "the most comprehensive, the best known, the most written about, and surely the most litigated federal environmental statute ever enacted. It may also be among the most important federal statutes for the protection of wildlife, yet it never so much as mentions the word 'wildlife.'"

Usually known by its acronym, NEPA, the law among other things requires federal agencies to conduct studies of all "legislation and other major Federal actions significantly affecting the quality of human life." For example, if the U.S. Army Corps of Engineers undertakes construction of a dam, NEPA requires the Corps to study the environmental impacts of several different alternatives to dam construction, including various modifications of the proposed plan and even a no-action plan in which no dam is built. The results of such studies are published in documents called environmental impact statements, which outline the proposed action, alternatives to it, and the likely environmental effects imposed by each. This serves several purposes. It helps avoid serious environmental harm, including pollution and other threats to people. It helps determine what measures might be taken to complete a project while avoiding environmental and social damage. And, by compelling an examination of various alternatives to a given project, it helps stimulate agencies to choose the best, least harmful, and most efficient courses of action.

Although NEPA's focus of concern is human life, the law does include protection of wildlife, as several court decisions have made clear. As one judge ruled in a 1972 case testing NEPA's authority, "Any action that substantially affects, beneficially or detrimentally, the depth or course of streams, plant life, wildlife habitats, fish and wildlife, and the soil and air 'significantly affects the quality of the human environment.'"

To comply with the act, the bureau in the late 1970s produced a single environmental impact statement covering its entire program on some 170 million acres of range. The Natural Resources Defense Council, a New York-based environmental group that specializes in legal matters, sued the bureau, arguing that a single statement was inadequate. The court agreed, and in the end the bureau was compelled to produce 141 environmental impact statements. The bureau is now more likely to consider environmental effects, including effects on wildlife.

Bigger changes arrived at about the same time. In 1976 Congress passed the Federal Land Policy and Management Act which, among other things, required the bureau to work more diligently for wildlife protection. For example, the law required the bureau to determine which of its lands might be set aside as federally designated wilderness areas in which no permanent development is allowed, ordered it to designate "areas of critical environmental concern" for the protection of wildlife and other natural values, and required it to use 50 percent of its grazing fees for range improvement, including wildlife-habitat enhancement. Nevertheless, rancher opposition to grazing reform, backed by the livestock industry's congressional minions, has ensured that little progress has been made in rangeland improvement during the past 50 years. Well over half of all bureau grazing lands remain in only poor to fair condition.

The Bureau Today

In conservation circles BLM sometimes is said to stand for the Bureau of Livestock and Mining. This is more frustratingly true than it is facetious.

Blame is not necessarily to be laid upon the average bureau employee, many of whom—particularly the field staff—are as concerned about the bureau's approach to land management and protection as any conservationist. This also is true of the employees of other federal land-management agencies. In general, the maligned career bureaucrats are not the bad guys. They are not derelict in their responsibilities nor professionally negligent. They often are the best allies—if not the only allies—that the conservation community enjoys within the agencies. Many foresters, range managers, botanists, ecologists, and wildlife biologists within the Forest Service, Bureau of Land Management, Fish and Wildlife Service, and National Park Service are as dismayed and chagrined over federal land policies as anyone. But their efforts to correct problems associated with federal policies often are thwarted by politicians and political appointees. During the Reagan and Bush years, appointees such as James Watt, Donald Hodel, Manuel Lujan, John Crowell, and Robert Burford erected obstacles to land protection and opened the doors to public-land piracy. The career bureaucrats who worked under them could do little more than attempt to put their own obstacles in the way of the appointees' obstacles.

At the Bureau of Land Management, the Bush and Reagan administrations appointed bureau directors wedded to the idea that public lands should be exploited as much as possible, preferably by their political cronies and friends. Interior secretary James Watt, who comes as close to overt ecological evil as is mortally possible, was the clearest example of this persuasion. He wanted to give the public domain to the states, who would turn it over to livestock raisers, miners, oil and gas developers, loggers—the usual clique of cash-now, consequences-later brigands.

These appointees had plenty to work with in the bureau, where a long tradition of ineffectiveness in land management dated to the very beginning, when policy matters were turned over largely to the rancher-dominated grazing boards. Little has changed in the bureau's demeanor, despite the advent of many new environmental protection laws such as the National Environmental Policy Act. On two critical issues, grazing and mining, the Bureau of Land Management has thrashed eternally in the stranglehold of commerical interests, and the public domain has suffered accordingly. The face of the West has been disfigured, in some areas perhaps permanently.

Approximately 177 of the 272 million acres managed by the bureau lie in 10 western states—Arizona, California, Colorado, Idaho, Montana, Nevada, New Mexico, Oregon, Utah, and Wyoming. The bureau administers substantial portions of several of these states, including 68 percent of Nevada, 42 percent of Utah, and 30 percent of Wyoming. Almost all of the remaining land administered by the bureau stretches across Alaska, an amount that will diminish to about 65 million acres as it is transferred into state and Alaska Native ownership in compliance with federal land-settlement agreements. A few hundred thousand acres are scattered over another 17 states.

The focus of the grazing issue is in the West, where roughly 23,000 livestock raisers lease public land for the use of 2.2 million cattle and 2.1 million sheep and goats. Nearly 20,000 of these leases are for lands managed by the bureau. The leases generally are good for 10 years and cost an average of $1.97 per AUM. A similar lease on private lands would cost $8 to $16.

The fees amount to a major subsidy for public-lands ranchers. If instead of $1.97 per AUM the federal government charged $5.20, about two and a half times the current rate, it could bring in an additional $60 million. Failure to bring in this additional amount is equivalent to a subsidy, over the 10-year life of a lease, of $26,000 per rancher. Keeping the fees four to eight times lower than those charged on private lands is thus a loss to the nation of tens of thousands of dollars per rancher.

But the loss is greater than mere fees suggest. A report by the General Accounting Office revealed that the bureau's grazing program in 1986 cost taxpayers $39 million in management expenses. That year, grazing brought in $14.6 million. If this $24.4 million loss is tacked on per lease holder, the subsidy calculated above jumps to $37,000 per rancher. And this still does not factor in the $25 million yearly that the federal government is spending to kill animals that livestock raisers believe are threats to cattle and sheep. Nor does it include the costs of various Department of Agriculture programs designed to assist ranchers, such as the emergency feed program that subsidizes feed costs during droughts and in 1988 handed out $140 million in emergency feed for livestock on land often too dry to support cattle and sheep without supplements. As Stanford biologist Paul Ehrlich said, quoted in the National Audubon Society TV companion book *Audubon Perspectives: Rebirth of Nature*, from which the figures above are derived, "Most of the ranchers in the western United States are on welfare, and their welfare is contributed to particularly by United States senators from the West who often sneer at welfare programs to help poor Black kids in Harlem but are happy to deliver enormous amounts of welfare, larger than any Black kid in Harlem ever dreamed of, to already-rich ranchers."

The livestock industry would have us believe that the ranchers are hardly "already rich." According to livestock association spokesmen, livestock raising is so marginally profitable that if fees were raised the tiniest amount, all 23,000 public-lands ranchers—who account for about 1 percent of all ranchers nationwide—would go belly up. This may be true for some ranchers, but not for all of them. A report by the House Committee on Government Operations showed that less than 10 percent of public-lands forage reaches livestock belonging to small operators. The other, much-subsidized 90 percent goes to corporate livestock operations owned by companies such as Getty Oil and Union Oil and to wealthy individuals such as J. P. Simlot, who not only is reported to be Idaho's wealthiest individual but also holds the record as the state's largest grazing permittee. A million acres of public land in Oregon is leased by a single entity. Is that single entity a hard-scrabble rancher? No, it is the Vail Ski Corporation.

Even at this late date it would seem premature to throw out those wealthy corporations if the financial loss that grazing puts on the federal books were balanced by some benefit to the American public. Unfortunately, the return for grazing's lost dollars is no better a deal than the return from below-cost logging. Ranchers claim that the public lands produce 20 percent of the nation's cattle. That is a sizable amount and a strong argument in behalf of grazers—or would be if government figures did not indicate that even a claim of 5 percent is something of an exaggeration. The figure is probably closer to 3 percent, or about 2.5 pounds of the estimated 77 pounds of beef eaten yearly by the average American. Even if the livestock raisers' claim of 20 percent were correct, fully 80 percent of our beef still comes from outside the West. If public-lands ranchers were to dry up and blow away, America's consumption of livestock probably would not even be affected. Other producers could absorb the loss.

Which is just as well, because drying up and blowing away is precisely what public-lands ranchers are on the verge of doing. The reason is overgrazing.

Overgrazing is what happens when more livestock are put onto a piece of land than the land can support. Because public lands are not the private property of the ranchers using them, ranchers often pack the range with too much livestock, seeking to make the largest possible profit in the shortest possible time. Moreover, much of western public lands is too arid to support constant use by livestock. The lands can survive long drought, but they cannot survive heavy grazing during drought.

As a consequence of overgrazing, most of the public land under bureau control is in unhealthy condition. A 1985 study by the National Resources Defense Council and the National Wildlife Federation concluded that 29 percent of bureau range is in poor condition and 42 percent in only fair condition. A scant 1.9 percent was rated as excellent, and only 27 percent as good. The bureau's own ratings differ just slightly from those reached by the two conservation groups. According to the bureau, 4 percent is in excellent shape and 18 percent is poor. The other ratings are nearly a match.

Public lands account for only about 2 percent of all feed consumed by cattle yearly. In terms of local regions, however, that 2 percent can be significant. Grazing permittees use nearly half the forage on bureau holdings, putting livestock into direct competition with wildlife.

Cattle and sheep do more than consume vegetation needed by the wild creatures for which the public domain is a final refuge from development. The presence of livestock brings with it several harmful effects. Demands by ranchers for government killing of wild animals perceived as a threat to livestock underlies the entire federal Animal Damage Control Program. Primary targets are coyotes, mountain lions, black bears, and prairie dogs. In a typical year, government agents kill about 80,000 coyotes, 200 mountain lions, nearly 10,000 black bears, and 125,000 prairie dogs. Ranchers claim that the predators kill livestock and that prairie dogs compete with livestock for grass. As a result, government agents kill badgers and coyotes in each of the 11 western states in which the animals occur, even though both predators feed on prairie dogs. Wyoming is the only western state in which government agents do not hunt down mountain lions, and Washington and Arizona are the only western states that have a federal truce on bobcats. Ironically, were animal damage control agents able to reduce these animals to low numbers, the animals probably would end up on the Endangered Species list, and taxpayers could invest millions more trying to save them. This is precisely what happened in the case of the grizzly bear, wolf, and black-footed ferret, all of which were nearly exterminated in the lower-48 states by control programs.

Ranchers have also blocked a wide range of wildlife-conservation programs, including efforts to reestablish the gray wolf in parts of the Southwest and in Yellowstone National Park, where they were wiped out at the behest of ranchers earlier in this century. Ranchers have attempted to block protection of grizzlies in national forests. Ranchers have even explicitly maligned wildlife as an obstacle to the raising of cattle, as if the native wild species of the West were somehow trespassing on public grazing lands. The Catron County Cattle Growers Association recently sent a letter to the New Mexico State Game Commission complaining that use of public lands by wildlife constituted a taking of rancher grazing rights "in violation of the fifth amendment to the United States Constitution."

The damage that overgrazing does to the West is particularly apparent along rivers and streams, areas that ecologists call *riparian zones*. Animals native to the arid West have adapted through the millennia to life with marginal supplies of water. Desert bighorn sheep can live up to three days without water in an area where temperatures may exceed 110 degrees in summer. Grassland rodents, such as the kangaroo rat, may go their entire lives without drinking water. But cattle need large quantities of fresh water, and in the arid West they find it by congregating around streams and other water sources. To get the 3,000 gallons per pound of body weight that a cow consumes in its lifetime, cattle stay close to water, trampling the ground around stock tanks into muck and wearing down stream banks. This widens the streams and sends mud into the flow. The water clouds and darkens, begins to absorb heat from the sun, and becomes a deathtrap to native aquatic species that need cool, clear water. Grasses around the stream are chopped into the soil. The combination of vegetative loss and bank destruction, as well as overgrazing in areas surrounding streams, leads to serious riparian degradation.

Some of this degradation is dictated by the ecological peculiarities of the arid West. When rain does fall, it often comes in short, heavy downpours. After lifestock remove the grasses that once absorbed the rain, holding it around roots and allowing it to seep slowly into streams, rainfall rushes over the earth, compounding the erosion and swelling streams to flood conditions. Because the streams have lost bank vegetation, the floods rush along the water course, further eroding the banks. When rains stop, the water quickly ebbs away, leaving a dry gulch. This has been the fate of many streams that once ran year round when fed water slowly by seepage from surrounding vegetation.

The extent of riparian damage in the West is hard to imagine. The Environmental Protection Agency estimates that nearly a third of all sediment reaching western streams is a direct result of cattle grazing. A 1975 Bureau of Land Management report on the effects of livestock grazing in Nevada found that grazing had damaged 883 miles of the 1,100 miles of riparian habitat administered by the bureau in the state. In 1988 an Arizona Fish and Game Department report concluded that less than 3 percent of Arizona's original riparian zones remain intact, while New Mexico has lost at least 90 percent of its riparian zones, primarily to grazing. Cottonwood/willow forests once sheltered most south-western streams, but cattle destroyed seedlings and saplings to such an extent that the mature trees died without reproducing. Today, only five extensive cottonwood/willow forests survive in Arizona. A 1988 General Accounting Office report declared that "poorly managed livestock grazing is the major cause of degraded riparian habitat on federal rangelands."

The loss of riparian habitat is critical to western wildlife. A 1990 study by the Environmental Protection Agency reported that 75 percent of terrestrial species in the Great Basin of southeast Oregon are dependent on or make some use of riparian habitat. More than 75 percent of all wildlife species in southeastern Wyoming are riparian dependent, as are fully half of the bird species in the Southwest. Riparian habitat is home to more bird species than all other types of western range vegetation combined.

The biological importance of riparian zones in the West makes their destruction an extinction machine. For example, 69 of New Mexico's 94 threatened vertebrate species are linked to riparian habitat, as are 81 of Arizona's 115 threatened vertebrate species. Of 32 fish species historically native to Arizona streams, five are now extinct and 21 survivors are listed as threatened or endangered or are candidates for listing. The cost of recovering these species must be added to the already high overhead of public-land grazing.

A late 1991 report by the General Accounting Office on grazing in the "hot desert" region provides a close look at how grazing is conducted on public lands administered by the Bureau of Land Management. The hot deserts are the Mojave, Sonoran, and Chihuahuan deserts, which lie in parts of California, Nevada, Utah, Arizona, New Mexico, and Texas. The Mojave is the least forgiving of the trio. Summer temperatures regularly exceed 120 degrees, and rainfall averages about 6 inches a year, coming mostly in winter. The region includes Death Valley. The Chihuahuan is the easternmost desert in the United States and gets 8 to 12 inches of rainfall yearly, generally in the form of pounding summer thunderstorms. The Sonoran desert is the land of cactuses, including the giant saguaro, that denizen of old western movies that looks like a man told to reach for the sky. Rain comes to the Sonoran in both summer and winter, totaling anywhere from 1.2 inches in the lowlands to 19 inches in the high country.

These three deserts, declares the report, "are among the least productive grazing lands in the United States. . . . more than 160 acres of land were sometimes required to support one cow for 1 month in southern New Mexico, Arizona, southwestern Utah, southeastern California, and most of Nevada. The average rate in this area was 16 acres per cow per month. In contrast, BLM lands in eastern North Dakota, South Dakota, southeast Wyoming, and northern Nebraska require an average of only 4.6 acres. . . ."

The phrase *least productive* can be interpreted to mean that these are the most delicate of western grazing lands, the lands least able to withstand grazing. How these most-delicate lands are managed is a measure of how more durable lands are handled.

The bureau has established 1,048 grazing allotments on nearly 20 million acres of hot desert. The 1991 report reached this conclusion about these grazing operations: "We found that domestic livestock grazing on BLM's hot desert allotments continues to impose the risk of long-term environmental damage to a highly fragile resource. In return, the grazing activity does not generate revenues to the U.S. Treasury, in the form of grazing fees, sufficient to cover the costs of managing the grazing program. . . . Livestock grazing in hot desert areas also poses a threat to several threatened and endangered wildlife species." Among the listed species in jeopardy are the Mojave desert tortoise, desert bighorn sheep, Sonoran pronghorn antelope, and Mearns quail.

Presently, about 102,500 acres in New Mexico's Caballo Resource Area, near White Sands, are degraded because key plant species not only are overgrazed but have been grazed during the wrong seasons. "Some areas," according to the 1991 report, "were found to be void of native vegetation and to contain highly erodible and severely compacted soils. As a result, undesirable plant species were invading, and use by wildlife was limited. These are clear signs that grazing in the hot deserts is reducing their biodiversity.

The livestock operations have no economic value to the nation, and even locally have little or no impact. The General Accounting Office calculated that from 1988 to 1990, only 1.6 percent of all U.S. cattle and no more than 3 percent of the nation's sheep were grazed in hot deserts. Ranching in Clark County, Nevada, produced less than 0.03 percent of county personal income and less than 1 percent of the total livestock sold in the state. The 33 ranches in the Lower Gila North area of Arizona contributed an estimated 0.32 percent to the total value of livestock and livestock products sold in three Arizona counties. Net income from profitable ranches was small—larger ranches averaged less than $4,000 in yearly profit. Most hot-desert livestock raisers told accounting office investigators that they stayed in ranching only because they liked the lifestyle enough to stick with it until they went broke. Many subsidized their ranching with other jobs.

Grazing damages the hot deserts at least in part because the Bureau of Land Management is not monitoring its allotments as it is required to do by law. A questionnaire distributed by the General Accounting Office to 14 of the bureau's hot-desert resource area offices revealed that the bureau is failing to monitor changes in range conditions on 48 percent of area allotments. Bureau staff admitted that they rarely ever count the number of livestock on allotments nor keep track of how long livestock are grazed on a given allotment. According to the 1991 report, "38 percent of the allotments for which monitoring data were being collected were not being evaluated. . . . Without proper evaluation of collected monitoring data, BLM does not know the impact of current grazing activity and is in no position to change the number of livestock grazing on public lands."

The General Accounting Office reported that shortcomings in monitoring resulted from a lack of staff in the wake of severe staff cuts in the years since President Reagan took office. For example, the number of full-time range conservationists in hot-desert resource areas dropped by more than 20 percent from 1983 to 1990. In some areas range conservationists were expected to monitor as much as 1.2 million acres each.

The conduct of grazing on public lands throughout the West is no better than it is on hot-desert allotments. In April 1992 the departments of the Interior and Agriculture released an 88-page economic report on the 27,000 farmers and ranchers who graze livestock on some 300 million acres administered by the Bureau of Land Management and the Forest Service. According to this report, livestock raisers pay an average of $9.66 per AUM on private lands, but only $1.92 per AUM on public lands. In the previous five years, the report noted, the gap between fees for private land and fees for public land grew by almost 75 cents. In 1990 the government spent nearly $74 million to administer its grazing programs and manage rangelands, but total grazing-fee receipts came to only $27 million after the deduction of state and county shares, yielding a loss of $52 million. In short, ranchers paid $1.92 per AUM, and the government spent $3.21 to provide each AUM. Quoted in the *Washington Post*, Representative Mike Synar, an Oklahoma Democrat and a leader in grazing-reform efforts, said that the 1992 report "underscores every one of our arguments supporting a fee increase; it demonstrates—convincingly—that fees are too low. . . . It's time to run federal rangelands more like a business."

Nevertheless, perennial efforts by congressional members such as Synar to bring grazing fees to a fair level have been repeatedly blocked by the livestock industry. In 1991 the House voted to bring fees closer to market rates, but the Senate killed the measure. The loss of revenue, of course, is in addition to the ecological toll taken by grazing's threat to biodiversity.

The grazing issue is in many ways a byproduct of the Old West. Ranchers are trying to preserve a nineteenth-century way of life in a twentieth-century world. They are not alone.

Public Lands Prospectors

Here is a description of hard-rock mining in Nevada:

We decided to sink a shaft. So, for a week we climbed the mountain, laden with picks, drills, gads, crowbars, shovels, cans of blasting powder and coils of fuse and strove with might and main. At
first the rock was broken and loose and we dug it up with picks and
threw it out with shovels, and the hole progressed very well. But
the rock became more compact, presently, and gads and crowbars
came into play. But shortly nothing could make an impression but
blasting powder. That was the weariest work! One of us held the
iron drill in its place and another would strike with an eight-pound
sledge—it was like driving nails on a large scale. In the course of an
hour or two the drill would reach a depth of two or three feet,
making a hole a couple of inches in diameter. We would put in a
charge of powder, insert half a yard of fuse, pour in sand and gravel
and ram it down, then light the fuse and run. When the explosion
came and the rock and smoke shot into the air, we would go back
and find about a bushel of that hard, rebellious quartz jolted out.
Nothing more. . . . One week of this satisfied me. I resigned. Clag-
get and Oliphant followed. Our shaft was only twelve feet deep.

If the techniques in this description sound a bit archaic, it is
because they concern events that took place around 1858. The
excerpt is from Mark Twain's *Roughing It,* an account of Twain's
brief bout of gold fever.

Roughing It was published in 1872, only seven years after the
Civil War and Abraham Lincoln's assassination. Ulysses S. Grant
was president, and George Armstrong Custer was still roaming
the West, four years away from his fate at the Little Big Horn. It
seems a distant world now, but it is not so distant for the Bureau
of Land Management. That year, 1872, was the one in which
Congress passed the law under which mining is still conducted
on public lands. The Mining Law has changed little since then.
The fees charged miners for claiming land are still exactly what
they were when the law was passed 120 years ago—$2.50 to $5
an acre. If a late nineteenth-century prospector could be resur-
rected today he would find that he could replace his pickaxe with
a jack hammer, his horse with a four-wheel-drive vehicle, his

sense of direction with a U.S. Geological Survey map, his woolen overcoat with some lightweight, Holofil-packed Gore-Tex. He also would find that he has to pay a few thousand percent more for bread, meat, and beans. But the per-acre price of his mining claim would remain the same, right down to the penny.

Some 20 years ago, secretary of the Interior Stewart Udall said that reform of the 1872 Mining Law was "the most important piece of unfinished business on the nation's natural resource agenda." According to Senator Dale Bumpers, that comment is still accurate today.

The Bureau of Land Management administers exploration and development of energy and mineral resources on some 570 million acres, including its own holdings and those of other federal agencies. The resources include a third of the nation's coal, 35 percent of its uranium reserves, up to 80 percent of its oil-shale and tar-sand reserves, and "world-class"—to use the bureau adjective—deposits of molybdenum, phosphate, sodium, lead, zinc, and potash. Anyone can lay claim to these resources for a fee of no more than $5 an acre, thanks to that apparently immutable 1872 Mining Law.

Under the terms of the law, any prospector can become a claim holder on public lands by investing at least $100 each year in developing a claim, which is an area of land thought to have mineral or energy value. The law stipulates the size limits of various types of claims. Claims can be held without time limit and with no payment to the government until the claim is patented.

Patenting can be done by any claim holder who presents to the bureau evidence showing that his or her claim is capable of commercial production. To do this, the claimant files an application for patent and posts and publishes a notice of the application. As a rule, the bureau issues a deed to the claim within 60 days. The prospector now owns the site. After that, even if all mining stops, the deed holder owns the claim. He or she can even sell it to someone else.

As a consequence, at least 80 percent of the nation's 1.2

million mining claims, covering approximately 20 million acres, are inactive, according to a 1990 study by the General Accounting Office. Or at least they are inactive as far as mining is concerned. A variety of nonmining activities are carried on at many of these claims. Some deed owners build vacation homes on them. Enterprising individuals have created marijuana farms on bureau lands in Nevada.

Investment-conscious deed holders have made millions from deeds that cost them a few hundred dollars. The government sold some 60 acres outside of Phoenix, Arizona, for $170, after which the land was turned into a resort and golf course valued at $60 million. An investor in Nevada filed several mining claims on lands likely to become part of a federal nuclear-waste dumpsite, paying the requisite $5 or less per acre, then reselling the lands to the government for $250,000. The Stillwater Mining Company has applied for a patent to 1,714 acres of national forest land in Montana, where it is mining platinum. The fee for the patent will be less than $8,600, but the value of the ore in the ground is estimated to be in excess of $30 billion. Near Breckenridge, Colorado—popular ski country—a patent is pending for 60 acres of national forest land worth an estimated $12 million. The cost of the patent, if approved, is $201. In the protected sand dunes region of Oregon, a family paid $1,950 for title to 780 acres, a tract whose mineral worth the General Accounting Office now estimates to be about $12 million. The accounting office reported that in 1987, 265 patent requests were pending on 80,000 acres lying in national forests and the public domain. A study by the accounting office of a dozen sites showed that patent fees would bring the goverment $16,000 for land worth between $14 million and $47 million in 1988.

If a deed holder does mine a claim and strikes it rich, no royalty fees need be paid to the federal government. This is another give-away of the 1872 law. Miners pay only the patent fees and nothing else. The loss to the public treasury has been immense. According to The Wilderness Society's Resource Planning and Economics Department, as reported in *Wilderness* magazine in 1992, between 1873 and 1988 more than 5 billion ounces of silver, more than 82 million tons of copper ore, and an estimated 289 million ounces of gold were mined from public lands. The total value of these minerals alone—forget tungsten, platinum, and the rest—was $363 billion when adjusted for inflation, using 1982 as the baseline. Nearly $6 billion worth of the three minerals came in during 1988 alone, with no royalties paid to the public.

On private lands, miners have to pay a substantial royalty to landowners. Even the federal government charges a 12.5 percent royalty for nonmetal resources such as coal, oil, and gas. Were it to require miners to pay the same royalty for metals, a production year equal to 1988 would have yielded $735 million to the public treasury from gold, silver, and copper alone.

The government gives away such public-lands riches because it is required to do so by law. The Bureau of Land Management is required to grant patents to anyone who provides proof of mineral deposits on a claim. The bureau is not so much managing land as doling it out. The Bureau of Land Giveaways, mandated as such by the Mining Law.

The costs are more than financial. In the story *A River Runs Through It*, transformed into a successful film in 1992 by Robert Redford, Norman Maclean wrote of his life-long involvement with fly fishing, something he and his brother, Paul, learned from their father. The book's descriptions of fly fishing in the 1930s shine throughout with the sound of mountain water and the chill of mountain air. "Paul and I fished a good many big rivers, but when one of us referred to 'the big river' the other knew it was the Big Blackfoot. It isn't the biggest river we fished, but it is the most powerful, and per pound, so are its fish." Maclean mentions in passing that near the Big Blackfoot's headwaters is a mine where a thermometer registered the lowest temperature ever officially recorded in the lower 48 states, nearly 70 below zero.

That mine today is a major contributor to the death of the Blackfoot River. A recent survey by the Montana Department of

Fish, Wildlife, and Parks revealed that populations of native fish, such as cutthroat and bull trout, have declined so drastically in the Big Blackfoot that they may soon cease to exist as viable stocks. Among other factors affecting the river, including over-grazing and logging, the mine is a primary suspect in causing the decline of Maclean's leanest, biggest, jumpingest fish. The area surrounding the headwaters of the river has not been mined since the 1950s, but abandoned claims continue to seep toxic elements such as zinc and arsenic into the stream. About 20 years ago, a settling pond bearing more than 100,000 tons of toxic mining wastes burst during heavy rain, spilling poisons that are still flowing downstream, contaminating the Blackfoot along an ever-expanding front.

The degradation that mining brings to the 44 million acres of public lands now covered by claims is almost immeasurable. According to the General Accounting Office, more than 424,000 acres of claims that have never been restored will absorb billions of taxpayer dollars in efforts to correct the environmental dam-ages and hazards they represent. For example, according to the accounting office, the biggest site on the Superfund list of high-priority pollution sites established by the Environmental Protec-tion Agency is a defunct copper mine in Montana. Mining com-panies excavated more than $2 billion from that mine before abandoning it. Taxpayers will spend an estimated $1.5 billion cleaning it up. Because of it, some 100 miles of the Clark Fork River—also once fished by Maclean—is riddled with mining toxins. Seepage from settling ponds—such as those at Warm Springs, Montana, which hold enough hazardous waste to fill a bumper-to-bumper line of dump trucks stretching from Valdez, Alaska, to Miami, Florida—now and then combines with toxins in river sediments to cause fish kills in the upper Clark Fork River.

The Montana copper mine is only one of dozens of sites on the Superfund list, only one of thousands of mining hazards across the nation. Cleaning up the Iron Mountain Mine in Cali-fornia will cost about $1.4 billion. At the Joshua Tree National

Monument, more than 2,000 abandoned openings are a danger for park visitors. In July 1991 a rock climber died from a fall into an abandoned, open mine shaft 225 feet deep.

Ecological problems associated with mining include sedimentation of streams from erosion and leakage of the deadly chemicals used in mining, such as cyanide. Sedimentation is a concern on valuable trout and salmon streams throughout Montana, Idaho, Oregon, and California. Mining under federal public-lands policies is even a threat to national parks, which are generally thought inviolate. According to the National Park Service, 2,100 claims, both patented and unpatented, lie in 130 units administered by the service, including Olympic National Park, one of the few strongholds of the ancient forests; Glacier National Park, with the largest grizzly bear population south of Canada; and Denali National Park, Alaska's premier park. Some 50,000 mining claims encircle Grand Canyon National Park like a besieging army. Restoring abandoned sites would cost the park service $45 million if all the work were done today, before costs escalate.

Meanwhile, new mines seem to be on the horizon. Noranda Minerals wants to dig two huge, open-pit gold mines only two miles from Yellowstone National Park, jeopardizing delicate alpine habitat and the integrity of the Absaroka-Beartooth Wilderness, which lies adjacent to the mine site. With its demands for new roads, to be heavily traveled by ore-bearing trucks, the mine threatens just about everything in the area, from streams to grizzlies to recreation. By law, however, the Bureau of Land Management can do little or nothing about it. The bureau can take action against a mine only *after* damage is done, not before. The Mining Law *requires* approval of mining proposals.

Clearly, then, the Mining Law must change.

Solutions, Anyone?

Change is afoot in Congress, though as with the legislative efforts to reform grazing policy, those designed to drag the mining industry kicking and screaming into the twenty-first century will likely be hard fought and long delayed. Nevertheless, in 1991 Representative Nick Joe Rahall and Senator Dale Bumpers submitted legislation to their respective congressional houses that would correct the failure of current mining law. The bills differ in some particulars, but both offer a chance to make significant changes.

Bumpers says that his legislation, by giving the federal government a 5 percent royalty on the gross value of all minerals found and imposing a new $100 holding fee, would bring in nearly $300 million yearly. His law would also "strengthen environmental regulations governing mining, require miners to post bonds, and provide funding for a new mine-reclamation trust fund."

Philip Hocker, president of the Mineral Policy Center, a private mining-reform organization headquartered in Washington, D.C., says, "In 1872, the Mining Law served an important function by helping to attract settlers out West. But today, the West is settled. The Mining Law has outlived all of its legitimate purposes and become a legislative zombie." It was Hocker's failed hope that in 1992, on the occasion of the Mining Law's 120th birthday, the nation would "give the Mining Law a decent burial."

Future legislative efforts, according to Hocker, must include giving the Bureau of Land Management and the Forest Service the right to deny mining applications if mining would cause unacceptable environmental damage. Miners should be required to clean up sites when they close down, and a fund should be established for the cleanup of abandoned sites. Annual rental fees should be initiated for the right to control mining claims in order to discourage speculators, and a royalty should be set on minerals that matches the 12.5 percent charged for coal, oil, and gas.

As with logging, the problems associated with grazing and mining as administered by the Bureau of Land Management are undermining the ecological integrity and biodiversity of our nation. They represent the theft of wild places from both the native species and the people who use them. The overwhelming influence of commercial interests in setting policies concerning the commercial use of public lands is clearly the villain here. This will remain unchanged as long as economic interests are given preference in ecological matters, for grazing and mining, though commercial activities, are nevertheless ecological matters. If properly managed, they can be conducted in some areas in such a way that they are both remunerative to the nation's coffers and pose no dangers to natural habitat. To bring this about will require the influence of both biological and financial experts in setting public policy. It is not unlikely that the latter's concerns eventually will be addressed in the fee structures for grazing and mining. But our society is still little prepared for understanding the critical need for considering biological factors in setting public policy.

It seems sometimes as if anyone who earns half a dollar in this nation believes he or she has performed some sort of civic duty. The big industries, such as grazing, logging, and mining, certainly attempt to give the impression that national service and industry profit are synonymous. But there is nothing of civic responsibility in their actions and motives. Every greed monger in the United States is endeavoring to make money. What we need is to leaven the profit-making objective with a sense of civic responsibility, a responsibility that requires more than maximum earning power. Responsible citizenship requires that we achieve our profits without undercutting the nation's economic strength or eroding its environmental integrity. Miners and grazers, among others, have failed miserably on both counts.

CHAPTER 7

Lands without Meaning: National Wildlife Refuges

≋

With over 800,000 acres, the [Charles M. Russell National Wildlife Refuge] is the largest grazing unit in the refuge system, and the range provides more in grazing fees than any other. One study found that much of the grazing is harmful to the refuge, with cattle competing with game animals for food and destroying nesting cover for birds. Due to pressure from the state government and affected ranchers, the Fish and Wildlife Service resisted efforts to reduce the grazing, and in at least several respects encouraged it.

Richard Tobin, 1990

The Fish and Wildlife Service does not own the subsurface mineral rights [at D'Arbonne National Wildlife Refuge]; oil and gas operators are drilling and producing natural gas on the Monroe gas field. . . . It is one of those refuges where you walk into it and you say, is this a national wildlife refuge? There are just gas wells everywhere.

Robert Robinson, General Accounting Office, at a 1989 joint congressional hearing on management of the National Wildlife Refuge System

~~~

Our national wildlife refuges date to the presidency of Theodore Roosevelt, and the agency in charge of them—the U.S. Fish and Wildlife Service—is really the oldest of the land-management agencies, though in its present form it dates only to 1940.

It began in 1871 as the congressionally ordained Commission on Fish and Fisheries, created to determine whether food-fish populations in lakes and coastal waters were declining and to come up with ways to protect them. Within a year, the first federal fish hatchery opened, putting the commission in the business of actually propagating fish. During ensuing years, the commission became increasingly involved in the protection of commercial fish species, including shellfish, and funded programs for the expansion of commercial fishing, such as attempts to locate new fishing grounds. In 1903 the commission was transferred into the Department of Commerce—a certain sign of the commission's commercial rather than biological emphasis—and renamed the Bureau of Fisheries. During the 1920s and 1930s it became involved in programs to protect commercial fish from dam projects, such as building fish ladders around dams, and continued to monitor commercial fisheries. In 1939, as part of President Franklin Roosevelt's persistent attempts to improve federal efficiency, the Bureau of Fisheries was transferred into the Department of the Interior, where Roosevelt hoped to consolidate all wildlife-related agencies.

Meanwhile, on an entirely separate track, Congress in 1885 had appropriated funds to the Department of Agriculture for a study on the economic effects of birds on farming and, in 1886, had created the Agriculture Department's Division of Economic Ornithology and Mammalogy. This division was assigned the task of surveying the nation's birds and mammals and reporting on how the creatures' eating habits and distribution affect agriculture and forestry. By the 1890s, in addition to its studies of wildlife and crop interrelationships, the division was surveying the distribution of a wide range of plants and animals. Increasing emphasis on these studies resulted in its rebirth in 1896 as the Division of Biological Survey, which was elevated to bureau status in 1905, putting it in a higher bureaucratic echelon.

At about the same time, President Theodore Roosevelt put the bureau on a course that would come to dominate Fish and Wildlife Service activities in the years ahead: He created the first federal wildlife refuge, encompassing 3.5-acre Pelican Island off the east coast of Florida. The island was shrouded in black mangrove thickets, making it vital to the survival of birds such as egrets and herons, which were hunted mercilessly for their plumes for use by the fashion industry. Roosevelt had no explicit legal right to create a wildlife refuge, but under the Forest Reserve Act of 1891 he could place forests in the public domain under federal protection. Pelican Island's mangroves gave him the excuse he needed. Subsequent legislation affirmed the president's authority to create refuges, and Roosevelt took full advantage of that authority. By the time he left office in 1909 he had created 51 refuges.

The National Wildlife Refuge System really bloomed in the 1930s, an outgrowth of concern over waterfowl. The history of this short period of explosive growth is a bit complicated, but shows clearly how federal land protection has been built brick by brick via the efforts of a few energetic and dedicated individuals.

During the droughts of the late 1920s and early 1930s, waterfowl numbers had declined drastically. A 1928 study by Aldo Leopold showed that waterfowl populations in the eight north-central states were declining because of poorly controlled hunting, failures in state and federal cooperative management efforts, and loss of wetlands to drought and drainage. Tighter restrictions on hunting solved the problem of overkill, but dealing with wetlands loss was more difficult. In 1934 President Franklin Roosevelt appointed Leopold to a committee that was supposed to devise a plan for wildlife restoration. Because of its emphasis on waterfowl, it was called the Duck Committee. Another key member of the committee was Jay N. "Ding" Darling, a Pulitzer Prize-winning political cartoonist, ardent duck hunter, and tireless conservationist.

After the committee published a report, based primarily on Leopold's ideas and calling for more research, improved state and federal cooperation, and a nationwide system of refuges where ducks and geese would find safety from hunters, Darling was appointed chief of the Bureau of Biological Survey. He quickly moved to implement Duck Committee goals by ushering through Congress an innovative law called the Migratory Bird Hunting Stamp Act, or Duck Stamp Act, which required all waterfowl hunters over 16 to purchase a special federal stamp before they could hunt. Funds from sale of the stamps were earmarked for acquiring refuge lands. These refuges were designed almost exclusively for the protection of waterfowl, a result of the close bond forged by the Duck Stamp Act between hunters and the refuge system. Not until 1956 did Congress expand the purpose of the wildlife refuges, authorizing the secretary of the Interior to acquire lands for the protection of all types of wildlife.

At the end of the 1930s the Bureau of Biological Survey was transferred into the Department of the Interior, where it met the Bureau of Fisheries. Love at first sight—the two agencies were joined in federal matrimony in 1940 to become the U.S. Fish and Wildlife Service.

Today, the Fish and Wildlife Service is the lead federal agency for wildlife conservation. It conducts research and administers a state and federal cooperative education system with stations located at land-grant colleges throughout the nation. Its law-enforcement division watches over illegal trade in wildlife products, including those coming into the United States through customs. It administers migratory-bird protection laws and, in that capacity, sets the length and bag limits of waterfowl-hunting seasons. Since passage of the Endangered Species Act of 1973, the Fish and Wildlife Service has been the federal agency most active in the recovery of endangered plants and animals. This law, widely recognized as the most powerful wildlife-protection law in the world, called for the creation of a list of species in danger of extinction or that threaten to become endangered if conditions do not change. It prohibited all U.S. citizens and government agencies from harming listed species and required the creation of recovery plans to restore populations of listed species. With the exception of marine species, which are handled by the National Marine Fisheries Service, the Fish and Wildlife Service is responsible for creating recovery plans for all listed species and for determining which species are eligible for listing.

Also among the service's endangered-species responsibilities is its role as advisor to other federal agencies. For example, if the Army Corps of Engineers plans to build a dam on a river that provides habitat for endangered species, or the Forest Service plans to log endangered-species habitat, the Fish and Wildlife Service is required to determine whether the actions will jeopardize any listed species. If the service issues a jeopardy decision, the action must be put off or modified to protect the species.

Management of the National Wildlife Refuge System is the Fish and Wildlife Service's biggest responsibility. Given that the refuges were created specifically for the protection of wild plants and animals, and given that the Fish and Wildlife Service is the federal agency specifically charged by Congress with the protection of wildlife, one might expect the refuges to be models of biodiversity protection. But neither the Fish and Wildlife Service nor the National Wildlife Refuge System can hold economic and political interests at bay. The refuge system has been thoroughly besieged and invaded.

Scant Refuge for Wildlife

Although Congress has never defined the purpose of the refuge system, the Fish and Wildlife Service more or less has. According to the service's *Refuge Manual,* which is the *Robert's*

Rules of Order for national wildlife refuges, the system is supposed to "provide, preserve, restore, and manage a national network of lands and waters sufficient in size, diversity, and location to meet society's needs for areas where the widest possible spectrum of benefits associated with wildlife and wildlands is enhanced and made available." To achieve this, the Fish and Wildlife Service has established four broad goals:

> To preserve, restore, and enhance in their natural ecosystems (when practicable) all species of animals and plants that are endangered or threatened with becoming endangered; to perpetuate the migratory bird resource; to preserve a natural diversity and abundance of fauna and flora on refuge lands; to provide an understanding and appreciation of fish and wildlife ecology and man's role in his environment; and to provide refuge visitors with high-quality, safe, wholesome, and enjoyable recreational experiences oriented toward wildlife to the extent these activities are compatible with the purposes for which the refuge was established.

The Fish and Wildlife Service establishes specific goals for each refuge, but the paramount, unified goal for the entire system is the management of wildlife and its habitat, with emphasis on the protection of endangered species and migratory birds. Refuges exist for no other purpose. They are not called upon to supply lumber or grazing lands, minerals or oil. They are required only to protect wildlife, with all the implications that holds for habitat protection and biodiversity—at least, that is the theory.

In the real world, beyond the pages of the *Refuge Manual,* the theory begins to crumble. A legion of secondary uses are permitted. A recent count by the Fish and Wildlife Service turned up nearly a thousand of them. All are required to meet a specific standard established by the National Wildlife Refuge System Administration Act of 1966, the very act that created the National Wildlife Refuge System by consolidating various types of federal wildlife sanctuaries into a single administrative unit. The act declared that the secretary of the Interior could permit the use of any refuge for any purpose provided that the uses were "compatible with the major purposes for which [the refuges] were established."

The compatibility of any proposed secondary use on any given refuge is determined by the refuge manager. According to the *Refuge Manual*, compatibility decisions are based on an analysis of the impacts that a specific secondary use is likely to bring to a refuge, particularly impacts on wildlife populations and habitat. The manual also requires refuge managers to review secondary uses periodically to ensure that they remain compatible with refuge goals.

Unfortunately, the authors of the *Refuge Manual* did not adopt Congress's clear message that secondary uses must be compatible with refuge purposes. Instead, they wrote that secondary uses "will not materially interfere with or detract from the purpose(s) for which the refuge was established." The phrase "materially interfere" leaves the refuges wide open to all sorts of secondary uses, particularly if the bureaucrats running the Fish and Wildlife Service and the Department of the Interior are graduates of the James Watt School of Public Land Grabs.

Concern about secondary uses resulted in two 1982 reports, one by the Fish and Wildlife Service and the other by the Department of the Interior. According to both, refuge managers feared that serious and widespread problems arising from secondary uses were directly affecting the refuges' biological integrity. The service report said that secondary uses were jeopardizing waterfowl on 85 percent of the refuges, wetlands on 79 percent, and endangered species on 41 percent. This was serious business. If the main purpose of the National Wildlife Refuge System was the protection of migratory birds, endangered species, and their habitat, then refuge administrators were failing miserably in their chief assignment. Wetlands, after all, are not only a vanishing ecosystem—the nation loses about 350,000 to 500,000 acres of wetlands yearly—but they account for about a third of the refuge system's 90 million acres.

Harmful secondary uses within the national wildlife refuges undermine our best chance for protecting wildlife and its habitat at the national level. These external threats have spawned all of our most seriously degraded refuges. In 1988 The Wilderness Society produced a list of the 10 most endangered refuges, and a brief look at it shows that external factors endangered them.

1. *National Key Deer Wildlife Refuge*. Significance: Established in 1957 in the Florida Keys, the refuge was designed to prevent extinction of the Key deer. This miniature subspecies of white-tailed deer, standing about 27 inches at the shoulder, was one of the first additions to the Endangered Species List, its numbers reduced by illegal hunting and loss of habitat. The refuge also provides habitat for bald eagles, ospreys, alligators, 450 plant species, and more than 250 bird species. External Threat: Urban development adjacent to the refuge is gobbling up deer habitat, and roadkills from increased traffic account for large numbers of deer killed each year, as much as 20 percent of the population. In 1978 the deer numbered 350 to 400 individuals, a number that has since dropped to fewer than 300. Local officials are pushing for construction of even bigger highways. The deer is not the only species at risk. Domestic waste is polluting refuge waters and increased boating activity is threatening feeding and nesting areas used by birds and other wildlife.

2. *Loxahatchee National Wildlife Refuge*. Significance: Created in 1931, Loxahatchee is the only protected portion of the northern Everglades and the only substantial remnant of it left. It is home to endangered wood storks and snail kites as well as roseate spoonbills, waterfowl, alligators, and various heron and egret species. It also provides habitat for some of the nation's rarest plants. External Threat: Urban and agricultural water demands have cut off the natural flow of water into the refuge. Its native sawgrass species are being rapidly replaced by cattails, eroding the integrity of the entire ecosystem. Chemical pollution brought in by agricultural runoff has led to high levels of toxins in birds and fish.

3. *Great Swamp National Wildlife Refuge*. Significance: This 6,900-acre refuge, established in 1960 just 26 miles west of New

York City's Times Square, houses some 300 vertebrate species, at least two of them endangered. It was established in 1961 after local residents, in a successful effort to block construction of a jetport on the site, bought up the land and donated it for creation of the refuge. External Threat: Great Swamp appears to be a pristine expanse of tall grasses and scattered strands, but it is heavily polluted by overtaxed water-treatment plants serving a rapidly growing part of central New Jersey. Effluents from the treatment plants flow into the refuge, bringing with them highly toxic PCBs, a well-known cancer-causing chemical. Fertilizers and pesticides washed by rainfall from farms, golf courses, and lawns pose a threat that the New Jersey Environmental Protection Agency says will intensify in years ahead. The Fish and Wildlife Service predicts that the 2,500 waterfowl hatched on the refuge each year will be cut in half by the mid-1990s as a result. Degradation of the refuge, which encompasses a 5-acre wetland asbestos dump bad enough to be a Superfund candidate, threatens urban water supplies because the refuge acts as a filter for the Passaic River, from which downstream communities obtain drinking water.

4. *Arctic National Wildlife Refuge.* Significance: Located on Alaska's arctic shore, this refuge includes the last strip of undeveloped arctic coast in the United States. It includes the coastal calving ground of the Porcupine caribou herd, some half a million animals that share the refuge with wolves, grizzlies, and occasionally polar bears. The herd is critical to the survival of Native Americans who hunt in the region. External Threat: The petroleum industry is pushing Congress to open the coastal portion of the refuge to oil and gas development. Operators want to drill as many as 100 wells, each of which will require 15 million gallons of freshwater and 35,000 cubic yards of gravel, most of it to be dredged from nearby streams. Though the activity is likely to diminish the breeding success of the caribou herd, it is unlikely to produce more than seven months' worth of oil, at present U.S. consumption rates.

5. *Lower Rio Grande National Wildlife Refuge.* Significance:

This refuge lies along some 200 miles of the Rio Grande in a region rich in wildlife. Its 525 vertebrate species and array of plants are rivaled in the United States only by the southern tip of Florida. About 90 percent of native brushland in the region has been wiped out by agriculture and other uses, a loss of habitat the 26,325-acre refuge was created in 1978 to stem. External Threat: The refuge consists of many small pieces, making it susceptible to the more than 100 pesticides sprayed yearly on adjacent farmland. Birds in the refuge have died after eating poisoned insects. Industrial and urban discharges into the Rio Grande and its tributaries are polluting refuge water supplies, and real estate development threatens some 8,000 acres of associated wetlands. Proposals for dams on the Rio Grande also threaten to drown thousands of acres of wildlands.

   6. *Yazoo National Wildlife Refuge.* Significance: This 12,000-acre refuge lies five miles east of the Mississippi and is part of the Yazoo Delta of northeast Mississippi. Its lakes, marshes, and bottomland forests provide critical winter habitat for waterfowl and other wildlife. External Threat: The refuge is so heavily contaminated by agricultural runoff that fish examined there in the early 1980s showed high concentrations of DDT, dieldrin, and toxaphene, all potent pesticides. Eggs of various waterfowl species have shown signs of contamination, and reproduction in herons has fallen to only a 55 percent hatching level. The Army Corps of Engineers has undertaken the largest drainage project in American history in the basin, a $2 billion scheme that will wipe out half of Mississippi's last 4 million acres of delta hardwood bottomlands. In 1986 the Corps bulldozed a 6-mile-long, 1,600-foot-wide swath of virgin oak and cypress trees within the refuge in preparation for draining more than 500 refuge acres. It has also undertaken a channel project that threatens Swan Lake, the refuge's main body of water. This project was authorized by Congress in 1936—the Corps never forgets a project—to limit agricultural flooding. Agricultural flooding is no longer a priority in the region, so the Corps justifies the project in behalf of urban flood control, even though independent experts say the project will not address that problem.

7. *Upper Mississippi River National Wildlife and Fish Refuge.* Significance: Will Dilg—founder in 1922 of the Izaak Walton League of America, a group that became one of the early leaders in water conservation—was instrumental in the creation of the refuge after his son drowned in this part of the Mississippi River while on a fishing trip. It runs for 260 miles down the river, from Wabasha, Minnesota, to Rock Island, Illinois, encompassing habitat critical to waterfowl, bald eagles, and 115 fish species. External Threat: More heavily used by recreationists than any other national wildlife refuge, the Upper Mississippi has a boat access ramp for every mile of river front, a level of human activity that diminishes its value for wildlife. Increased construction of docks and other facilities is also damaging wildlife habitat. Soil erosion from development and farming is causing extensive sedimentation. When sediment is dredged from area rivers and streams, the spoil—laced with a variety of chemical toxins from farm and urban runoff—is dumped on the refuge. This obliterates wildlife habitat, changes drainage patterns, and creates concentrated hot spots of contamination. Inappropriate public activities, such as illegal firewood cutting and off-road-vehicle use, are also damaging wildlife habitat, but limited staff can do little to step up law enforcement.

8. *Chincoteague National Wildlife Refuge.* Significance: Located on Virginia's Eastern Shore, this coastal refuge is home to more than 250 bird species and is important to waterfowl during migration. More than 70 percent of threatened piping plovers nest at Chincoteague. It is also home to the endangered Delmarva fox squirrel. External Threat: More than 1.5 million visitors come yearly to the refuge, primarily for summer beach activities. This threatens delicate sand-dune vegetation and shorebird nesting areas. Heavy traffic jeopardizes the Delmarva fox squirrel, whose activity around trees near refuge roadways makes it susceptible to roadkills.

9. *Stillwater National Wildlife Refuge.* Significance: Lying about 75 miles east of Reno, Nevada, this refuge is especially important to waterfowl, including tundra swans, cinnamon teal, and canvasback and redhead ducks, as well as pelicans and a

variety of shorebirds, such as avocets and black-necked stilts. External Threat: Because Stillwater lies at the terminus of two river systems extensively used for crop irrigation, it receives all its water from a U.S. Bureau of Reclamation irrigation project. This water, which drains from farmlands, is laced with toxins leached from agricultural soils, including arsenic, boron, selenium, and lithium. The water also contains pesticides from farmlands and mercury from nearby abandoned silver mines. Mercury levels in area fish are up to four times the maximum considered safe for human consumption. The refuge has been subject to bird and fish die-offs related to contamination. Irrigation has absorbed so much of the region's water that area marshes, including those on the refuge, are vanishing.

10. *Kesterson National Wildlife Refuge.* Significance: Kesterson lies in California's Central Valley, a region that provides habitat for the bulk of the waterfowl that migrate along the Pacific Coast. About 90 percent of the valley's original wetlands have been drained for agriculture, compounding the refuge's importance for ducks, geese, and other wetland birds. External Threat: The refuge has garnered massive amounts of press since the early 1980s, when refuge managers discovered that it has become a toxic dump deadly to the birds and other wildlife it was supposed to protect. The problem begins on surrounding agricultural lands, where irrigation runoff leaches selenium, a natural component of local soils, from the earth. The water is drained into Kesterson, where the selenium accumulates in the tissues of animals that feed there. Selenium is highly toxic in concentrated doses, and on Kesterson it has built up to such high levels that it poses a serious threat to refuge birds. Many are hatching deformed young, such as chicks without eyes or with twisted beaks, as a result of selenium poisoning. Many birds die outright. The highest selenium concentration ever found in a living fish was recorded at Kesterson. In 1984 refuge personnel began using explosives to chase away birds. Two years later, the Bureau of Reclamation shut off the flow of contaminated water, but pollution problems from toxic buildup continue.

The Wilderness Society's list is just a hint of how external threats, driven mostly by economic factors, are jeopardizing the National Wildlife Refuge System. The definitive study of the moment, published by the General Accounting Office late in 1989, gives a more precise measurement of the extent of the problem.

The General Accounting Office undertook its study at the request of Representative Mike Synar, an Oklahoma Democrat who is chairman of the House Environment, Energy, and Natural Resources Subcommittee. Synar's interest was spurred by alarming signs of habitat degradation within the National Wildlife Refuge System, notably the persistent decline of waterfowl populations nationwide during the past decade despite intensive management efforts in their behalf. Synar asked the General Accounting Office to determine whether the refuges were being managed in line with their legally established purposes and whether those purposes were being met—questions arising from his concern about incompatible uses.

General Accounting Office investigators took four approaches to fulfilling their mission. They sent a questionnaire to the managers of the 444 refuges that existed as of March 31, 1988 (the number now exceeds 450 and is growing), visited and prepared in-depth case studies on 16 wildlife refuges, held extensive discussions with Fish and Wildlife Service staff, and reviewed service policies and procedures concerning the refuge system, with an emphasis on those involving compatibility decisions.

Compatibility, or, Is It Really a Refuge If the Air Force Is Bombing It?

Investigators for the General Accounting Office found that at least one secondary use is occurring on 92 percent of all refuges. "Refuge managers believe [the *Refuge Manual* compatibility standard] is often not being met, and as a result many harmful uses are occurring," the investigators reported. "It is not possible to precisely measure the effect of these uses on the refuges' performance because FWS does not identify each refuge's wildlife enhancement and production potential. While the effect cannot be quantified . . . there is no doubt that the consequences of harmful secondary uses are substantial."

The investigators divided secondary uses into three types: public uses, such as hunting, fishing, hiking, and picnicking; economic uses, such as grazing and mining; and military uses, such as practice bombing by the Air Force and ground training by the Army. "Because demand for secondary uses is so heavy," the investigators reported, "more than 70 percent of refuges have at least 7 different categories of secondary uses occurring on them and more than 30 percent have at least 14 different uses occurring. A few refuges have more than 20 secondary uses."

Demand for secondary uses was, and still is, steadily increasing. In 1988, 44 percent of refuges with public uses reported an increase in use, while demand for economic uses increased 31 percent and for military use, 27 percent.

Secondary use does not necessarily mean *harmful* use. A secondary use can be benign. However, uses that refuge managers believed harmful were reported on 254 refuges, 59 percent of all refuges. Eighty-eight of these refuges reported only one harmful use, while a full dozen reported more than 10.

Harmful uses took a variety of shapes. On the Des Lacs National Wildlife Refuge in North Dakota, refuge staff kept lakes at high water levels to provide recreational boating opportunities even though doing so severely reduced effective wetlands management for migratory bird nesting, which was Des Lacs' primary purpose, and cut the birds' reproductive success in half. The high water levels were maintained at the direction of the Fish and Wildlife Service's chief in Washington, D.C., in response to pressure from local officials who did not want to see recreational activity reduced.

At Browns Park refuge in Colorado, livestock grazing disturbed nesting geese and ducks. In 1989 the Fish and Wildlife Service, after years of concern, initiated only minimal grazing reductions. The protests of local ranchers blocked meaningful changes.

D'Arbonne National Wildlife Refuge in Louisiana was created in 1975 "to protect, enhance, and perpetuate bottom-land hardwood habitats, and manage associated shallow impoundments for the benefit of wintering migratory waterfowl," yet gas development and production jeopardize the survival of the endangered red-cockaded woodpecker and other species found there. By the mid-1980s some 30 gas operators had established 165 wells, destroying wildlife habitat through soil and water contamination with brine. The hardwood forests that the refuge was designed to protect—part of a mitigation plan for environmental damages caused by an Army Corps of Engineers navigation project on the nearby Ouachita River—have been falling steadily since 1984. That year, a local gas extractor proposed drilling 58 new gas wells on about 500 refuge acres, resulting in one well per 8 acres and requiring the stripping of all trees and vegetation from one acre for each well. Fish and Wildlife Service biologists determined that this would drive away the red-cockaded woodpecker unless specific measures were taken to protect its habitat. When the gas operator refused to cooperate, the service went to court, only to have a district court judge rule against it on the grounds that the service did not own the refuge's subsurface mineral rights. The service could do little or nothing to control gas extraction. According to the refuge manager, within two years the gas operator had improperly installed surface and underground pipe and gas lines, provided inadequate financial compensation for habitat destruction caused by unauthorized travel routes, and destroyed D'Arbonne's future viability through unabated salt-water contamination at numerous well sites.

One of the most outrageous cases of a harmful secondary use occurs on Cabeza Prieta National Wildlife Refuge, which lies in the Sonora Desert of southwestern Arizona, hard against the Mexican border. This is hot, dry country rarely visited by the casual traveler. The main road through the refuge is called *El Camino del Diablo*, the Devil's Roadway.

The refuge may seem barren and uninhabitable to the average urban dweller, but to the rare desert bighorn sheep and the endangered Sonoran pronghorn antelope it is home. Of course, they are made of stern stuff. The bighorn can go without water for several hot summer days with no ill effects, and in this region sometimes needs to.

Despite its aridity, the refuge frequently reverberates with the rumble of rolling thunder. This is not the drumbeat of rain storms, however, but the blast of military rockets, bombs, and sonic booms. The Air Force uses the refuge as a practice site for low-level flying, aerial gunnery, rocketry, electronic warfare, and tactical maneuvering and air support. The refuge manager told General Accounting Office investigators that he was concerned about the effect that the bombing and other activities had on the pronghorns and bighorns, but that he had no evidence to support his concerns since no study on the issue had been completed. Even if one were, he still might not be able to stop the bombing runs. Although the refuge was created in 1939 for the conservation of wildlife resources and for the improvement of public grazing (which was phased out in 1982 because the land was too dry for livestock), some 825,000 of the refuge's 860,000 acres are overlain by the Barry M. Goldwater Air Force Range, originally created in 1942 as the Luke Air Force Range. Congress, half a century ago, gave the military the right to bomb the refuge, which in effect means that, officially, the bombing is not an incompatible use, regardless of how harmful it might be.

A refuge manager's assessment of a secondary use as harmful depends on the specific refuge and how the use is conducted. For example, small-game hunting was permitted on 162 refuges at the time of the General Accounting Office study. Eleven percent of managers thought it was harmful, but 89 percent thought it was not. Although 85 percent of managers whose refuge was open to mining thought mining was harmful, 15 percent thought it was not. Overall, however, certain activities were more likely to be assessed as harmful than others. More than half of all refuge managers faced with mining, off-road-vehicle use, airboats, military air exercises, waterskiing, and large power boats thought these uses, though officially labeled as compatible, were harmful.

According to the investigators, some uses that seem benign may still be harmful to primary refuge purposes. For example, on 20 percent of the 192 refuges on which it occurred, picnicking was thought to be harmful because it diverted staff from higher-priority purposes and required them to spend considerable time preparing and maintaining facilities, picking up trash, and ensuring visitor safety. At Desoto National Wildlife Refuge, north of Omaha, Nebraska, waterskiing and power boating caused declines in waterfowl nesting. By creating wakes and rough water, they cut away at weed beds that provided food for wildlife and helped stabilize lake bottoms. After the refuge manager garnered enough local support to ban the activities, lake clarity improved and fish and waterfowl populations increased.

Refuge managers, of course, want to stop harmful secondary uses. However, they are prevented from doing so by a variety of outside influences. Roughly 70 percent of all harmful uses discovered by the General Accounting Office were caused by two factors. The first is local officials and politicians who pressure Fish and Wildlife Service administrators to continue certain harmful uses. For example, refuge staff at Des Lacs invested a considerable amount of time proving that high water levels were harming waterfowl. Nevertheless, the Fish and Wildlife Service director brushed aside their concerns when local public officials said they wanted lake draw downs blocked because waterskiing was economically important, a local golf course needed the water, and the value of nearby homes would suffer.

The second factor concerns land title. In many cases, the Fish and Wildlife Service is powerless to stop harmful uses because it lacks full ownership of or control over refuge lands, waters, and resources, as at Cabeza Prieta and D'Arbonne. This generally represents a failure on the part of Congress to purchase all rights to land acquired for refuges.

Problems posed by harmful uses are compounded because

refuge staff often do not monitor the effects of secondary uses even though required to do so by the *Refuge Manual*. Refuge managers told General Accounting Office investigators that they ignore the requirement because the Fish and Wildlife Service has never established a set of formal policy guidelines for compatibility requirements. To top it off, during the 1980s the Fish and Wildlife Service failed to collect financial data showing that the costs of managing secondary uses were not interfering with each individual refuge's primary goals. This, too, is a critical shortcoming because, refuge managers told the investigators, "Although not quantified, the costs of secondary uses are high" and they "draw a significant portion of limited refuge funding away from wildlife protection and enhancement activities."

A Conservationist Perspective

The General Accounting Office completed its report in September 1989. Two years later the National Audubon Society, The Wilderness Society, Defenders of Wildlife, and the National Wildlife Refuge Association jointly published a brief document showing that nothing had changed. Based on data from a Fish and Wildlife Service report published the previous June, the document indicated that approximately 60 percent of the 478 units in the National Wildlife Refuge System bore at least one of the 836 harmful activities occurring in the system. Military activity was reported on 96 refuges. Among them was the Tiajuana Slough refuge in southern California, near and over which Navy pilot trainees fly some 350,000 sorties yearly. Cabeza Prieta was still being bombed. Oil and gas extraction was considered harmful to 30 of the 42 units on which it occurred. Oil and gas exploration—which endeavors to increase the extent of extraction—was considered harmful to nearly half of the 64 refuges on which it occurred. Other harmful activities included motorized water sports, grazing, off-road-vehicle use, logging, sewage dumping, and mining.

Professional conservationists working in behalf of the refuges are consistent in their interpretation of refuge problems and in their perception of what will solve them. Ginger Merchant, executive vice-president of the National Wildlife Refuge Association, says that in the refuge system's early years conventional wisdom taught that the best way to protect the refuges was to keep them in the background of public interest, out of harm's way. But as the amount of wild places available to the public has dwindled, the public has been drawn to the refuges. This has been particularly true since Congress opened the refuges to hunting in 1949. But administrators were not prepared for burgeoning public use of the refuges. "The Fish and Wildlife Service has backed into this increased public awareness and use of refuges and as a result has not cultivated the kind of public constituency and support that they need," Merchant says. This has left the refuge system understaffed and underbudgeted. The service, she says, has never even sought proper funding. The National Park Service, for example, requested a $920-million budget for 1993, while the Fish and Wildlife Service asked for only $172 million for the refuge system, though it is larger than the park system. The refuge system has fallen far behind in general maintenance. Merchant says the backlog on maintenance for 1992 was expected to reach $357 million. Compatibility problems arise because the *Refuge Manual* is so inconsistent in outlining permissible activities that virtually anything can be allowed.

The refuges are "lands in search of a meaning," says William Reffalt, who became director of The Wilderness Society's National Wildlife Refuge System Program in 1983 after 23 years in the Fish and Wildlife Service, including six years in refuge field offices and two years as chief of the Division of Refuges. He believes that legislation presently in Congress could give the refuge system its meaning by clarifying issues such as compatibility, which has never been adequately defined. "Also," he says, "Congress has never said what the refuges are for. Many in the Fish and Wildlife Service think it's for waterfowl, and land acquisition is mostly for waterfowl." But, he says, the refuge system needs to consider much broader purposes, setting the protection of biodiversity as its goal. Congress also needs to step in to keep other agencies, such as the military, from "trampling on the refuges," Reffalt says.

What is needed, says Jim Waltman of the National Audubon Society, is a refuge organic act, referring to a category of law that established the broad purposes, mandates, and operations of federal agencies. Echoing Merchant and Reffalt, he says that the refuges are supposed to be managed in a way that is consistent with their purpose, but that this purpose has never been defined. The Fish and Wildlife Service has an understanding of the purpose, but Congress has never established it legislatively.

Congress may do so soon. Senator Bob Graham, a Florida Democrat whom Reffalt calls "a modern-day Theodore Roosevelt" because of his consistent support of conservation issues, has introduced a bill that clearly would establish the purpose of refuges as, in part, the protection of wildlife, wildlife habitat, and wildlife communities. It also would strengthen protection against incompatible use. As already mentioned, the *Refuge Manual* defines a compatible use as one that "will not *materially* interfere with or detract from the purpose(s) for which the refuge was established" [emphasis added]. Graham's bill takes a less ambiguous approach. Under the terms of the law as now written, a secondary use cannot be permitted unless it "will contribute to the fulfillment of the purposes of the System and the refuge or will not have a detrimental effect upon fulfillment of the purposes of the System or the refuge." In addition, the secretary of the Interior is required to make "a determination that funds are available for the development, operation, and maintenance of such use." And finally, "Unless the Secretary [of the Interior], in consultation with the Director [of the Fish and Wildlife Service] determines that there is sufficient information available to make a reasoned judgment that a proposed, continued, or expanded use of a refuge is compatible with the purposes of the System and the refuge, the Secretary shall not permit the use."

Reffalt says, "I think if we can get this legislation passed, then in the next century we'll finally have a refuge system that protects the whole fabric of American wildlife." By requiring better refuge planning, the act will help conservationists identify necessary funding levels. "Planning," says Reffalt, "tells us greenies what the refuge system needs to do. Then we can go out and fight for the dollars."

A panel of experts drawn together by Defenders of Wildlife for a study of the refuge system summed it up succinctly in 1992:

> The National Wildlife Refuge System, we firmly believe, is a centerpiece of federal efforts to conserve wildlife habitats. The system urgently needs reform, however. We recommend swift congressional action on an organic act for the nation's federal refuges. This act must set forth a clear, comprehensive, and far-sighted mission for refuges. A stronger and more visible refuge agency should be administered through ecologically defined bioregions. It must have congressional backing for a tighter process of screening proposed secondary refuge uses that threaten refuge functions. Congress must require and support much improved planning and a coherent, expanded research program on federal wildlife refuges. A critical component both of planning and of future acquisition of additional marine, freshwater, and terrestrial units of the system is an increased consideration of external threats to refuge wildlife and the specific steps that can be taken to mitigate them.

Those external threats are the central problem of refuge protection. Social, political, and economic pressures subject even dominant-use lands designed to protect biodiversity to a variety of conflicting and even damaging uses. In many cases, activities on lands miles away from refuges are affecting refuge integrity, as when farming in California's Central Valley leads to the poisoning of Kesterson and when pesticide spraying on surrounding farms affects the Lower Rio Grande. The pervasive influence of outside forces on national wildlife refuges highlights the inadequacy of mere boundaries as protective devices in today's human-dominated world. This is equally clear on three other types of dominant-use lands: national parks, marine sanctuaries, and federally designated wilderness areas.

CHAPTER 8

Playgrounds for the People: The National Parks

If we are going to succeed in preserving the greatness of the national parks, they must be held inviolate. They represent the last stand of primitive America. If we are going to whittle away at them we should recognize at the very beginning that all such whittlings are cumulative and that the end result will be mediocrity. Greatness will be gone.

Newton Drury, director of the
National Park Service, 1940–1951

It is only in very recent years—less than a century in fact—that an attentive attitude toward undisturbed and unutilized nature has begun to emerge. It is surprising that in the long history of man's conquest of the earth there is no evidence of sustained effort on the part of any people to preserve native landscape for its own sake, until our own national park system began to take form late in the nineteenth century.

A. Starker Leopold, 1957

≋

The federal government became involved in land protection as long ago as 1832, when the Arkansas Hot Springs won status as a reserve. Some 30 years later the federal government bequeathed the Yosemite Valley to California for use as a park (the federal government later took it back). But despite these dabblings, federal land protection did not begin in a big way until Yellowstone was created in 1872.

In the first half-century after Yellowstone, Congress created nearly a dozen more national parks. But these were created more for the protection of scenery than for the protection of wildlife. Consequently, our national parks usually lie in areas with dramatic vistas but with limited value to wildlife. For example, virtually all of the early parks were located in western mountains, which though beautiful generally provide poor-quality wildlife habitat. Winters are hard and the plant foods needed by deer, elk, moose, bison, and other herbivores are relatively scarce, limiting their populations. The high country's restricted numbers of hoofed animals means that the larder is comparably bare for predators, restricting their populations, too. Nevertheless, it was these remote—and economically unimportant— alpine regions that Congress sought to protect in the first parks.

Much of the protection, like that of Yellowstone, was accomplished at the behest of the railroad industry, which wanted parks as tourist destinations. For example, Glacier National Park was won for the public by the Great Northern Railroad, headed by Louis Hill. Hill shepherded the idea for the park through

Congress and, once the park was created, quickly built a chain of lodges within Glacier.

Lack of concern for the biological integrity of the parks might explain why, for the first 44 years after Yellowstone was created, no special agency was established for park management. Congress turned over administration of several early parks to the Army, which did an inconsistent job of meeting its park responsibilities. Moreover, private citizens continued to treat the parks as if they were still part of the frontier, suitable for all manner of exploitation, from hunting to logging.

Enactment of the National Park System Organic Act of 1916 was Congress's proposed cure for these problems. The act created the park service and declared that the fundamental purpose of the parks is "to conserve the scenery and the natural and historic objects and the wildlife therein and to provide for the enjoyment of the same in such manner and by such means as will leave them unimpaired for the enjoyment of future generations."

The first director of the National Park Service was Stephen Tyng Mather, a 47-year-old entrepreneur who had become a millionaire by tireless promotion of his household cleanser, Twenty Mule Team Borax. In photographs taken during his years as director his hair is short, parted on the left, and graying. Even when posed for the camera in the out-of-doors, surrounded by trees or on a dock beside a boat at Yellowstone Lake, he usually is trussed up in coat and tie, a fedora clapped to his head. In some photos he wears a long, wool, urban overcoat that hangs to the tops of his laced hiking boots. He looks thin-lipped and grave and altogether indistinguishable from the suited and behatted businessmen, bureaucrats, and politicians photographed beside him.

But in life he must have been much different from the average run of commercial and political figures. Horace Albright, who would work with Mather for 15 years and succeed him in office, wrote in his history of the early park service that "Mather was unlike anybody I had met since coming to Washington. He was exuberant, warm, yet had an aura of authority about him. . . . He was forty-seven. I was only twenty-four, and a bit in awe of him. He was like a wound spring. His reactions were sharp and unguarded. . . ." Ironically, this man who would spend the last years of his life defending the nation's wild places had inherited his surname from Cotton Mather, the old Puritan minister who had set his parishioners a'tremble with stories of devils and dragons at large in the wilderness.

Mather's ascent to the directorship began with a letter solicited from him in 1914 by Franklin K. Lane, the secretary of the Interior. Lane had met Mather in Chicago through a mutual friend. At that time, each park was run as practically a separate unit, with little or no interaction among park superintendents. The military was still in charge of some of the parks. The Interior Department, ostensibly the government's park manager, had only two people in Washington, D.C., assigned full-time to park administration. The park system encompassed nearly 5 million acres, but its annual budget hovered around $20,000. The field staff for all the parks and national monuments numbered fewer than 100, most of them untrained local residents employed only during the summer.

Mather had a long familiarity with the protected lands that ultimately entered the park system, beginning with a 1905 Sierra Club outing to the heights of Mount Rainier. During the ensuing years, Mather climbed many other high western peaks and visited a variety of national parks. When Lane asked him for a letter expressing his assessment of the parks, Mather complied, describing the generally poor condition of the parks and complaining of the low-quality food and lodging he had found at Yosemite National Park. Lane promptly urged Mather to come to Washington, D.C., and take over park management. Mather, who had no government experience, was reluctant to take the job, but he was finally persuaded to do so. He was sworn in on January 21, 1915, and promised to stay for one year.

He stayed for nearly 14, however, working as park service director until illness forced his retirement in 1929, a year before his death. He put into the parks all the manic energy and imagination that he had put into his business. He also put into it his money, making loans to concessioners for improvements to park facilities, personally paying nearly half the salaries of upper-level staff, and even buying additional lands for the parks.

At first he focused the bulk of his considerable energy on enactment of a law that would establish the purpose of the parks and create a park service to administer them. The fight for such a bill had been going on for at least five years before Mather stepped in. He was faced with fierce opposition. Western ranchers were opposed to formalizing the parks because they feared they would lose grazing privileges. Some senators and representatives were opposed to expanding the federal bureaucracy and budget. The Forest Service adamantly opposed the creation of a park service, certain that it would create a constituency for the parks and turn some national forest lands into parks. Though he had been fired as Forest Service director by President William Howard Taft in 1910, Gifford Pinchot was still a formidable enemy of the parks, which conflicted with his conception of proper land use.

Undeterred, Mather, by the end of 1915, was holding regular meetings with influential men committed to passage of a national park organic act. Among them was Representative William Kent, a Californian who in 1908 had given the federal government the forested land that became Muir Woods National Monument; Gilbert Grosvenor, the founder of the National Geographic Society; Enos Mills, a writer who was instrumental in the creation of Rocky Mountain National Park; and Frederick Law Olmsted, Jr., whose father had designed New York City's Central Park. All would have input into the writing of the park organic act that Kent would introduce in the House, with the language outlining the fundamental purpose of the parks coming verbatim from a letter Olmstead had written in November 1915 to the American Civic Association, which had led lobbying for the bill since 1910.

Mather and his colleagues chaperoned the law through Congress, promising to keep the new agency small and compromising on the use of the parks for grazing. President Woodrow

Wilson signed the bill at around 9 P.M. on August 25, 1916. Congress did not appropriate any funds for the freshly minted National Park Service until the following April, a month before Mather was appointed as the service's first director.

Mather had definite ideas about how he wanted the parks developed, he worked hard to initiate them, and—as did Pinchot with the national forests—he established a standard for park management that still dominates today. In the process, he pushed himself over the edge, suffering two nervous breakdowns brought on by exhaustion.

One of the strains he faced was the concession industry. Concession operations within the parks were in shambles. For example, in Yellowstone, already considered the crown jewel of the park system, tent camps were stuffed into sites established for permanent camps. Food service was so bad that during a one-day inspection Mather's assistant, Horace Albright, found 20 cases of ptomaine poisoning in a single camp. Concessions were operated by a snarl of competing companies. Wrote Albright in *The Birth of the National Park Service,* "When Mather had taken over the parks, Yellowstone had one concessioner running the five hotels, two lunch stations, and one stagecoach line, two others running permanent camp systems, another two concessioners running stagecoach lines, and several running traveling camps."

Despite his concern over the shoddiness of park concessions, Mather did not want to run out the concessioners. He believed that he had to build up visitor numbers to ensure support for the parks in Congress, and he was committed to park development as a means for attracting visitors. His vision of how the parks should be maintained came from his travels in Switzerland, where the most popular mountains were strung with cog railways for the transport of visitors. Mather wanted lodges for comfortable billeting and roads to attract drivers of the increasingly popular automobile. He wanted the parks to be user friendly.

He triumphed on all counts. After fighting pitched battles with concessioners who had strong allies in Congress, he succeeded in revamping the concession system. He permitted only one concession company per park, turning the parks into mini-monopolies. This streamlined the administration and monitoring of concessions and also encouraged concessioners to invest in the parks. His penchant for automobile promotion increased park visitation even though it drove a stake through the heart of the railroads. In 1916 trains brought 14,251 visitors to Yosemite National Park. Two years later, trains carried fewer than 4,000, while automobiles transported 26,700. Park visitation was up, but the train lines were languishing.

Mather was also instrumental in expanding the National Park System into the East. He won from Congress authorization for the first eastern national parks: Great Smoky Mountains on the Tennessee–North Carolina border and Shenandoah in Virginia. He also fought off efforts to permit major developments within western national parks, including a plan to drown beneath a reservoir some 10,000 acres of meadow and forest in Yellowstone. He also repaired some of the damages of the past. For example, he was offended by a sawmill in Glacier National Park that was supposed to have been removed following construction of a railroad lodge. When his orders to remove the sawmill were ignored, he personally blew it up with dynamite.

When he died in 1930, the National Park Service was on the verge of a sea change. Although the 1916 organic act called for the protection of wildlife, it was passed in an era when even experts thought in terms of "good" and "bad" animals, much as the Forest Service thought in terms of good and bad trees. Consequently, park administrators sought to protect "good" animals, such as elk, deer, and bison, and to get rid of "bad" animals, such as wolves and mountain lions, which traditionally ate "good" animals. As a result, the gray wolf disappeared entirely from Yellowstone by 1926.

This approach to the natural world began to change in 1929 when biologist George M. Wright, who had worked as a temporary ranger in Yosemite National Park, became the first park service scientist and put the service in the vanguard of modern wildlife management. Not only did he succeed in reducing its predator-control activities, but, using his large family fortune, he personally funded a two-year survey of the wildlife in all the parks. This was crucial to park success, because the status of wildlife within the park was changing so rapidly that it would soon be impossible to determine what original conditions had been and how to protect them. Wright's survey provided some of the first substantial information ever gathered on species such as the trumpeter swan and the elk. In 1933 Horace Albright, who had been appointed director in 1929, created a new wildlife division and made Wright its head. But Wright died prematurely the following year, and the service regressed, again undertaking activities such as predator control.

Albright, like Mather, was a true believer in the value of constructing visitor facilities and expanding the park system. This cause was taken up by subsequent directors after Albright stepped down in 1933. Even during the Depression, when the park service budget was cut in half, park facilities continued to expand. The Civilian Conservation Corps, one of Franklin Roosevelt's federal programs for returning the unemployed to work, put up buildings, bridges, and other facilities, doing in 10 years, some said, the work of half a century. Not everyone viewed this with equanimity. The National Parks Association, founded with Mather's help in 1919 to monitor the park service, protested the civilization of the parks. The association also was alarmed when the park service took over administration of human-made recreation areas, such as a variety of reservoirs. But if it seemed that expansion was pulling the park service away from the protection of wildlands, other developments brought it back. In 1937 the service took over control of Cape Hatteras National Seashore, the first of many coastal stretches protected from development for public enjoyment.

Park protection wavered during World War II, when the National Park System was enlisted in the global conflict—war is hell even for national parks. Some parks were used as military training grounds and others as sources of timber; the Grand

Canyon was squeezed for copper and Yosemite for tungsten. In Washington State, the site of some of today's bitter fights over logging, the timber industry attempted to open Olympic National Park to clearcutting. Loggers had been after the trees ever since failing to stop creation of the park in 1930. Claiming that the park's giant spruce trees were vital to airplane construction and waving the demagogic flag of hypocritical patriotism, the loggers begged the park service for cutting privileges. To no avail. Secretary of the Interior Harold Ickes said "the virgin forests in the national parks should not be cut unless the trees are absolutely essential to the prosecution of the war, with no alternative, and only as a last resort. Critical necessity rather than convenience should be the governing reason for the sacrifice of an important part of our federal estate." Ironically, the park service located spruce in Canada and Alaska that were sacrificed instead.

Soon after the war, the park service became embroiled in a combative turning point in the history of the conservation movement when an attempt to drown parts of Dinosaur National Monument in northwestern Colorado united the environmental community as never before and showed it the way to the legislative future, creating the superstructure and the methods that would yield the great environmental advances of the 1960s and beyond, including the Endangered Species Act and the Clear Air and Clean Water acts.

It began in 1950 when Newton Drury, the park service director, discovered that the secretary of the Interior had approved a plan to build two dams—one across a deep, narrow gorge on the Green River at a place called Echo Park, and the other at a rapids called Split Mountain Gorge—which would back up water into Dinosaur. The Echo Park dam alone would have created a reservoir 107 miles long, inundating much of Dinosaur's multihued, rocky canyons.

Drury mounted a defense of the park in opposition to the secretary of the Interior—his boss, Oscar Chapman. Drury argued that within the national parks "no resources should be consumed or features destroyed through lumbering, grazing, mining, hunting, water control developments or other industrial uses. This is a cardinal point, which park agencies and executives have learned they must adhere to as closely as possible. . . . If we are going to succeed in preserving the greatness of the national parks, they must be held inviolate."

The dam-building Bureau of Reclamation was the most powerful agency within the Department of the Interior at that time, and Chapman backed the agency's dam project and began looking for a replacement for Drury. Drury concluded that Dinosaur was a lost cause and left federal service in 1951, subsequently turning up as head of California's Division of Beaches and Parks and later with the Save-the-Redwoods League, which he had founded in 1918.

After Drury stepped out of the fray, private conservation groups stepped in. Their leadership actually began the previous year, when historian, conservationist, and author Bernard DeVoto exposed the Bureau of Reclamation plan in an article for the July 1950 *Saturday Evening Post*. Public opinion rushed to Drury's side. By then, however, Chapman had approved the dam.

Congress, however, had not yet provided funds for it, and it was in the congressional arena that the conservation community, including The Wilderness Society, the National Audubon Society, the Sierra Club, and the Wildlife Management Institute, mounted its offensive. The fight eventually boiled down to the dam at Echo Park, and even though the Truman and Eisenhower administrations supported the Echo Park dam, the fight continued for years, primarily because the public was aligned against the dam. In 1954 mail to the House of Representatives during debate on Echo Park was 80 to 1 against the project. This support was rallied by the conservation groups, which heavily publicized the importance of Dinosaur as well as the shortcomings of the dam site. David Brower, who was then head of the Sierra Club and remains today a leader in the conservation cause, undercut the entire argument in favor of the dam when he proved that engineers at the Bureau of Reclamation had miscalculated the amount of water that the Echo Park reservoir would store. He showed that other dam sites that would not harm the park would both hold more water and lose less to evaporation. His reasoned arguments began to crumble the edifice of support for the dam that the Bureau of Reclamation had built in Congress.

Alfred Knopf, chief of the publishing firm that bears his name, also played a significant role in behalf of Dinosaur. Influenced by DeVoto and inspired by the lives of people such as John Muir, he had a deep interest in conservation issues. Working with literary figure and conservationist Wallace Stegner to bring out quickly a book in support of Dinosaur, he squeezed into only three months the usual year-long publication process that turns a manuscript into a completed book. *This Is Dinosaur: Echo Park Country and Its Magic Rivers,* replete with dramatic photos that glittered with the monument's natural beauty, was handed out to every member of Congress. Eventually, the hard work and support paid off. In 1955 Congress dropped the Echo Park dam proposal.

Schemes such as the proposed dams resulted from the National Park System's lack of an overall management plan and from the need for an updating of park goals and objectives. Concern over park management heightened during the dam debate and was compounded after 1956, when Conrad Wirth, Drury's replacement, won from Congress a billion-dollar appropriation for a program to expand and enhance the National Park System. This program, called Mission 66, was a 10-year plan that was supposed to make the parks capable of handling 80 million visitors yearly. Unfortunately, by the time the plan was concluded in 1966, park visitation had already surpassed 80 million. That Mission 66 would fall short of equalizing park capacity with park visitation was apparent long before then.

This management glitch in part led to the appointment in the early 1960s of a park service advisory board, headed by Aldo Leopold's son A. Starker Leopold, to examine park management. The panel produced in 1963 an advisory document that has guided much of park-management policy for roughly the past 30 years. It urged park administrators to seek to preserve the parks in a state representative of "a reasonable illusion of primitive America." This included a return to natural cycles. For example, natural fires, which play an important role in maintaining certain ecosystems, would be allowed to burn as they would have before European settlement. In response to the Leopold Report, the park service has endeavored since the 1960s to maintain the parks in or to restore them to a condition approximating that found when Columbus arrived.

In addition, when it became clear in the early 1960s that Mission 66 would not bring the parks to a level sufficient to serve the present, let alone the future, Congress passed the Land and Water Conservation Act of 1964, which funds the purchase of more park lands by using money raised from park fees, a tax on motorboat fuel, receipts for oil and gas leases on the outer continental shelf, and the sale of excess federal property.

This was a critical breakthrough for the park service because scarcely any land had been added to the park system since the 1930s—22.9 million acres of its 23.8-million-acre domain had been acquired before World War II. The fund brings in nearly $1 billion yearly and accounts for almost all land acquisition made since 1964.

Meanwhile, Mission 66 was not an unmitigated failure from the viewpoint of the Mather school of park management. It resulted in the construction or upgrading of 2,000 miles of roads and the erection of 144 visitor centers.

Construction of roads and visitor centers, however, is not necessarily the best approach to conserving scenery, wildlife, and natural and historic objects, as called for in the 1916 organic act. Development both inside and outside the parks poses a continuing threat to their ecological integrity.

The World of Columbus Today

Attempting to keep the parks in as pristine a condition as the twentieth century will allow is becoming increasingly difficult as the century draws to a close. A growing problem is the parks' immense public appeal. According to the National Parks and Conservation Association's annual report on the national parks, nearly 268 visitors crowded the nation's parks in 1991, the most recent year for which figures are available. In Alaska and the Pacific Northwest, visitation was up by almost 9 percent from the previous year. It had decreased only in the Southwest, but that drop was less than 1 percent. Visitation is expected to reach 360 million by the end of the decade and half a billion by 2010. "The consequence of this popularity," declares the report, "mirrors the ills of large urban areas: traffic congestion and gridlock, the degradation of both cultural and natural resources, and human conflict. As the number of visitors increases, so does the damage to our national parks."

The report provides several examples. In Grand Canyon National Park, the banks of the Colorado River are showing signs of overuse by river runners, while an estimated 750,000 tourists fly over the canyon each year in chartered aircraft, disturbing the thousands of visitors on the ground. In Yosemite, hikers along stretches of the Merced River have worn away ground vegetation and exposed the roots of trees. Park officials say the trees will probably collapse into the river.

About 95 percent of park visitors arrive by private vehicle, and the bulk of them never get more than a hundred yards from roads. Air pollution intensifies because of heavy vehicle traffic in some parks. Yellowstone pulls in more than 3 million vehicle-riding visitors yearly, while Great Smoky Mountains National Park on the Tennessee–North Carolina border sees nearly 9 million hauled in yearly. In 1988 the National Park Service reported in its study of air quality in the parks that air pollution—not all of it vehicle related—reduced the visibility of scenic vistas 90 percent of the time at sites monitored in the lower 48 states. "Even at the Grand Canyon National Park, the color and textual detail of the canyon are nearly always impaired to some extent by manmade haze." Visitors who travel the skyline drive over the Blue Ridge Mountains of Shenandoah National Park, about two hours west of Washington, D.C., will find that air pollution lends a grayish haze to distant views. Between 1945 and 1985 air pollution reduced visibility by 40 percent at Maine's Arcadia National Park, where high peaks overlook the Atlantic.

Heavy visitation increases wear and tear on park facilities, adding to the service's budgetary burden in a time when parks have received minimal support from recent administrations. Maintenance of facilities was a low priority for 12 years under Reagan and Bush, so "there is a backlog of repair, maintenance, preservation and public health and safety projects that exceeds $2 billion," according to the parks association report. For example, 60 percent of Yellowstone's roads are in need of repair. Shenandoah, with more than 2 million visitors yearly, suffers an equipment-replacement backlog of $1.7 million, but in 1991 its budget included only $77,000 for this item. One of the main visitor pathways in Grand Canyon National Park passes within a few yards of an abandoned uranium mine that emits low levels of radiation, but is separated from public intrusion by only a chain-link fence.

The national parks also face serious threats from activities on lands outside the parks. Three national park units in coastal Alaska continue to be jeopardized by the aftermath of the *Exxon Valdez* oil spill that dumped 11 million gallons of oil into Prince William Sound in 1988. The trustee council charged with allocating funds from the settlement of a lawsuit over the spill has ignored the effects of the spill on grizzly bears and wilderness habitat in favor of restoring specific species, particularly commercial salmon. At Great Smoky Mountains, construction of a 108-acre solid-waste landfill has been slated for a site three miles from park boundaries, raising the potential for the seepage of toxic wastes into the park. It was approved over the objections of not only the park service, but also the Forest Service and the North Carolina Wildlife Resources Commission. The park is already threatened by severe air pollution in the form of a chemical haze that clouds park air 90 percent of the time. Most of the pollutants come from industry smokestacks on the Tennessee side of the park and have been blamed, according to the National Park and Conservation Association's 1992 report, "for endangering 27 species of native trees and plants in the park, including tulip poplar, sassafras, sweet gum, and black cherry trees."

Yellowstone's geyser system, one of only two left in the world after eight others were permanently destroyed by underground geothermal development, faces threats from a geothermal development project on land adjacent to the park, owned by a survivalist splinter group, the Church Universal and Triumphant. The church also owns the wintering ground for the park's pronghorn antelope herd. Although the park houses the pronghorns for nine months of the year, the private land is essential to the animal's survival during the other three months. If the area is disturbed in such a way that the pronghorn are locked out of it or avoid it, the park could lose the herd.

Concessioners—those banes of Stephen Mather's early park years—are still a problem, placing a burden on taxpayers while turning a profit for themselves in a way that the mining and logging industries must admire. The fee structure for concessioners is so low that on average, according to the parks association, a concessioner pays the federal government only 2.5 percent of gross revenues. Many pay much less. When investigators for the General Accounting Office, at the behest of Representative Mike Synar, examined 31 concession contracts, they found that in most cases concessioners paid little or nothing to use public facilities.

For example, the popular restaurant at Mount Vernon, George Washington's home on the Potomac, is a public facility administered by the National Park Service. The concessioner who runs it under contract reported gross revenues of $4.3 million in 1990 but paid a monthly rent of less than $115. At Grand Canyon, a concessioner who runs a luxury hotel that is public property and rakes in $50 million in gross revenues yearly paid no rent in 1990, but did put $11,250 into a maintenance fund. An art studio in Yosemite National Park with reported annual revenues of $2 million pays only $265 in yearly use fees for six public buildings. At nearby Sequoia National Park, a concessioner makes $11 million yearly through use of 391 public buildings administered by the park service and pays no rent. The largest park concessioner pulls in $83.5 million in gross receipts from operations in 19 public buildings, paying a rent of only $19,271.

The accounting office investigators, in their 1992 report to Synar, showed that concessioners earned $531 million in 1990, from which the government received $11 million in franchise fees in addition to rent. The parks association says that "park officials concede that the agency has no reliable estimate of how many buildings and facilities it provides to concessioners or the estimated value of the facilities. This makes it impossible for [the park service] even to gauge whether or not the fees it charges are fair."

The parks association in 1992 undertook a survey of California state park franchise fees and found that they range from 3 to 45 percent of gross concession receipts. According to the association, if the national parks had assessed only 10 percent in 1990, it could have taken in nearly $60 million—four times its actual receipts. But even if the funds do come in, they will not go to the park service but into the general fund for paying the national debt.

Funding losses are an old park service problem. The first park director, Nathaniel P. Langford, quit in disgust over lack of funds from Congress. Today, the park service, as characterized by the National Parks and Conservation Association, is a $3 billion agency with a $1.2 billion budget. One side effect of this budgeting shortfall has been a decline in staff quality. Only slightly more than 60 percent of park rangers have a four-year college degree, and they are often forced by burgeoning visitation to act more as policemen than as experts in natural history. Since Reagan's election in 1980 park staff has become increasingly overburdened. In 1980, the ranger-to-visitor ratio was 1 to 59,432. In 1991 it was 1 to 81,526. From 1987 to 1989 the number of seasonal rangers fell from 4,079 to 3,662. Chances of a park visitor seeing a ranger are only one in four. The parks association says, "The lack of adequate staffing jeopardizes visitor safety as well as the protection of the parks' natural and cultural resources."

In 1992 the park service requested an $8 million budget increase so it could hire 350 seasonal rangers in 1993. The House responded with a $2 million increase, the Senate with $4 million.

Politics, of course, can be a problem for any agency, and perhaps that is as it should be. But in the case of the national parks, politics seems to have crossed the line. "Overt and covert political intrusion threatens the very existence of our parks," declares the parks association's 1992 report on the park system. "Strong lobbyists for property rights, timber, mining, grazing, and other big-business interests have crippled the ability of dedicated National Park Service staff members to carry out their mission to protect and preserve the parks for future generations."

For example, when Lorraine Mintzmyer, director of the park service's Rocky Mountain Region—the highest position ever held by a woman in the park service—produced a 60-page document in 1991 urging the park service to focus on outside threats to the parks and calling for a comprehensive management program for Yellowstone National Park that would encompass the seven national forests that surround the park and that are used by park wildlife. She immediately came under indictment by the Bush administration. Apparently, Bushites did not want the integrity of the park to be purchased at the cost of reduced logging on the national forests, which nets the government about minus $21 million yearly. The Bush administration, at the behest of conservative western lawmakers, whittled the 60-page ecosystem management plan down to 10 pages of platitudes about the need to strike a balance between resource development and protection. The park service transferred Mintzmyer to Philadelphia, where she soon resigned.

That same year, Secretary of the Interior Manuel Lujan, Jr., failed to include in testimony before Congress a report by the park service indicating that plans by the Church Universal and Triumphant to undertake geothermal development outside Yellowstone would jeopardize the park's geyser system. Instead, he told Congress, which was studying the issue, about a U.S. Geological Survey report suggesting that development might not harm the geysers. House Democrats promptly accused Lujan of attempting to manipulate Congress by suppressing the park service's strenuous objections to the plan.

Politics enters on yet another level. Of the roughly 360 units administered by the National Park Service, only 50 are national parks. The rest include battlefields, historical sites such as Mount Vernon and Independence Hall, and other sites with little or no wild value. Many historic sites have been dumped on the park service by members of Congress who hope that the service will develop the sites and turn them into profitable tourist attractions for local constituencies. This drains funds that the service is supposed to use to protect national parks.

One way to solve this and other problems is to remove the park service from the Department of the Interior and reorganize it as an independent agency. As part of this reorganization, the battlefield national monuments and other units lacking in natural-resource value would be placed in a separate agency that will focus on American heritage sites. Only the national parks would be left in the reorganized and independent park service, which could then focus on the various perplexing tasks of wilderness protection in parks to which nearly 300 million visitors come each year.

The parks association does not go so far as to suggest breaking up the units administered by the park service. But it does call "for the creation of an independent, autonomous National Park Service to insulate the agency from the political pressures it faces, and to allow its resource-protection mandate to be considered more clearly in debates over the federal budget. . . . While this solution is not a panacea, it is a crucial first step in addressing the threats to our national parks."

Perhaps the biggest threat to the parks, as well as to all other areas set aside for the protection of wildlands and wildlife, is fragmentation. National parks, forests, and wildlife refuges are becoming increasingly isolated in a world of development. This is a bigger problem that requires perhaps more extensive changes than a mere reorganization of an existing agency. It is the subject of a chapter that lies ahead. Before that discussion begins, however, the following chapter looks at the last of the federal categories of land protection.

CHAPTER 9

New Kids on the Block: Designated Wilderness Areas and National Marine Sanctuaries

꘍

Wilderness is a resource which can shrink but not grow. Invasions can be arrested or modified in a manner to keep an area usable either for recreation, or for science, or for wildlife, but the creation of new wilderness in the full sense of the word is impossible.

Aldo Leopold, 1949

As a rule the nations that have wilderness do not want it, and those that want it do not have it.

Roderick Nash, Wilderness and the American Mind

On January 2, 1901, Florence Marshall, the wife of wealthy New York City constitutional attorney Louis Marshall, gave birth to a boy she and her husband named Robert. Apparently she passed on to him a genetic brevity of life. Florence would live only 43 years, and Robert and his older sister Ruth only 38 years. But in those years Robert would scatter his footprints over much of North America and leave behind a legacy that should, depending on the vagaries of the political world, endure through the centuries.

The family lived in a brownstone on Manhattan's East 72 Street. On school-day mornings, Louis Marshall would assemble his children, who would eventually number three boys and one girl, and hike with them to their school on the far side of Central Park. As they walked, he would often point out various tree species and blossoming flowers and talk about the cultivation of trees. These were subjects of deep interest to Louis Marshall, who was not only a co-founder of the American Jewish Committee, head of New York State's Immigration Commission, and a defender of civil liberties and minority rights who often litigated in the Supreme Court, but also an ardent advocate for the protection of wild places. He served as chairman of the board of trustees of Syracuse University's College of Forestry and was an active defender of both Central Park and the Adirondack Forest Preserve, which today, as Adirondack State Park, encompasses 6 million acres in the mountainous heart of New York State, the largest park in the lower 48 states. In 1915 Louis Marshall, at the state constitutional convention, fought for preservation of a clause guaranteeing that the Adirondack reserve would remain "forever wild."

Louis gave his children every opportunity to absorb his interest in wild places. It took root deeply in two of the four. George, the youngest by five years, would work throughout his life on conservation issues and become the only individual to serve as president of both The Wilderness Society and the Sierra Club, though professionally he would always remain an economist.

The other, Robert, who would spend the first 21 summers of his life at the family's camp on Lower Saranac Lake in the Adirondacks, became the most ardent and persistent conservationist of the litter. Immersing himself in forests, mountains, lakes, and wilderness lore, he turned into an avid—really a maniacal— hiker. By the time he was 21 he and George had climbed all 46 peaks in excess of 4,000 feet elevation in the region surrounding the Saranac summer house. And he did not merely climb peaks, he darted over them at breakneck speed. In the summer of 1930 the brothers and their guide scaled a record nine peaks in a single day, breaking the previous record of six set in 1894. It was nothing for Robert to hike 30 miles in a single day. In fact, while in college he determined that he would finish one day-long 30-mile haul in each state. While still a student, he knocked down 62 miles in a single day then, a few years later, broke his record by covering 70 miles in 36 hours. One of his eccentricities was the keeping of a log that showed how many miles each hike covered in what amount of time, with mileage and time for each hike broken into small segments.

Photographs of Bob taken in the 1930s show a tall, lean figure whose high forehead is topped with wavy, dark hair. He was marginally homely, with a slight puffiness beneath his eyes and with ears he might have borrowed from H. Ross Perot. In an age in which hikers wore heavy, thick-soled boots, he was said to have favored canvas sneakers. He was at home in the wilderness and, in his own words, possessed an "abnormal fear of girls."

In his youth, Marshall spent many hours in New York City

lamenting a certain cruelty with which fate had victimized him—he had been born too late. His thoughts turned often to Lewis and Clark, the explorers that Thomas Jefferson sent out in 1803 to traverse the Louisiana Purchase and the first whites to report extensively on the wonders of the West, its vast bison herds, its grizzlies, its myriad of elk and deer and wild sheep and pronghorn antelope. Marshall longed to travel as they had into an untrammeled wilderness, and he was convinced that he had been born a century too late for such "genuine excitement." His reveries about Lewis Clark, he would write in a 1930 essay published posthumously in a 1951 issue of *Nature* magazine, "ended in terrible depression."

His longing for vast wilderness, his father's influence, and his education as a forester at Syracuse University, Harvard, and Johns Hopkins all conspired to make Bob Marshall into perhaps the most effective of the early defenders of wilderness. In the late 1920s and early 1930s he spent three years as a forester in Montana and 13 months above the Arctic Circle exploring the blank spots he had found on a map of Alaska. In 1933 he became director of Forestry for the Office of Indian Affairs, a position he held for four years until he became chief of the Forest Service's Division of Recreation and Lands. In both capacities he fought for protection of the nation's few remaining wilderness areas, urging the government to keep them untouched by the machinations of human society.

Designated Wilderness—
How Many Brahms Symphonies Do We Need?

Marshall had a strong perception of the importance of wilderness to modern society. He believed that expeditions into the wilderness promoted health and stamina, as well as a sense of independence and self-sufficiency. The wilderness, he believed, compels us to rely upon our own innate survival skills, making us into stronger individuals.

More important, wilderness, he believed, provided respite from the corrosive effects of society and civilization. He wrote that we need the adventure of the wild to escape the banality of society. Civilization leads to repression, he wrote, but in the wild we can shed social bounds and be free, a balm to troubled psyches. He also believed in the aesthetic value of wilderness, in the importance of its beauty to human life. As Roderick Nash writes of Marshall in *Wilderness and the American Mind*, "He felt wild scenery compared to the great works of art. When asked how many wilderness areas America needed, he replied, 'how many Brahms symphonies do we need?'"

Marshall could find support for his ideas in literature old and young. Henry David Thoreau, writing in the mid-nineteenth century, presaged Marshall's observations about the need for wilderness:

> At the same time that we are earnest to explore and learn all things, we require that all things be mysterious and unexplorable, that land and sea be infinitely wild, unsurveyed and unfathomed by us because unfathomable. We can never have enough of nature. We must be refreshed by the sight of inexhaustible vigor, vast and titanic features, the sea-coast with its wrecks, the wilderness with its living and its decaying trees, the thunder-cloud, and the rain which lasts three weeks and produces freshets. We need to witness our own limits transgressed, and some life pasturing freely where we never wander.

And Marshall, with his inquiring mind, can scarcely have missed Sigmund Freud's examination of the pressures of society in *Civilization and Its Discontents:*

> During the last few generations mankind has made an extraordinary advance in the natural sciences and in their technical application and has established his control over nature in a way never before imagined. . . . Men are proud of those achievements, and have a right to be. But they seem to have observed that this newly-won power over space and time, this subjugation of the forces of nature, which is the fulfillment of a longing that goes back thousands of years, has not increased the amount of pleasurable satis-

faction which they may expect from life and has not made them feel happier. From the recognition of this fact we ought to be content to conclude that power over nature is not the *only* precondition of human happiness, just as it is not the *only* goal of cultural endeavor. . . . And, finally, what good to us is a long life if it is difficult and barren of joys, and if it is so full of misery that we can only welcome death as a deliverer?

Freud, in the same book, observed that "Beauty has no obvious use; nor is there any clear cultural necessity for it. Yet civilization could not do without it." In later pages he wrote, "We require civilized man to reverence beauty wherever he sees it in nature and to create it in objects of his handiwork so far as he is able"— truly a Marshallian juxtaposition of nature and art.

Marshall was not a mere theorist. His passion for wilderness compelled him to find practical means for protecting wilderness. In 1934 he worked with other conservation notables, including Aldo Leopold, to create a conservation group dedicated to winning government protection for wilderness areas. On January 21, 1935—only a few days past his 34th birthday—he and his colleagues published a brochure announcing that "for the purpose of fighting off the invasion of the wilderness and of stimulating . . . an appreciation of its multiform emotional, intellectual, and scientific values, we are forming an organization to be known as the WILDERNESS SOCIETY." Marshall contributed $1,000 to help with start-up costs and turned down the presidency in favor of Robert Sterling Yard, who had served as publicity chief for Stephen Mather and later had headed the National Parks Association, created with Mather's help as a National Park Service watchdog.

While The Wilderness Society attempted to persuade Congress to protect wilderness, Marshall worked within the bureaucracy. In 1937 he won the designation of 16 wilderness areas on Indian reservations. In the Forest Service he promoted the need for wilderness designations, knowing that the national forests included the most extensive wilderness acreages in the United States. He created regulations specifically for the protection of national forest wilderness areas.

On November 30, 1939, Marshall was little more than a month from his 39th birthday. He met in Washington with Robert Sterling Yard in a Wilderness Society financial and editorial planning session. After dining that evening with a friend, he boarded the midnight train for New York City, bedding down for the last time in the berth of a Pullman car. Somewhere between New York and Washington, the heart that had pounded through more than 200 day-long hikes of 30 miles, more than 50 of 40 miles, and several in excess of 70 miles, gave out. In his will, he left a $400,000 trust to The Wilderness Society "to increase the knowledge of the citizens of the United States of America as to the importance and necessity of maintaining wilderness conditions in outdoor America for future generations."

In 1940 the Forest Service remembered him with the creation of the Bob Marshall Wilderness Area in Montana. The same year, the service adopted the wilderness-protection regulations that were largely his creation.

But wilderness protection was slow in coming. As part of a federal make-work policy, the Civil Conservation Corps during the 1930s had punched roads, often unnecessary, into potential wilderness tracts, and when World War II broke out demand for natural resources pushed wilderness considerations into the shadows. In the late 1940s Aldo Leopold, in *A Sand County Almanac*, wrote:

> In the Rocky Mountain states, a score of areas in the National Forests, varying in size from a hundred thousand to half a million acres, are withdrawn as wilderness, and closed to roads, hotels, and other inimical uses. In the National Parks the same principle is recognized, but no specific boundaries are delimited. Collectively, these federal areas are the backbone of the wilderness program, but they are not so secure as the paper record might lead one to believe. Local pressures for new tourist roads knock off a chip here and a slab there. There is perennial pressure for extension of roads for forest-fire control, and these, by slow degrees, become public highways. Idle CCC camps presented a widespread temptation to build new and often needless roads. Lumber shortages during the war gave the impetus of military necessity to many road extensions,

legitimate and otherwise. At the present moment, ski-tows and ski-hotels are being promoted in many mountain areas, often without regard to their prior designation as wilderness.

Progress in wilderness protection, as Marshall would have defined it, did not really begin until the late 1950s. It was directly influenced by the fight over Echo Park dam in Dinosaur National Monument. The Echo Park incident was a milestone in modern conservation. It showed the environmental community that conservation issues enjoyed widespread support among the American people and that support could be rallied. It taught professional conservationists how to reach the public and how to cooperate with one another in a concerted campaign.

With the recent experience of Echo Park uppermost in his mind, a quiet, scholarly man named Howard Zahniser, noted in conservation circles for his light wit and satiric poetry in iambic pentameter, decided the time was ripe for progress in wilderness protection. He knew that the conservation community could not persist in fighting one battle after another over individual pro-jects such as Echo Park. The nation needed, he believed, a single law that would give congressional approval to wilderness pro-tection—a Wilderness Act.

This belief fit his professional objectives, because he was the executive director of The Wilderness Society, for which he had worked since 1945. Enlisting the aid of people such as George Marshall, Bob's brother, he drafted in 1956 a bill for creation of a national wilderness system that would protect the nation's last roadless areas from any form of permanent human intrusion and development. The bill was subsequently introduced in the House and Senate, and a fight was joined that would last for eight years.

The bill went through 66 incarnations and was the subject of nine separate hearings and more than 6,000 pages of testimony. The usual forces were arrayed against it. The Forest Service knew that the bulk of the wilderness areas would lie in the national forests and wanted no part of a plan that might reduce logging. The National Park Service was insulted by the implication that they were not already doing everything possible for wilderness, although Zahniser pointed out that the park service was a great builder of roads, lodges, and other facilities inimical to wilderness. Ranchers, loggers, miners, and other developers were also opposed to the bill.

But the American public seemed to like the plan. When the Senate conducted hearings on the bill in the Southwest and on the West Coast, it received 1,003 letters in favor of the bill and only 129 against it. A much revised Wilderness Act was finally passed by the Senate on April 10, 1963, by a vote of 73 to 12. On April 28, 1964, Zahniser, who had attended every congressional hearing on the bill, made his last appearance in behalf of wilderness, testifying before the House. Like Bob Marshall, he was weak of heart. He died on May 5, at age 58, still fighting. The following July, the House passed the bill by a vote of 373 to 1, and in September President Lyndon Johnson signed it into law. It is ironic that three of the leading advocates of wilderness protection—Marshall, Leopold, and Zahniser—did not live to see the law enacted. Leopold, the oldest of the trio, would have been 78 had he lived.

Under the terms of the law, in language penned by Zahniser, a wilderness area is one "where the earth and its community of life are untrammeled by man, where man himself is a visitor who does not remain." Federally designated wilderness areas can be created only by an act of Congress. Once an area is designated as wilderness, no permanent facilities or new roads are to be built in it. Motorized vehicles are permitted only for special purposes, such as search and rescue missions. A wide variety of activities are permitted, such as hunting, fishing, research, camping, back-packing, cross-country skiing, and horseback riding. In some particularly sensitive areas, even some of these activities are banned. In the West, only large pristine areas with no development or signs of development, such as past logging, are eligible for wilderness designation, although exceptions are made. For example, some western wilderness areas do have old roads and even private inholdings. Nevertheless, once a new road is cut into an area, the area is withdrawn from wilderness consideration. Much of the Forest Service's eager road building centers on eliminating roadless areas. In the East, where development has had a more profound effect than in the West, wilderness areas are more loosely defined. In the Eastern Wilderness Act of 1973, Congress permitted the designation of areas that had been developed in the past but had recovered sufficiently to offer a wilderness experience.

But, of course, wilderness protection is not all that simple. To get the law passed, Zahniser and others had to compromise on the terms of the bill. One of the big compromises permitted exploration for minerals, oil, and gas to continue at the discretion of the secretary of the Interior until the end of 1983. Any mining claim established by then could be developed at any time in the future. When the discretion is placed in the hands of someone with James Watt's ethics, wilderness protection becomes meaningless, as it did during his brief stint as Interior secretary. He attempted to open designated and potential wilderness areas to development. It took congressional action to curb his plans during the months before his proclivity for impolitic public discourse forced his resignation.

Under the law, the various federal land-management agencies were to study their holdings and recommend areas for designation. Over the years, however, the agencies have attempted to stall the process, leading to lawsuits brought by conservation groups to compel compliance with the law. Developers and their congressional lackeys still oppose wilderness designation, though it would little threaten development plans. At the very most, the Wilderness Act could lead to wilderness designation of some 60 million acres in the lower 48 states, a total equal to less than 3 percent of the area covered by the lower 48. Research has shown that wilderness designation of this land will have little effect on resource development. Most wilderness areas are at high-elevation, where the least valuable forest grows. Only about 20 percent of the nation's oil and gas onshore reserves lie on public land, and only about 1 percent lie on wilderness areas.

Today, nearly 30 years since passage of the Wilderness Act,

the wilderness system includes some 95 million acres, 57.4 million of it in Alaska. In the lower 48 states, the wilderness system is still 22 million acres short of the goal of 60 million that Zahniser sought.

The protection offered by wilderness designation is critical to vanishing wild places. According to figures in the proceedings of a 1990 Forest Service conference, "Preparing to Manage Wilderness in the 21st Century," only about 200 million acres of remote, or very remote, lands remain in the United States out of an original 2.4 billion acres. The surviving remnant accounts for only 8 percent of the area lying within U.S. borders. In the lower 48 states, no more than 1.8 percent of the original wilderness is protected by federal designation, though that number skyrockets to all of 4 percent if Alaska is included. If the nation cannot protect this scant amount of wild space and still survive economically, then the nation is in trouble so deep that putting oil-well rigs and mines into wilderness areas will not save it. Nevertheless, the agencies in charge of wilderness designation have proved reluctant through the years to move with alacrity in this matter of wilderness protection.

Making the World Safe for Wilderness

Wilderness areas are the odd balls in this survey of federally protected lands because they are not the province of any particular agency. The Forest Service, the National Park Service, the Bureau of Land Management, and the Fish and Wildlife Service were all instructed by Congress to determine which of the lands they administer should be considered for wilderness designation. They have responded to the occasion with varying results.

"There are some real differences between the agencies and how they see wilderness management," says Jay Watson, The Wilderness Society's specialist on wilderness issues (as have many of the larger groups, the society has gotten involved in other issues, notably protection of the national forests and the public domain, and has specialists working on them). Watson has been with the society for seven years. Prior to coming to the Washington, D.C., headquarters he was in the California/Nevada regional office. Before that, he was a wilderness ranger for the Forest Service. In between he was a wilderness backpacking guide for a nonprofit group that worked with 10- to 17-year-olds. He quit the Forest Service and signed on with the backpacking group after he became involved in an effort to win wilderness designation for half a million acres in California's Trinity Alps. The Forest Service wanted to designate only 250,000 acres, and Watson found it increasingly difficult to settle the implicit philosophical differences. While working as a backpacking guide he testified on behalf of the California Wilderness Act and met the local Wilderness Society representative. Within a couple of years, his career at the society had begun.

"The best, the most comprehensive wilderness program is in the Forest Service," Watson says. He suspects that this is largely because the service has been in it longer than the other groups. The next best is the bureau's. Both the service and the bureau have full-time wilderness-area managers in Washington.

The National Park Service is a bit problematic, he suggests. The park service does not differentiate between wilderness and nonwilderness areas in the parks. Park staff call it back country and front country. The service has wilderness rangers and law-enforcement officers, but it lacks a wilderness leader in the Washington headquarters, does not have a separate wilderness program, and has never created a wilderness component in its annual budget.

On the last point, the Forest Service and the bureau do only a little better. Their wilderness personnel are housed in the agencies' recreation programs, giving them little bureaucratic clout. Watson believes that they and the park service need to create separate programs to ensure that wilderness receives proper planning, management, and budgeting. This is particularly true for the Forest Service, since 16 percent of its domain is wilderness.

The Fish and Wildlife Service, says Watson, is the big hold-out. Service staff do not see wilderness protection as part of their mandate, even though they could carve about 63 million acres of wilderness out of their lands, with 60 million of it in Alaska. The Fish and Wildlife Service's wilderness staffer in Washington is "stretched" more than his counterparts in the other agencies, says Watson, making it hard for him to focus on specific wilderness matters.

Funding for wilderness designation and management has been elusive. Increases in the wilderness budgets of the Forest Service and the Bureau of Land Management have resulted from congressional interest and public support and have had "precious little to do with the Bush administration," Watson said. Nevertheless, the bureau is "hostile to wilderness" and persistently attempts to cut its wilderness budget. Recently, in a time when the bureau should be "gearing up for wilderness management because of increased designations on its lands," Watson said, "the Washington office was downsizing, cutting its staff of seven in wilderness to two." The Forest Service was taking a similar approach, diverting into other programs roughly 40 percent of the funds budgeted for wilderness, which to begin with accounts for only 1 percent of the entire service budget. Watson says that agencies often shift funds within a program but that in this case the shift is "a blatant abuse of agency discretion." Watson believes this would not happen if the service's wilderness chief were co-equal, rather than subordinate, to other program chiefs.

These two approaches to wilderness backsliding, which Watson says were indicative of actions being taken "at the highest levels of these agencies," signaled to Congress, notably Bruce Vento, that the situation needed correcting. Vento's means for making that correction is a bill that would strengthen wilderness management. Called the National Wilderness Management Act, the law would create leadership for wilderness within each agency. Making wilderness management the leaders' sole responsibility would increase their accountability and pull wilderness protection out of the Forest Service and bureau recreational programs. The bill would also set up a national wilderness monitoring system to track trends in the condition of wilderness areas and would establish a public education program on wilderness. It would also collect baseline data on wilderness resources and coordinate the wilderness activities of the various agencies.

This legislation, says Watson, "is an absolute must." Without it, he says, the agencies will not give wilderness the attention needed to develop a coherent national wilderness system.

The wilderness system will come up again in the discussion of fragmentation in the next chapter. Before that, we will examine briefly the youngest of federal land-protection endeavors.

Marine Sanctuaries

With a nineteenth-century confidence in the limitations of humanity's technological prowess, Henry David Thoreau could write of the ocean as if it would always remain beyond human influence:

> We do not associate the idea of antiquity with the ocean, nor wonder how it looked a thousand years ago, as we do of the land, for it was equally wild and unfathomable always. The Indians have left no traces on its surface, but it is the same to the civilized man and the savage. The aspect of the shore only has changed. The ocean is a wilderness reaching round the globe, wilder than the Bengal jungle, and fuller of monsters, washing the very wharves of our cities and the gardens of our seaside residences. Serpents, bears, hyenas, tigers rapidly vanish as civilization advances, but the most populous and civilized city cannot scare a shark far from its wharves.

Today, because of uncontrolled fishing, shark populations the world over are collapsing. Research during the past 10 to 20 years has revealed that many shark species have low reproductive rates, close to that of whales. We know what whaling did to whale populations, and evidence from shark populations that dwindled after heavy fishing indicate that commercial fishing is doing much the same to the sharks that swim past our wharves and even farther out to sea.

The sea itself bears our mark. It shows up in the toxins found in the tissues of Atlantic coastal bottlenose dolphins, the sleek creatures cavorting on the waves off popular East Coast beaches. Their tissues bear the greatest concentration of toxins ever found in a mammal. Their population died off by half in the mid-1980s, cause still unknown. The suspect is immune-system suppression caused by pollutants. A marine biologist working for the National Audubon Society has compiled anecdotal evidence from elderly fishermen which indicates that the dolphin population throughout the northern Atlantic may be on the edge of failing. The same holds true for swordfish populations off Long Island, which were recently so common that fishermen encountered several each day in areas where today none are seen.

Little wonder that fish populations are shrinking. Commercial fishermen throw away millions of tons of fish every year, vast quantities that they had not targeted for catch or that are not legal size. The National Marine Fisheries Service estimates that more than a billion pounds of fish, equal to 10 percent of the entire U.S. commercial catch, are dumped overboard each year by Atlantic and Gulf of Mexico shrimp fishermen alone. Every pound of shrimp represents a loss of 9 pounds of red snapper, mackerel, sea trout, and other edible species.

And then we have the problem of pollution. In all, U.S. citizens and industry dump about 16 trillion gallons of sewage and industrial waste into American rivers and coastal waters every year. Some of it is dumped intentionally, such as the 9 million tons of sewage sludge that New York and New Jersey drop offshore each year. Some of it is uncontrolled seepage—21 million barrels of waste annually from such sources as industrial effluents and rainfall that washes chemicals and solid wastes from city streets.

As a result, 40 percent of all U.S. shellfish beds, poisoned by toxins, have been closed to fishermen. The striped bass that in 1973 produced a commercial catch of nearly 15 million pounds in New York Harbor is now off the market because it is polluted with toxins such as cancer-causing PCBs. Around some parts of

Puget Sound off Washington State, signs have been erected in seven languages warning that crabs, shellfish, and bottomfish may be unsafe to eat. Beaches as far apart as those in southern California and New Jersey have been shut down because of locally high levels of coliform bacteria from fecal matter.

The National Marine Sanctuary Program represents part of an effort to stop the degradation and overfishing of our coastal waters, including those of the Great Lakes. It was brought into existence by the Marine Protection, Research and Sanctuaries Act of 1972, sometimes called the Ocean Dumping Bill. The law was an outgrowth of public concern over oil spills, particularly the infamous 1968 Santa Barbara Channel spill, and the dumping of wastes, notably nerve gas and oil waste dumped off Florida. Only a portion of the law, called Title III, dealt with creation of protected marine areas. Title III declared that the secretary of Commerce "may designate as marine sanctuaries those areas of the ocean waters, of other coastal waters where the tide ebbs or flows, of the Great Lakes and their connecting waters, which he determines necessary for the purpose of preserving or restoring such areas for their conservation, recreational, ecological, or esthetic values."

Under the law, the National Marine Sanctuary Program is administered by the Sanctuaries and Reserves Division of the National Oceanic and Atmospheric Administration (NOAA, pronounced Noah) in the Department of Commerce. According to regulations issued in the 1970s, any citizen or organization can nominate a site for consideration by NOAA as a sanctuary.

The first sanctuary was not created until 1975. This was the Monitor National Marine Sanctuary, which lies 16 nautical miles southeast of North Carolina and was established to protect the wreckage of the USS *Monitor,* the prototype for the Civil War ironclad ships, which went down in a gale on December 31, 1862, with 16 sailors aboard. The sanctuary covers an area one mile in diameter over the wreckage. The next sanctuary—Channel Islands, some 1,252 nautical square miles off the coast of southern California designated for the protection of birds and marine mammals—was not created until September 1980. Three more followed in January 1981 as the Carter administration packed up and left town.

The Reagan administration—no surprise—strongly opposed the marine sanctuary program. Congress kept the program from starving financially during the eight-year reign, a period in which only one tiny sanctuary was created—Fagatele Bay, covering 0.25 square nautical miles of a coral reef ecosystem off American Samoa. Since then, six more sanctuaries have been added to the system.

Unfortunately, the national marine sanctuaries remain little known and little heralded. They have received little support from the public or from a cross-section of the more influential conservation groups. Consequently, the marine sanctuaries program faces problems that by now will have a familiar ring.

Perhaps the most salient problem is a lack of clear purpose. Their mission as stated in the 1972 law was general enough to allow broad agency interpretation. As a result, writes marine-policy-consultant David Tarnas, in a 1988 article for *Coastal Management*, emphasis has been placed increasingly on multiple-use. The first agency regulations, published in 1974, said that multiple-use "may be permitted" after careful investigation on a case-by-case basis. Five years later, a new regulation said that human use "will be allowed." In 1983 yet newer regulations, presumably reflecting the anything-goes philosophy of land use during the Reagan years, declared that the sanctuaries "will provide for multiple public and private uses." Finally, in 1984 Congress attempted to clarify the multiple-use question with an amendment. Among other purposes outlined for the sanctuaries was facilitation "to the extent compatible with the primary objective of resource protection, all public and private uses of the resources of these marine areas not prohibited pursuant to other authorities." All in all, this sounds much like the compatibility approach that is applied to national wildlife refuges.

The creation of national marine sanctuaries for the protection of coral reefs, marine mammals such as sea lions and whales, and a vast array of fish and other oceanic species has been opposed by various commercial interests. Perhaps foremost among them is the oil and gas industry, which has feared since the beginning that the sanctuaries would affect offshore oil development, even though the sanctuaries cover less than 0.1 percent of the outer continental shelf. The industry challenged in court NOAA's authority to ban oil and gas development within the Channel Islands and Gulf of the Farallones national marine sanctuaries off California, but the courts upheld the protection. Some commercial fishermen have also opposed specific sanctuary designations, but in general they have not been ardent opponents. In the case of Looe Key National Marine Sanctuary off southwest Florida, fishing improved in surrounding waters after sanctuary staff imposed a fishing ban around Looe Key's coral reef.

The most pervasive problem confronting the marine sanctuary system is lack of funding and staff. According to a report issued in early 1991 by the Marine Sanctuaries Review Team, a panel of experts convened by NOAA's assistant administrator for Ocean Services to review the sanctuaries program, the program has been hampered by an annual budget of $4 million that "does not begin to meet the needs of the sanctuary program in place today. . . ." Added the panel, "An adequate budget for the Florida Keys National Sanctuary alone would be $7–8 million. The California sanctuaries, as a group . . . should probably receive a similar level of funding." The panel concluded that the program needed a budget "on the order of $30 million."

The panel also recommended that the sanctuary program be expanded to include all the various types of marine ecosystems found in U.S. waters. Each individual sanctuary should be large enough, the panel urged, to allow sanctuary staff to create zones within which various activities would be restricted. For example, a core zone might be closed to human consumptive use, offering a place where fish and other sea animals are safe from commercial and sport fishing. Outside this zone, certain low-impact uses might be permitted, and so on to the sanctuary boundary. To ensure that staff are prepared for their task, the panel recommended improved training as well as cooperation with other agencies.

The panel also recommended that Congress again clarify the sanctuaries' purpose, adding, among others, the need "to identify and designate a representative network of biogeographically representative ecosystems to ensure the continuing biodiversity of our coastal and marine areas, linked to an international system of biosphere and wilderness reserves aimed at maintaining the diversity of the Earth's natural living communities." In addition, Congress should also make it part of the sanctuaries' mission "to maintain, restore and enhance the diversity of the biological resources by providing places of refuge for exploited species that depend upon these areas to survive and propagate themselves." In short, the panel would like the sanctuaries to become part of a linked system of protected areas designed to protect biodiversity in part through the sheltering of various species used by commercial and recreational interests. If adopted, this recommendation would give the infant sanctuary system a strong position in the realm of public-land and biodiversity protection. We can be certain, however, that commercial interests will fight the new concept every step of the way, as they have with logging, public-domain regulation, refuges, and other public lands.

The very newness of the marine sanctuary program works against it. Its position within the Department of Commerce suggests that it will always be lost amidst greater commercial concerns. Until the program builds a strong constituency, as Marshall and Zahniser did for wilderness, it will be engaged in an uphill battle for federal dollars and congressional support. The time may soon come when it will be necessary to give responsibility for marine sanctuaries to an agency more concerned about the goals and necessities of wildland protection.

The need to protect the medium above the terrain is more manifest in marine sanctuaries than it is in terrestrial reserves. Sanctuary managers must protect the integrity of the sea that flows over the ocean floor as well as the floor itself and all its denizens. It is as if the administrators of Yellowstone had to worry not only about mountains, plains, and streams, but also about the air above the park.

Though, of course, they do. One of the knottiest problems facing wildland administrators is the sticky question of outside influences on the integrity of protected lands. This is a serious problem for marine sanctuaries because coastal sites can be jeopardized by events occurring miles away and deep inland. For example, when farm runoff floods into rivers that then carry agricultural pesticides and other toxins downstream and into bays, estuaries, and the ocean itself, a marine sanctuary may ultimately be steeped in the chemicals. Similarly, national parks are influenced by the substances that the winds bring to them. Ozone levels harmful to humans have been recorded in three national parks near urban areas in southern California and Indiana. Hazardous levels have been recorded even in relatively remote parks, such as Acadia National Park on the coast of Maine, Joshua Tree National Monument in the southern California desert, and Sequoia National Park, high in the Sierra Nevadas. About 70 percent of Great Smoky Mountains National Park's eastern white pines show evidence of damage from high ozone levels, as do more than half the eastern white pines in Acadia. Shenandoah National Park is on the brink of an acid-rain debacle. About half its streams are likely to begin losing fish populations if acidity rises only slightly, and the ability of the soil to balance the acidity of local rainfall could reach its end within 40 years.

The boundaries with which we have attempted to protect wild places are no longer effective. Their ability to sustain wildness is illusory. They are a nineteenth-century artifact that, in the twentieth century and beyond, are becoming part of the problem, breaking up wild places into fragments that cannot sustain the biodiversity within them.

PART THREE

A New Agenda
for Biodiversity

CHAPTER 10

The Shattered Cradle: Fragmentation

≋

The National Parks do not suffice as a means of perpetuating the larger carnivores; witness the precarious status of the grizzly bear, and the fact that the park system is already wolfless. Neither do they suffice for mountain sheep; most sheep herds are shrinking.

The reasons for this are clear in some cases and obscure in others. The parks are certainly too small for such a far-ranging species as the wolf. Many animal species, for reasons unknown, do not seem to thrive as detached islands of populations.

Aldo Leopold, A Sand County Almanac

Habitat fragmentation is the most serious threat to biological diversity and is the primary cause of the present extinction crisis.

B. A. Wilcox and D. D. Murphy, 1985

≋

At the heart of our land and wildlife problems lies the fact that in the late twentieth century—in a world of computers, space travel, and electronic imaging, in a nation of 250 million people and 140 million automobiles in which it is impossible to get more than 20 miles from the nearest road—we are still protecting wild places much as we did in the years when Clagett, Langford, and Theodore Roosevelt were at work. Congress, the White House, the state wildlife agencies, and even private conservation groups are continuing to draw boundaries around wildlands with the presumption that everything that lies within those boundaries will be safe and sound. Study after study has shown that this approach is not working, yet we rarely trifle with the idea that our initial premises might be wrong, that we started out at square one and blundered off in the wrong direction, like Truman C. Everts at the start of his 37 days of peril in 1870s Yellowstone. And as with Everts, life is at stake—the life of our parks, refuges, and forests and the survival of hundreds, perhaps thousands, of species, all at the cost of billions of tax dollars.

Carving Up the Planet

The Earth has been a great cradle of life, the only planet in the solar system that ever nurtured unliving chemicals into breathing, scurrying, running, crawling, flying, swimming, deeply rooting, eating, drinking, fighting, warring, loving, hating, ever-evolving, endlessly striving creatures. But the Earth, as if some tragic figure from classical Greek drama, possesses a fatal flaw. The mindless decisions of natural selection led inexorably to the creation of intelligent life, but to one of only limited intelligence, one geared, as biologist Paul Ehrlich has asserted, to responding quickly and adapting beautifully to immediate problems, but relatively unaware of slower, long-term troubles such as habitat degeneration and species losses and, therefore, hard-pressed to do anything about them.

Granted by nature a profound technological capability, human intelligence nevertheless seems mortally destitute of introspection and self-restraint. In us, life seems finally to have produced a creature capable of destroying Life, and we seem to be exercising that capability with increasing intensity. We have become experts at prolonging the survival and increasing the comfort of individuals, but we have become inept at surviving as a species. While we worked at being hunters and gatherers of wild foods, the survival of our species seemed ensured for millions of years. But many human societies during the past 15,000 years or so switched to acquiring food through agriculture, and immediately the environmental costs started to mount. Through changes in water flow, concentration of natural soil toxins, and the removal of forests, agriculture created deserts in large parts of the Middle East, Asia, and North Africa, wiped out the native forests of Europe, and toppled kingdoms and empires whose economic bases were destroyed. It threatens to do the same in the New World, especially now that agriculture depends so much on the chemical industry, steeping croplands in toxic fertilizers and pesticides. Perhaps high-tech agriculture as a means of life is only possible for a few millennia. Of even shorter duration may be the promise of the Industrial Revolution. Our highly industrial society, though created only within the past two centuries, already seems to threaten much of life and society as we know them. As a viable adaptation to the demands of survival, industry as it has been conducted may be suitable only for a very few centuries.

Perhaps we are a biological experiment gone awry, nature's

Frankenstein monster, nature's folly. Perhaps we are only a fascinating blip on the evolutionary graph. Perhaps the real secret to survival is possessed by insects and lizards and other creatures less adept at modifying their environment. The key, of course, is whether we can learn soon to develop and practice the self-restraint that is becoming an increasingly critical adaptation to survival in the techno-modern world.

At present, humanity's 5 billion individuals consume an estimated 40 percent of the Earth's net primary productivity or photosynthetic products, both of which are scientific jargon for plants. If the population doubles in the next century as predicted, will our consumption double too? Could we survive it? Could the planet?

Our consumption of plant life takes many recognizable forms—logging on the national forests and grazing by livestock on the public domain spring readily to mind. Destruction of forests and grasslands for mineral and petroleum extraction count too. Roughly 99 percent of U.S. tall-grass prairies have been lost since settlement, as have half the nation's wetlands, including marshes and swamps that help cleanse from rainfall the various toxins with which industry has imbued the Earth.

In our efforts to protect wildlands from the onslaught of society, we have put boundaries around quantities of forest, mountain, lake, seashore, grassland, and desert. The total of our protected lands equals about 9 percent of the entire United States, a fragment of the once vast natural ecosystem. And that tiny fragment is itself broken up and scattered across the continent in a sprinkling of even tinier fragments, each one largely isolated from the others, surrounded by the alien rush of development.

"Habitat fragmentation is considered by many biologists to be the single greatest threat to biological diversity," wrote Reed Noss, a biodiversity-conservation specialist, in the 1991 book *Landscape Linkages and Biodiversity.* Fragmentation is the breaking up of natural habitat into smaller pieces or isolated units. It is the chopping up of habitat into such small pieces that it can no longer provide native species with adequate food, water, or shelter.

If you are observant, you can see fragmentation and its effects all around you. In the late 1980s I lived in suburbs in New
Jersey and the Hudson River Valley while working for the National Audubon Society in New York City. One winter night as I
drove through suburban Morristown, New Jersey, I nearly col-
lided with a white-tailed deer that darted from a backyard, across
the icy two-lane, and into a field increasingly closed in by housing and malls. The doe was eeking out a living in habitat
chopped up by development, a victim of fragmentation. So too
was a buck that bolted, tongue lolling out of gaping mouth,
among morning rush-hour traffic near Croton, New York, one
recent autumn, trapped on a narrow wooded strip between
bumper-to-bumper cars and the parking lot of a corporate office
building. So too was a doe I saw killed near Yonkers, New York,
as she bounded across a four-lane highway for scant refuge in a
narrow copse.

Last Fourth of July weekend I spotted a hen mallard and five
hatchlings waddling along the shoulder of the Washington, D.C.,
Beltway, an eight-lane segment of interstate highway. To her
right were whizzing lanes of traffic, to her left a concrete road
divider waist high to a grown man. I suspect that she had nested
in a small, marshy pond that lay farther down the road between
the two sides of the interstate. She had been safe there from
predators and other dangers until the eggs hatched and the time
came to move the hatchlings. Now she was trapped with her tiny
young in the asphalt median of a highway corridor.

After I spotted her it took a good 10 or 15 minutes to get back
to her because of the arrangement of the exits and entrances to
the Beltway. I had hoped to catch the young and somehow re-
unite them with their mother in safer surroundings, which I
knew would be something of a problem. But by the time I
reached her the problem was solved. She was dead, pressed flat
by rubber tires, as was one of the hatchlings. The four survivors
were huddled together against the concrete road divider. After
chasing them along the shoulder and across four lanes of heedless traffic, I caught three of them and turned them over to a
ranger at a local national-park facility. The fourth disappeared

into some undergrowth. They too were victims of fragmentation, hatched on a pond in a tiny patch of marsh smaller than an average suburban backyard.

I live now in northern Virginia outside Washington, D.C., where the suburbs are growing fast. Pastures 10 years ago now sprout housing developments, and the roads that serve the home dwellers are being ever widened. Early last summer, in the town where I live, a large wooded tract that had provided nesting habitat for birds, hiding places for raccoons and opossums, and homes for salamanders and other amphibians was stripped to earth to make way for townhouses with a view of the Potomac River. It was only a small fragment of woods, like many other small fragments of woods in northern Virginia, which now are fewer in number by one in my community. A year before I had driven past a construction site outside Washington where a wood was being knocked down by bulldozers, red earth baking in the sun, the fallen trees and shrubs piled together and burning, black smoke rising. I was reminded of similar scenes in Costa Rica. We lament the waste of Latin American rainforests while all around us in our own nation wildlife habitat is cleared, burned, and fragmented.

These anecdotal stories prove nothing in the scientific sense. But they are indications of a major wildland problem, and the extent and the seriousness of that problem are well documented.

The Effects of Fragmentation

One of the most thoroughly studied examples of species declines induced by fragmentation concerns creatures that even urban dwellers see almost daily—songbirds. Many songbirds prefer to nest in large stands of forest. The deep interiors of these forests permit the birds to avoid forest edges. Some forest-interior birds refuse even to fly across open fields. When forests are fragmented, these species decline in the face of a variety of threats. Some of their avian competitors favor forest edges, where trees meet open land, and overwhelm the interior species. A 1978 study cited in Reed Noss's technical paper, "A Regional

Landscape Approach to Maintain Diversity," found that interior birds forced to nest in edge habitat laid fewer eggs and were subject to increased predation. Noss cited other studies that showed migratory bird numbers dropping significantly and species diversity changing after a transmission line corridor split a deciduous forest in Tennessee.

Songbird species that comprise 80 to 90 percent of the birds breeding in extensive tracts of eastern deciduous forests account for less than half the birds in small, isolated forest fragments. Forest-interior bird species in the Midwest breed only in patches of forest larger than 60 acres. Surveys of songbird populations conducted since 1948 around Washington, D.C.—where wooded lands are being fragmented by housing and commercial development—have turned up declines in such forest-requiring species as the Kentucky warbler, American redstart, Acadian flycatcher, hooded warbler, ovenbird, yellow-throated warbler, red-eyed vireo, and wood thrush. Not all the blame can be placed on the fragmentation of North American forests, however. In West Virginia's Cheat Mountains, where forests have not been cut, a survey conducted since 1947 started turning up songbird declines in the 1960s. The species that declined there, as well as the first to decline in the Washington, D.C., area, were those that migrate yearly to Latin America, where their rainforest habitat is being rapidly fragmented. Many songbird migrants today are being hit by fragmentation in both their Latin American and North American habitats.

In a 1989 technical paper entitled "Conserving Diversity in Cosmopolitan Faunas," Fritz Knopf, a biologist with the Fish and Wildlife Service's National Ecology Research Center, revealed further examples of wildlife population declines caused by fragmentation. He reported that 12 of 21 species native to the Sonoran desert in southeastern Arizona were absent from residential urban areas where the habitat had been cut up by housing developments. Of the bird species native to the creosote-bush habitat upon which the residential area was built, none were found.

Michael Soule, chairman of environmental studies at the

University of California in Santa Cruz and a past chairman of the Del Mar, California, Planning Commission, studied the effects of fragmentation on wildlife living in 37 isolated tracts of chaparral in San Diego, California, and reported his findings in the summer 1991 issue of the *Journal of the American Planning Association*. Chaparral is a dense, scrub vegetation that, along coastal southern California, rarely grows more than 9 feet high and usually is less than half that. Soule's study focused on bird species left in remnants of chaparral after development. Most of the development was in canyons separated by steep hills. The surviving fragments of native habitat lay on the hillsides.

The "chaparral-requiring" (CR) birds, as Soule calls them, monitored in the study were the black-tailed gnatcatcher, roadrunner, California quail, California thrasher, rufous-sided towhee, Bewick's wren, and wrentit. Soule found that most canyons lose at least half of their CR birds within 20 to 40 years after they become isolated by development. Larger canyons continued to support up to six species, while on average only half the canyons of less than 125 acres supported as many as one CR bird species after 40 years. A fragment's proximity to larger stands of chaparral habitat did not affect the survival of its CR birds. Apparently, the birds are reluctant to cross disturbed areas, such as housing developments and roads, to get to new habitat. The study also found that native mammals, such as rodents, rabbits, and hares, disappear even more rapidly than do the CR birds, to be replaced by house mice and black rats, those persistent cohabitants of humanity. Soule also found that chaparral-requiring birds disappeared in a predictable sequence based on body weight and on average abundance of the species in its typical habitat.

In Florida, as Larry Harris reported in *Transactions of the North American Wildlife and Natural Resources Conference 1988*, forests are being cut at the rate of 150,000 acres yearly, with clear effect on black bears. As forested regions shrink, so does the bear population. Black bears inhabit 75 percent of Florida forests in excess of 100,000 acres and located near a much larger wild area. But the bears inhabit less than 10 percent of natural areas smaller than 1,000 acres.

Species that do survive in fragmented areas may end up as reduced populations that fall victim to inbreeding. In addition, human activity brings with it a variety of non-native species that often outcompete the natives. Studies in England show, for example, that free-ranging house cats take a significant toll on local birds and small mammals.

Fragmentation also makes wildlands more vulnerable to disasters. For example, in presettlement America, fires were a natural part of forest ecology, creating openings in the millions of acres of forest that cloaked much of the eastern half of the continent and large portions of the West. Wildlife within a burned area could filter into surrounding unburned forest. But now that forests, particularly ancient forests, are restricted to relatively small units of protected lands, wild creatures are much more vulnerable to fire. A large fire or conflagration that might have done insignificant damage to old, uncut forest could today, if it damaged a large enough proportion of an isolated forest reserve, make the area unable to support native wildlife, leaving them with nowhere to go. Similarly, a large forest could withstand windfall—the knocking down of trees by high winds—because this sort of damage is never extensive. A small stand of forest, on the other hand, could be wiped out by windfall. In the Pacific Northwest, the forest fragments that the Forest Service leaves on mountainsides to reinforce its claim that it no longer conducts large clearcuts are extremely vulnerable to windfall.

The Causes of Fragmentation

Noss, in a 1987 paper entitled "Protecting Natural Areas in Fragmented Habitats" published in the *Natural Areas Journal*, outlines the causes of fragmentation. Acknowledging that agricultural and urban development are obvious causes, he focuses first on roads, which

> by themselves can be significant fragmenting factors. Not only do roads isolate some species that depend on interior habitat and/or are unwilling to cross open areas, . . . but they create artificial edges that encourage invasion by weeds and opportunists such as

the brown-headed cowbird [which parasitizes songbird nests] and serve as direct sources of mortality to many animals. . . . Perhaps the most insidious effect of roads is that they create access for humans to log, mine, develop, poach, "go four-wheelin'," and otherwise harass and disturb species and their habitats.

Research has shown that the number of roads in a given area of wolf habitat is the best indicator of the number of wolves in the area. If roads exceed more than .93 miles for every square mile of habitat, wolves disappear. "Considering the history of habitat fragmentation and road building in North America," writes Noss, "it is not surprising that the range of the wolf, outside of Canada and Alaska, is only about 5 percent of what it was in 1700." Similarly, studies in Utah and Arizona have shown that individual mountain lions avoid roads, particularly roads with hard surfaces, and seem to prefer home ranges with lower than average amounts of roads, no recent timber sales regardless of whether the area was logged, and few or no human domiciles.

Data from Florida, reported in the Defenders of Wildlife book *In Defense of Wildlife: Preserving Communities and Corridors,* indicate that, with the exception of white-tailed deer, roadkills take the lives of more of the state's remaining large mammals than any other cause. Since 1981 roadkills have been responsible for nearly two-thirds of all deaths of Florida panthers, an endangered species that numbers fewer than 50 individuals. Roadkills are also the major cause of death for the endangered Key deer and the American crocodile.

Roads slice up wildlife habitat. A multilane road with a concrete divider can form an impenetrable barrier for many wildlife species. Amphibians, snakes, lizards, turtles, and small mammals are likely to find it impossible to cross from one side to the other of a forest or grassland bifurcated by a highway. A river, a mountain, or an entire ocean could not more effectively isolate the animals on either side of the road. This can lead to inbreeding and reproductive failure at the same time that the roads are boosting mortality, a double-barreled assault on wildlife populations. It is impossible to determine how much damage roads do to wildlife. For example, no data exist to show the effect of dividing most of the length of Long Island, New York, with major highways or the effect of cutting up entire states into biological districts bounded by superhighways. However, the estimated 100 million animals killed yearly on roads give some sense of the magnitude of wildlife losses.

The most obvious cause of fragmentation is land use, including heavy grazing, mining, timber production, housing, dam construction—virtually any of the uses to which human society puts land in its pursuit of that 40 percent of all plant growth.

Our system of public-land protection has tended to compound the effects of fragmentation nationwide. When we protect public wildlands, putting boundaries around them, we permit surrounding lands to be developed, making protected lands into islands.

Fragmentation and Public Wildlands

Any discussion of the effects of fragmentation must begin with William Newmark's study of U.S. and Canadian national parks. In 1987 he published in *Nature,* one of the world's leading scientific journals, an article entitled "A Land-bridge Island Perspective on Mammalian Extinctions in Western North American Parks." The title is a bit opaque, perhaps, but the article's theme is clear: Our parks offer dangerous ground to large wildlife.

Newmark looked at the fate of carnivores, hoofed animals, and rabbits in 14 national parks in the western United States and Canada and discovered that 43 percent of the study species had become extinct. "Only the largest western North American park assemblage, the Kootenay-Banff-Jasper-Yoho park assemblage (20,736 sq. km), still contains an intact historical mammalian assemblage." In other words, 13 of the 14 parks studied had lost some of their mammals.

Most important, he found that the older and smaller a park is, the more species it loses. Small park size speeds the rate of extinction because smaller parks start out with smaller, and therefore more vulnerable, wildlife populations. If animals on surrounding private lands are killed off, the park animals become isolated from others of their kind. The parks become prisons, disrupting a full range of natural behaviors. Young animals are unable to disperse in search of unoccupied territories and mates and may die without reproducing. If animals within the park are lost, they cannot be replaced by individuals from other areas. Migratory mammals may be unable to reach seasonal feeding grounds outside the parks.

Extinction occurs at different rates for different species. Large predators are particularly vulnerable because they need a lot of land and a lot of prey. Other species vanish more slowly. Newmark believes that more park mammals will become extinct.

Noss, in the *Natural Areas Journal,* offers an explanation for the failure of public wildlands to protect wildlife adequately, summing it up in two words: inappropriate boundaries. "Most 'protected' areas of any size were not selected on the basis of ecological criteria and do not comprise intact ecosystems," he writes. "Legal boundaries rarely coincide with the ecological boundaries necessary to maintain ecological processes or the species with the largest home ranges. . . . Also, because most natural areas are not adequately buffered from intensive land use (such as agricultural fields, clearcuts, intensive rangeland, strip mines, and housing subdivisions), adverse factors . . . readily penetrate in from the boundaries. . . ."

Biologist Allen Cooperrider, writing about biodiversity conservation on western range lands in *Landscape Linkages and Biodiversity,* an excellent overview of fragmentation edited by Wendy Hudson of Defenders of Wildlife, states plainly the central problem of federal land protection:

> Current preserve systems in the United States are of limited effectiveness by themselves because most were not established to preserve biological diversity. . . . Most of the national parks and monuments of the nonforest West . . . were designated because of their spectacular geological features. Similarly, until recently most designation of wilderness areas and wild rivers has been based upon the

desirability for primitive recreation such as backpacking and canoeing. This policy has resulted in a disproportionate number of alpine [high-mountain] wilderness areas and white-water wild and scenic rivers.

"A second major problem," writes Cooperrider, " . . . is that many preserves are not large enough to maintain viable populations of target species, much less self-sustaining ecosystems. Our oldest and largest national park in the West, Yellowstone, is not large enough to contain viable populations of many species, thus necessitating the need for management based on the 'Greater Yellowstone Ecosystem.' "

An additional problem is the choices that were made when federal agencies determined which areas would be protected. The federal government, without intending to do so, followed a two-tiered process in determining which lands would be protected. First, it gave away or sold off as much of the public domain as possible. This ensured that the best land went into private hands, since the best lands were bought up quickly while the least desirable lands were left in federal hands. Next, the government, beginning around the turn of the century, established several types of public-land categories. Those with the best potential for commercial exploitation were put into multiple-use agencies. Thus, the Forest Service received the prime, low-elevation forest lands and the National Park Service the mountaintops. No attempt was made to protect a representative sample of native ecosystems. During most of the process, none of the experts of the time knew enough to even suggest that this be done. As a result, the lands we do protect, however well or badly, constitute only a portion of the continent's different types of ecosystems.

Reed Noss discussed this in a paper called "What Can Wilderness Do for Biodiversity?" published as part of the proceedings of a 1990 Forest Service conference on the federal wilderness program:

How well have we succeeded in representing American ecosystems in designated wilderness today, more than one-quarter century after passage of The Wilderness Act of 1964? Of 261 major terrestrial ecosystems . . . 104 (40%) are not protected in the 36 million hectares [88.9 million acres] of the National Wilderness Preservation System. . . . In general, the most productive habitats have been appropriated for intensive human uses, leaving behind 'rock and ice' as potential wilderness. . . ."

Matters quickly deteriorate when we look at the size of the wilderness areas that the government has set aside. Noss notes that "If we apply Schonewald-Cox's . . . criterion of 1 million ha [hectares; 1 hectare is 2.47 acres] as the size above which a protected area is relatively self-sustaining, only 5 ecosystem types (2% of the 261 Bailey-Kuchler ecosystems) in the United States and Puerto Rico are represented adequately in designated wilderness, and all 5 of these are in Alaska. If we apply a less demanding criterion of 500,000 hectares, only 11 ecosystems (4%) are represented." Wilderness areas in excess of 100,000 hectares account for 50 of the 261 recognized ecosystems, and half of those are in Alaska. East of the Rockies, only four ecosystem types—less than 2 percent of the total—in excess of 100,000 hectares are protected in designated wilderness.

What is true for wilderness areas is true, also, for our national parks. As Newmark wrote in 1987, loss of mammal species "indicates that virtually all western North American national parks were too small to maintain the mammalian faunal assemblage found at the time of park establishment." In short, our federal agencies have protected too little and too few types of wildland. Even the least developed of our protected wildlands— the last refuges for many wildlife species—are becoming wildlife prisons, trapping many species within areas too small to sustain them and isolating them from other populations of their own kind.

Happily, given a suitable social and political will, the solution to these problems is within reach.

CHAPTER 11

Picking Up the Pieces: Gap Analysis and Wildland Corridors

≈

Practical conservation programs have traditionally focused on individual species populations, particularly game species, . . . but also rare ones (for example, endangered species laws). This emphasis ignores the ecological maxim that species exist as functional components of larger systems, and that we cannot "manage for" certain species without affecting many other components of the system.

Reed F. Noss and Larry D. Harris, 1986

Our parks have been shedding species the way a lump of uranium sheds alpha particles.

David Quammen, 1988

≋

Formulating a remedy to fragmentation begins with seeking out ecosystems that are not being protected. These are the lands most likely to suffer further degradation and, through increased fragmentation, to become endangered-species hotspots. State and federal agencies have never initiated a concerted effort to locate these lands, which accounts for the gaping holes in our wildlands system. However, a cheap and easy method for locating the missing pieces is already available

Gap analysis is a process for identifying unprotected species or wild communities by the indirect evidence of plant life.

Plants are the foundation of virtually all known ecosystems. We speak of rainforest ecosystems, and desert ecosystems, and marsh and swamp ecosystems. These adjectives describe plants or relatively consistent associations of plant species. We do not speak of grizzly ecosystems or sidewinder rattlesnake ecosystems. Plants are to an ecosystem as walls and roof, floor and foundation are to a house.

Any given ecosystem is populated by animals that are adapted to it. This means, in effect, that the animals are adapted to the environment that the plant life and climate offer them. Remove the plants, cutting away the superstructure of the food web, and the ecosystem collapses.

The close link between the plant life of an ecosystem and the types of animals found in the ecosystem permits biologists to make a logical inference: If a map shows that a given area is covered by a certain type of plant community, by a certain type of ecosystem, then biologists can presume that a certain variety of animals are found there. For example, if a map of New York State shows a lake and marsh, biologists can make certain presumptions about the species of fish, insects, salamanders, mammals, birds, and other animals found there. They also know that the area will not include species of the western mountains, such as bighorn sheep, or creatures of the desert, such as Gila monsters. Similarly, they know that the Sonora Desert will not house ruffed grouse, a woodland species.

Gap analysis begins with the presumption, then, that if you know which ecosystems lie within a given area, then you know which wildlife species live there. So gap analysts begin with satellite maps that show vegetative cover. From this they can delineate the ecosystems that exist in the area covered by the map and make presumptions about the species living there.

The drawback to this is that it is, at heart, presumptuous. In many cases, the only data we have about animal distribution come from the old Bureau of Biological Survey wildlife censuses. Gap analysis is supposed to improve on this system, and yet the presumptions so critical to gap analysis are derived from the very system it is supposed to be improving.

Nevertheless, short of actually going afield and surveying every species on the ground, as well as under and above it, gap analysis is the best process we have for determining what ecosystems and which species can be found where. As explained by J. Michael Scott, one of the leading gap-analysis advocates in the nation, and two of his colleagues in *Landscape Linkages and Biodiversity,* "While habitat specificity varies between species and classes of vertebrates, habitat is a powerful predictor of the distribution of many smaller mammals and birds, as well as reptiles and amphibians."

To refine the process, gap analysts focus on the three best-documented groups: vegetation, vertebrates, and butterflies. By mapping the distribution of these groups with the aid of satellite technology, gap analysts can map the ecosystems of any given region. They then overlay the ecosystem map with a map of protected lands. This shows which ecosystems lie within protective boundaries. Scott and his colleagues explain the value of this: "An analysis of [vegetation, vertebrate, and butterfly] distribution relative to current nature reserves, national parks, wilderness areas, and the like would yield an assessment of the current level of protection of national biodiversity . . . and suggest management alternatives to fill the gaps in the network of reserves."

Gap analysis has been used in Hawaii, Oregon, Idaho, and California and has highlighted some serious shortcomings in traditional conservation plans and procedures. In Hawaii, for example, researchers found that existing preserves included few areas high in species richness and even fewer areas with high densities of endangered species. In other words, the areas with the highest biodiversity and the most endangered species lay largely outside the protected areas. In California, gap analysts found that the protection of some 31 different vegetation types was very uneven. Less than 1 percent of species-rich riparian zones were protected, but 95 percent of alpine zones—the infamous but scenic rock and ice—were. In Idaho, 42 percent of known vegetative types were unprotected. In one 7,000-square-mile area, 14 of 23 vegetative types had no protection.

Identifying the holes in the protective net permits land managers to recognize areas that need protection *before* they are damaged further or suffer greater species declines. This saves money. Scott observes, for example, that irrigation in California's southern San Joaquin Valley years ago led to the destruction of most of the native habitat and added to the endangered species list three animals found only in the San Joaquin Valley—the San Joaquin kit fox, the giant kangaroo rat, and the blunt-nosed leopard lizard. If, decades ago, the developers of the San Joaquin Valley irrigation project had had access to gap analysis, and had they been compelled to meet the guidelines established by modern environmental laws, they could have initiated land-use plans that would have avoided the costly crisis management inherent to endangered-species protection. "It is especially clear in densely populated areas like southern California that unplanned development of wildlands can lead to costly and contentious conflicts between environmentalists and developers," says Scott. "Once they reach a crisis stage, these conflicts are usually resolved in a confrontational climate, leading to much expense and dissatisfaction for all parties."

Gap analysis offers a cheap solution. The entire nation can be analyzed within six years for only a penny an acre. The process can even help predict where habitat will be lost in the future, allowing land managers to undertake preemptive measures that avert costly species declines. This helps not only conservationists, but also developers who, by using gap-analysis data, can avoid being dragged into court when they inadvertently take actions that jeopardize wildlife. The program will help to protect species while they are still common, before they ebb away and end up on the endangered species list. This makes wildlife protection both more successful and less burdensome to federal and state budgets.

As Scott and other gap-analysis proponents point out, the bottom line in conservation is not how many species we save from extinction in the next decade, but how many will survive the next century or more. No one, Scott says, has analyzed the distribution of plant and animal species in a way that identifies the number occurring on existing preserves or the number that could be saved through intelligent land-use planning. Without this data biologists and land managers cannot determine which areas need to be protected in order to ensure the survival of 98 percent, or 90 percent, or even 50 percent of today's species.

Gap analysis, which the Fish and Wildlife Service is gradually applying across the nation, offers the promise that biologists and public-land managers will soon be able to identify the types of lands that need protection, permitting them to fill up the holes in the system. But fragmentation studies have shown that merely putting a boundary around a plot of land will not adequately protect the wildlife within. Consequently, once ecosystems in need of protection are identified, we have to go beyond traditional management boundaries.

Building Bridges

The best way to maintain wildlife and ecosystems, writes Michael Soule emphatically, is *to minimize habitat fragmentation*. The means for doing this in our heavily fragmented world is protection of ecological bridges or corridors between protected wild areas.

Ecological corridors have a long and venerable history. During glacial periods, when seas were low, land bridges linked now-isolated parts of the world. Indonesia was once linked to Malaysia, Alaska to Siberia. Animals and people traveled across the bridges. The first settlers in the Americas came across the land bridge that spanned today's Bering Strait many thousands of years ago. Similarly, the concept of ecological bridges uniting protected wildlands is the most viable remedy for fragmentation.

Florida provides a good example of corridor potential. The State of Florida, in conjunction with The Nature Conservancy, a private conservation group that since 1951 has worked to protect biodiversity by purchasing natural lands and managing them or turning them over to government agencies, has initiated a statewide corridor plan. It will link Everglades National Park at the southern end of the state with Okeefenokee Swamp in Georgia on Florida's north border.

The system begins in Everglades National Park. As outlined in Chapter 1, the park has been languishing for years because of disruptions in the water flow that maintains the Everglades ecosystem. Park staff recognize that these troubles cannot be relieved within park borders. The park requires ecosystem management, a plan that encompasses the Everglades and surrounding regions.

This is being sought by the Save Our Everglades project initiated by Senator Bob Graham when he was governor. This project intends to undo many of the developments that fragmented

South Florida. It will revise water flows to make them fit more closely the natural regimen. It will provide an ecosystem management plan of which the park will be a part. It will attempt to restore as much as possible the original course of the Kissimmee River, which was straightened by Army Corps of Engineers channelization projects. The Corps will design a system of openings in a canal that cuts through a large marsh north of the park and elevate parts of U.S. Highway 41, permitting water flow and animal traffic beneath it. Water flow from the canal will be fed in a sheet across the park and a new, 107,000-acre addition to it. These measures will help keep the park wet during annual dry seasons and reduce flooding during months of heavy rain.

The effort to put Everglades National Park back together again will serve to restore the southern end of Florida to a condition more closely matching what was found there in 1900 than what was found there in 1990. But if nothing more were done, the park would still become an isolated trap for wildlife. However, the state and The Nature Conservancy are working to end that isolation. They are attempting to locate and purchase the largest remaining blocks of essentially unbroken wildland with low road density. These areas will provide a string of core reserves—large, protected areas with a natural or nearly natural diversity of species. Then, a third category of land will be added to these ecological hot spots—corridors.

These corridors will include strips of wildland that will lie between and connect core reserves. Riparian strips probably will be the most common connecters. The rivers provide deeply wooded corridors and are frequently traveled by large mammals, such as the Florida panther. The state has been spending about $100 million yearly to purchase land for the network, including sites along the Suwanne River and a nearly 100,000-acre coastal corridor that stretches along the Gulf of Mexico in Florida's Big Bend.

In some cases, corridors will be little more than underpasses built beneath major highways. Underpasses permit wildlife to negotiate roads without the risk of being hit by motor vehicles.

The State of Florida is building underpasses beneath the Interstate 75 extension that spans the southern part of the state, providing safe crossing for Florida panthers, black bears, mink, otters, and alligators, among others. Data from Glacier National Park in Montana suggest that the corridors will help. In Glacier, road underpasses permitted mountain goats to reach mineral licks, increasing their success rate at crossing the road from 74 percent to 100 percent.

The Florida wildlands network is a harbinger of a new approach to wildlands protection. It goes beyond traditional protection of isolated units of wildland and instead creates a network of wildlands hundreds of miles long. This permits a freer flow of wildlife across the state, reducing the risk that species will become isolated into dwindling populations. A project similar to the Florida network is under way to restore the forest of the Ohio Valley and rebuild its wilderness. This project will use corridors along the river to link remaining stands of forest in Ohio, West Virginia, and Kentucky, permitting the movement of wildlife across the entire area.

Conservation biologists define two broad categories of corridors. Line corridors are narrow, following, for example, a fence line or hedgerow. Strip corridors are wide enough to maintain the characteristics of a particular ecosystem within their interiors. For example, a forest corridor through cut-over land would be a line corridor if only a few trees wide, but a strip corridor if wide enough to maintain true forest interior habitat in its center. This is critical to use of the corridor by interior species. According to Blair Csuti in *Landscape Linkages and Biodiversity*, edge effects can typically be measured 200 yards into a forest and sometimes as much as 600 yards. This would suggest that a forest corridor less than a mile wide would fail to contain interior habitat.

But width ensures more than interior habitat. A corridor also needs to be wide enough to prevent severing by a single catastrophe. For example, a forest corridor should be large enough to keep it from being cut asunder by windfall.

Corridors are critical components of ecosystem planning,

permitting animals to move about widely in search of food, water, and mates. They help prevent inbreeding and allow migratory animals to move between seasonal habitats. However, they must be carefully planned because, like all silver linings, they are attached to a cloud. We have limited control over the species that will use corridors. Thus, poorly conceived corridors can serve as pathways over which non-native species can move into areas for which they were not predestined, as it were, by nature. The invaders may disrupt their new habitat, outcompeting native species and eliminating them.

The ideal arrangement for protected lands, then, would involve a series of large units of wildland linked by strip corridors wide enough to maintain interior habitat. If possible, several corridors would link each unit as backup in case a corridor is destroyed by some catastrophe, natural or otherwise. The corridors would be arranged as much as possible to avoid an influx of non-native species. The large wildland units would be managed in concentric zones. The interior would be, to use Newton Drury's word, inviolate, protected strictly for wildlife and wild value. Buffer zones outside the core zone would be subject to increasingly intensive human use.

For example, in the Yellowstone Ecosystem, the park would form the core area. Adjacent parts of the national forests would be added to it, with gradually increasing human use through and beyond the forests to private land. Federal purchase of private lands north of the park would link it to more northerly national forests and, ultimately, to Glacier National Park, which presently links to protected land in Canada. If we wish to dream big dreams we might imagine an immense bioreserve network that stretches from Alaska's arctic coast through Canada, the United States, Mexico, and Central America clear to Tierra del Fuego. A branch from the east would link with this network in Texas or Mexico after passing from northeastern Canada and the eastern United States. This international ecosystem reserve would restore the Americas' broken cradle of life.

But back in the real world, we face grave difficulties merely adopting the gap analysis/corridor approach to wildland protection here in the United States. What we are talking about here is ecosystem management, not fragment protection, and it is quite a break with tradition. The federal land-protection agencies, as the previous chapters suggest, have become welded over the years to various management traditions. The Forest Service clearly remains committed to the logging policies of past generations even though the pressures on national forests have shifted dramatically over recent decades. The Fish and Wildlife Service ignores its roles in wilderness protection because nothing in its bureaucratic tradition prepared it for such an activity. The Forest Service in the past opposed the creation of the National Park Service because it feared a potential rival. Similarly, today's old-line bureaucrats are lethargic in adopting an ecosystem approach to wildlands protection. They prefer to remain in the familiar world of discrete preserves where individual species, particularly certain popular endangered species, win the bulk of protection efforts.

The agencies have not been alone in this process. They have been backed by the nation's private conservation groups, which also have typically cast boundaries around sites in need of protection and put management emphasis on individual species. The hunting and fishing groups have wanted government agencies to focus on game reserves and species such as deer and wild turkeys, and the true conservation groups have tended to focus on blocks of wildland in conjunction with endangered species. The reason for both is obvious: Hunters and fishermen want more game, and the conservation groups need to garner public support, which generally is easier to accomplish if a land-protection issue can be boiled down to a single attractive species, such as the northern spotted owl.

There is nothing wrong with either approach, unless they harm overall conservation goals. Which in some cases they do. Deer management, for example, relies in many parts of the nation on creating openings in forests. This creates forest edge, with harmful effects on some birds. It can also affect many forest-dependent species, such as the pine marten, a sort of squirrel-hunting tree weasel.

Similarly, the use of popular, attractive endangered species as drawing cards for public support tends to yield conservation programs that focus heavily on popular, attractive endangered species. As a result, the federal government spends millions of dollars yearly on such high-profile species as the gray wolf, grizzly bear, and California condor. Meanwhile, less appealing but equally important species—usually bloodless, cold-to-the-touch, but biologically significant species that include dozens of insects, shellfish, and reptiles—are ignored.

To a biologist, of course, the protection of the endangered Cumberland monkeyface pearly mussel—a real species on the federal list—is equal in importance to the protection of the California condor. A biologist knows that the streams of North America were once crowded with clams and mussels. Early settlers in Ohio reported freshwater clams as big as dinner plates that paved the bottoms of clear-running streams. But the streams no longer run clear, and many of the shellfish species have disappeared or become endangered. Their decline is not only a sign of ecological disintegration, but also a loss of a vital riparian component, for shellfish helped filter debris from the streams. Their loss compounds the damage European settlement has done to our waterways.

Nevertheless, public support is far easier to rally for big and impressive creatures. Logically, therefore, the conservation community focuses on the most appealing species, often ignoring the bigger question of ecosystem protection. Since the private groups generally play the leading role in keeping government land-management agencies abreast of the times, it is critical that the groups begin to emphasize the need for ecosystem rather than single-species management. At least one organization, Defenders of Wildlife, has undertaken to put biodiversity protection and ecosystem management on the national agenda, and presumably others will soon join the effort.

Some conservationists, adamant about the need for ecosystems management, want to scrap the endangered-species program or at least give up on management-intensive, and expensive, species such as the California condor. This faction of the conservation community urges the Fish and Wildlife Service to apply medical triage to endangered species protection. Medical triage is used during times of war when medical resources are scarce. Only patients likely to respond to treatment are given aid. No treatment is given to patients likely to survive without treatment or likely to die without a massive effort. With triage in mind, some conservationists suggest that seemingly hopeless species—and no one has ever defined this term—be left to extinction.

Of course this is ludicrous. We can never, with the certainty of medical science, predict which species will fail and which will not. Moreover, speaking objectively, we have an apples and oranges analogy here. Triage advocates are comparing the loss of an individual to the loss of a species. But the loss of an individual member of a species is not biologically significant. The loss of an entire species is.

We cannot play God by selectively wiping out species through inaction (though when it comes to playing God, we always seem comfortable with destroying life and taxed by nurturing it). Each lost species represents a decline in local and global biodiversity, and it is this decline that all the works and endeavors of conservation seek to avoid. We should attempt to protect and preserve every species that needs it, even if we think its survival unlikely. We lack the knowledge to determine which species will inevitably fail and which we can save. Better to err on the side of life than on the side of oblivion. Moreover, we should not pass on to future generations a diminished biodiversity. They may have skills and abilities yet undreamed, and it behooves us to ensure that they do not have less to work with than we had.

Rather than draw analogies with medical triage, let us seek metaphors in the legal system. The funds we expend on endangered-species management are the fine we are required to pay for past crimes and misdemeanors against nature. The result will be that future generations can, perhaps, gaze into the skies of California—and perhaps of Oregon and Washington State—and see soaring on whistling wings the California condors that our efforts in behalf of the endangered have bequeathed to them. Isn't this a nobler goal than letting the largest bird on the continent vanish, leaving future generations to wonder why we deprived them of this marvel?

The conservation community should not waste time providing the world with justifications for disgarding endangered wildlife. It should focus on finding more funds for biodiversity protection and more means for bioeducating the world, creating a place where wildlife and wildlands are better understood and more highly valued. Special efforts to protect endangered species should continue, as should work on hunted and nonhunted species. But they should be placed within the context of ecosystem protection. We should not use management techniques that boost species such as deer, but fragment the forest ecosystem. Our attempts at the protection of wildlife and wildlands should be fundamentally, and at heart, ecosystem management. Other efforts should not be dropped, but should be integrated into ecosystem planning.

Noss and Harris corroborated the need for ecosystem management in a 1986 article for *Environmental Management* when they wrote, "We cannot consider our parks and preserves as closed, self-supporting systems, but rather as parts interacting within still larger systems." Ecosystem management and sound biodiversity protection require that we stop managing national park fragments and national forest remnants and that we eschew management techniques that splinter the natural environment.

Yet fragment protection is precisely what federal management was set up to do, has done, and does do. To pull our protected wildlands out of this morass will require reorganization of federal goals and methods. The way to this goal has been paved, somewhat, by proposed legislation presently languishing in Congress.

CHAPTER 12

Ethics, Economics, and Ecosystems

We have this concept of growth, of enhanced exploitation of resources . . . that we cannot seem to get away from. Each of us wants more, feels he or she needs more—more money or simply greater opportunity to get more resources. There is no counterbalancing notion of "enough."

Niles Eldredge, The Miner's Canary, *1991*

Never doubt that a small group of thoughtful, committed citizens can change the world; indeed, it's the only thing that ever has.

Margaret Mead

～

On April 21, 1948, a trash fire at a farm in Wisconsin's Bar-
aboo Hills escaped across neighboring grasslands, surging toward hundreds of newly planted pines on a nearby farm.

The planter of those pines was Aldo Leopold, one of the
leading conservationists of his day and the father of modern
wildlife management. He spotted the fire at about ten thirty that
morning, at first watching its smoke without alarm, then realiz-
ing that it posed a threat to his trees. He, his wife, and his daughter grabbed shovels, a hand pump, buckets, and other fire-
fighting gear and drove to the front of the fire. The wife and
daughter were left at their car with instructions to keep the fire
from crossing the road and to call for help from a nearby rural fire
department.

As more area residents joined the fire fight, Leopold took his
hand pump and moved beyond sight of the others to a spot along
the road where the soaking of unburnt grass would have slowed
the spread of the flames. If this was Leopold's plan, it was cut
short by sudden pain in his chest. He must have known that his
heart was giving out, for he seems to have brought his fire
fighting to an abrupt halt, putting down the pump, lying on his
back with his head pillowed by a clump of grass, and crossing his
hands over his chest. There he died quietly between earth and
sky, as close to the forces of nature as were the many wild creatures to which his life had been devoted. Before his neighbors
found him, the ebbing fire swept over his body.

Leopold left behind a manuscript of unpublished essays

called "Great Possessions." This collection embodied perhaps the clearest call ever made for the protection of wildlands. Eventually it would be published as *A Sand County Almanac* and become one of the most eloquent of environmental books, speaking with consummate wisdom—and selling briskly—down to the present day. Upon Leopold's death, however, its future was in doubt. In November 1947 Alfred A. Knopf had turned down the book with a letter to Leopold, portions of which are reproduced in *Aldo Leopold: His Life and Work* by Curt Meine: "What we like best is the nature observations, and the more objective narratives and essays," wrote Knopf editor Clinton Simpson. "We like less the subjective parts—that is, the philosophical reflections, which are less fresh, and which one reader finds sometimes 'fatuous.' The ecological argument everyone finds unconvincing. . . .

"In short, the book seems unlikely to win approval from readers or to be a successful publication as it now stands."

A week before Leopold died, however, editors at Oxford University Press agreed to publish the book. They told Leopold that if he could revise the manuscript over the summer, they would have the book in stores by the fall of 1949.

With Leopold gone, the orphaned book appeared about to vanish. But within days of Leopold's death, conservation writer Joe Hickey, whom Leopold had asked to review the manuscript, sent a letter to Leopold's family offering to help get the book into print. With modest revisions, and entitled *A Sand County Almanac*, the manuscript was published late in 1949. It was an instant success among critics and became a classic of conservation literature. In the mid-1960s, when it was republished as a paperback, it immediately captured the heart of the conservation movement created in the wake of Rachel Carson's *Silent Spring*. With Henry David Thoreau's *Walden*, it is perhaps the most frequently quoted conservation text ever penned, a perfect marriage of sublime writing and environmental insight. Even now, nearly half a century after it was first published, it provides a foundation for much current environmental thought and concern.

The most important theme to emerge from Leopold's *Alma-*

nac was the need for an ecological ethic. "The first ethics dealt with the relation between individuals; the Mosaic Decalogue is an example," he wrote in the *Almanac,* drawing upon ideas he had first propounded in a 1933 speech to the Southwestern Division of the American Association for the Advancement of Science. "Later accretions dealt with the relation between the individual and society. The Golden Rule tries to integrate the individual to society; democracy to integrate social organization to the individual.

"There is as yet no ethic dealing with man's relationship to land and to the animals and plants which grow upon it. . . . The land-relation is still strictly economic, entailing privileges but not obligations."

Leopold observed that ethics regulate the constraints that individuals must put upon their behavior as part of a community of interdependent elements. Ethics keep us from putting personal interests before those of the community. Thus far, the community is conceived in terms of other people. "The land ethic," he wrote, "simply enlarges the boundaries of the community to include soils, waters, plants, and animals, or collectively: the land."

Leopold was not naive about how difficult it would be to bring this about. "Obligations have no meaning without conscience," he wrote, "and the problem we face is the extension of the social conscience from people to land. No important change in ethics was ever accomplished without an internal change in our intellectual emphasis, loyalties, affections, and convictions. . . . Perhaps the most serious obstacle impeding the evolution of a land ethic is the fact that our educational and economic system is headed away from, rather than toward, an intense consciousness of land." To initiate the process of social evolution leading to a land ethic, Leopold wrote, we must "quit thinking about decent land-use as solely an economic problem. Examine each question in terms of what is ethically and esthetically right, as well as what is economically expedient." He followed this with two statements that succinctly delineate the land ethic and that have become a credo among conservationists. An action, he wrote, "is right when it tends to preserve the integrity, stability, and beauty of the biotic community. It is wrong when it tends otherwise."

Even now, despite our national forests, parks, and wildlife refuges, our state parks and recreation areas, our national monuments and wilderness areas, we have not succeeded in creating a land ethic. The predominant approach to land protection today is still based upon economic exploitation. Our nation was conceived as a business and dedicated to the proposition that all people can turn a profit if given enough land. The earliest explorers and settlers came here in search of gold, spices, furs, timber, and farmland. Commerce compelled the settling of the continent, and this nation—as all nations—is run even now as a business. Despite vast political differences, all nations share the desire for a large gross national product.

As commerce overspreads the world, wild creatures and wild places will dwindle if no restraint is placed upon human developmental activities. Virtually any wild area can be developed for profit. Only by resisting the urge to win every potential profit—by declaring that in wide cross-section of wild places natural balances will take precedence over checkbook balances—can we protect and conserve the world's wildness.

Accomplishing this level of social and economic restraint requires the development of a land ethic, as outlined by Aldo Leopold. But wildlands and wild species are sinking rapidly, and ethics evolve slowly. Adequate protection for biodiversity cannot wait while society develops the intellectual and emotional means for producing a true land ethic. Business—as it is conducted today—is gobbling up the planet, leaving the natural world in life-draining fragments all over the nation, all over the globe. Think of the familiar signs of ecological and biodiversity degradation that we have seen in recent years, recounted in books, magazines, television, and newspapers—the falling of forests worldwide, the turning of once fertile grasslands into deserts, the pollution of rivers, streams, lakes, and seas, the pollution of air and soil, the contamination of foods taken from land and water, the pollution of our own lungs and bloodstreams by various types of air-borne toxins—all of which represent the inroads of unbridled business upon the natural realms of the globe.

Business interests tell us we must strike a balance between economics and the protection of the environment. The environmental community, they say, goes too far in seeking protection of forests and grasslands. The truth is that the conservation community is becoming far too remiss in defense of biodiversity, too "reasonable" in the sense desired by the business community. Too often, professional conservationists acquiesce in striking balances. But how do we strike a balance in the protection of wetlands, which nurture a variety of species from insects and amphibians to fish, waterfowl, and humans? Are we in balance if we give up half of the nation's wetlands and protect half? But half of the original 200 million acres of U.S. wetlands already are gone, replaced by human development. People shop in malls, live in houses, grow crops, and pursue other economic activities on fully half the area once covered by wetlands. Is an even split between development and nature a balance? Then we need to stop destroying wetlands now.

Is a fifty-fifty split a fair balance in the use of our forests? If it is, then the corporate world is correct: Attempts to protect virgin forest today are way out of balance. Well over 90 percent of the nation's once-virgin forests have been cut. The conservation community is trying now to preserve less than 5 percent of the original forest. How much of the 5 percent will the logging companies require before they agree that we have struck a balance?

Would we balance the protection and exploitation of American grasslands and prairies if we put half of them into production and half into protection for native species? Would we be in balance if we developed 60 percent, or 75 percent? Would we be in balance if we developed 85 percent of native grasslands and protected 15 percent? Then again the developers are right: Conservationists are far out of balance in their desire to protect prairies and plains. An estimated 99 percent of native American grasslands are already in production.

Too many of our businessmen are economic junkies ever in need of a financial fix. Each succeeding generation of real-estate developers and corporate executives and oil and gas engineers and miners and loggers looks at the nation's protected wildlands, protected *public* lands, and says that it wants its share, that we must strike a balance. In their efforts to be reasonable and realistic, politically sophisticated and pragmatic, the conservation groups often agree that we have to give up some wildlands to human need. How many generations can give up 50 percent or 90 percent or even 10 percent before, in some future generation, nothing is left to give up, to be reasonable about?

We cannot strike balances that both seem reasonable in our time and provide meaningful protection for wild places and biodiversity down through the decades and centuries. The balances we strike must be balances for the ages, for millennia to come. We cannot think in terms of fiscal years or human lifetimes, because too much of nature marks its life in centuries.

The demands that business places upon the natural world are essentially elitist and self-serving. They appropriate great gulps of the world to satisfy the appetites of a handful of hirelings. The interests of how many logging-industry executives are served by the cutting of public forests? A few million? Certainly not. A few thousand? No. A few hundred? Perhaps. A few score? Quite likely. Meanwhile, our national parks, among the most protected of our public wildlands, serve the interests of nearly 300 million people yearly. As population grows, the amount of people served by public wildlands will burgeon. Are we to reduce our wildlands through commercial consumption for the benefit of a few company men and women when we could instead protect those lands for millions upon millions of people down through the years?

More than 80 percent of U.S. oil reserves are on private land. Some 85 percent of all lumber comes from private land. Well in excess of 90 or 95 percent of all meat products come from private land. In the process of converting roughly 95 percent of the nation's wildlands into production we have created a power-house for satisfying human needs. *Our* future does not depend on the public lands, but the future of biodiversity and the integrity of the natural world—ultimately vital to human survival—does.

Yet we lack an ethic that will bridle our business interests in their pursuit of every potential profit. Social evolution has not taken us to the exalted position for which Leopold had hoped. And when ethics fail, we are forced to fall back upon laws.

Expanding Environmental Protection

We know that all public wildlands are beset with internal management problems, threatened by powerful political pressures exerted by private business, and subject to corrosive geographic arrangements that deplete them of species. Not only are the public wildlands themselves fragmented, but so is their management, split among several agencies that have varying degrees of commitment to land protection and exploitation. Moreover, the federal land-protection system suffers from bureaucratic redundancies that inflate budgets, duplicate staff, and complicate the processes of land protection. The Forest Service, Bureau of Land Management, Fish and Wildlife Service, and National Park Service are all supposed to create staff divisions for the protection and management of designated wilderness areas. Both the Bureau of Land Management and the Forest Service are managing forest lands for logging. All the agencies, at one level or another, are protecting lands for wildlife. This leads to an immense amount of bureaucratic babble and confounds the entire management process.

To protect adequately the wildlands in their charge, the various agencies need to develop ecosystem management plans that integrate the various wildland reserves into a single network built of reserves connected by corridors. This requires that the agencies break down traditional bureaucratic barriers and work together. But how efficient is cooperation likely to be among agencies with old bureaucratic animosities? How will agencies with widely varying and sometimes antagonistic management goals achieve meaningful cooperation over entire ecosystems and aggregates of ecosystems? And what talent for and commitment to ecosystem and biodiversity protection are brought to the table by agencies such as the Forest Service and the Bureau of Land Management—agencies that traditionally have lain tucked in the pockets of commercial interests such as logging and mining and whose personnel are trained to emphasize land development rather than biodiversity management?

Federal efforts at biodiversity protection are fragmented and lack a single, comprehensive guiding principle. The United States has no national conservation policy. Its efforts at biodiversity protection are haphazard and dictated too often by industries working with selected minions in federal agencies that are already oriented to land use rather than land protection.

The remedy, short of developing an ethic, is enactment of a law that will outline and establish a clear national policy for the protection and maintenance of biodiversity and provide a fundamental program for implementing it.

Some approaches to this are already in the air. In 1991 Representative James Scheuer, a New York Democrat; Representative Gerry Studds, a Massachusetts Democrat; and Senator Daniel Moynihan, another New York Democrat, sponsored biodiversity bills in Congress. The various bills would likely merge into one before Congress enacted any of them. What they would probably do, merged, is declare biodiversity protection a national goal, create a national biodiversity strategy, establish a biodiversity research center, provide research grants, and earmark up to $50 million for three years of work on the protection of habitats as well as the protection of unlisted plants and animals. This is an important beginning, signaling that the nation recognizes the need for biodiversity protection and elevating it to a goal. But it is short on specifics and action, focusing for the moment (bills change as they move through Congress) on research.

Defenders of Wildlife, a Washington-based conservation group that emphasizes biodiversity protection among its programs, advocates a more down-to-earth plan. A Defenders policy document called *Putting Wildlife First: Recommendations for Reforming Our Troubled Refuge System,* outlines a plan for a National Wildlife Habitat System, recommending that:

1. Congress establish a National Wildlife Habitat System (NWHS) for federal lands, making all federal landholding agencies part of a national effort to protect dwindling wildlife habitats.
2. All federal agencies managing habitat-system units be required to participate in bioregional conservation coordination meetings, called and hosted at regular intervals by regional heads of participating agencies on a rotating basis.
3. Congress direct the secretaries of Interior and Agriculture to initiate a two-year study of the feasibility of inviting state and private-landholder participation in the National Wildlife Habitat System.
4. Planning for incorporation of the habitat system into hemispheric and global conservation efforts begin immediately.

This seems a reasonable and conservative suggestion, a modest proposal. Nevertheless, one outside observer—William Reffalt, the former chief of the National Wildlife Refuge System presently working for The Wilderness Society—says he does not think this proposal would make it through Congress. The proposal would, for example, make wildlife protection the dominant use of any national forest lands put into the wildlife habitat system, a measure sure to be opposed by Forest Service foresters and the powerful logging industry. Wilderness areas would also go into the habitat system, he says, arousing the ire of wilderness advocates who fear the areas will lose their purity. "The agencies would be nervous as hell, because this is like saying that multiple use doesn't work." Reffalt said.

If so modest a proposal is likely to be squelched, then we may as well go off on a different tack and try to come up with a plan to reorganize federal wildlife protection completely, if only as a starting point for discussion among the lawmakers and lobbyists endeavoring to better our protection of biodiversity.

An Immodest Proposal

If you live and work in the Washington, D.C., political arena, you quickly acquire an instinct for political pragmatism. You tend to look not for the solutions that are needed, but for the actions that stand some chance of being implemented. Politics, according to the old saw, is the art of the possible.

But another old saw declares that if you reach for the stars you may not quite touch them, but you're not likely to come up with a handful of mud, either. To determine precisely what is possible, you often have to begin with a larger vision. Consequently, this proposal is not leavened with pragmatism. Why stack the deck against your own goals and objectives? Anyway, if John Muir and the other early conservationists could envision and win the creation of wilderness reserves in a world that did not have any and little wanted them, then certainly we should be able to come up with an ambitious and comprehensive plan for managing reserves that already exist.

The nation is in need of a national conservation plan. Initiating such a plan cannot be left to the land-management agencies because they are too fragmented and their management goals too varied to permit readily the creation of a comprehensive national conservation plan. The plan needs to be created by Congress in the form of a National Biodiversity Policy Act.

As in the biodiversity laws sponsored by Scheuer, Studds, and Moynihan, the act would make biodiversity protection a national goal. To facilitate this, the law would need to create a new land-protection agency whose sole mandate is the protection of natural biodiversity within the lands it manages. This would avoid the management fragmentation and contradictions of the various agencies that now dominate wildland protection.

The new agency would seek to enhance and protect natural biodiversity by creating a network of connected wildlands. Its primary initial goal would be the selection of core wildlands and the acquisition of corridors to connect them. The lands that make up the core zones would come primarily from existing public lands. Where possible and when needed, the agency would acquire private lands—including all subsurface and other rights—at a fair market value. All lands would be selected through gap analysis and other standard land-evaluation techniques.

All present and future designated wilderness areas would become part of the ecosystem/biodiversity network, as would national parks, monuments, recreation areas, and wild and scenic rivers with significant wildland value. The National Park Service would be left in charge of lands of historical significance and other non-wildland units. National Park Service staff assigned to the units put into the new network would be shifted into the new agency to the extent possible.

The new agency also would be directed to evaluate the National Wildlife Refuge System and select units that would make useful additions to the new ecosystem/biodiversity network. Emphasis would be placed on selecting units that represent natural wild values.

All remaining ancient forests on the national forests and the public domain would be added to the new network for eternal preservation. Logging henceforth would be limited—if you can call it limiting—to the more than 90 percent of public and private forest lands already in production. However, some cut-over lands on national forests may be added case-by-case to the new ecosystem/biodiversity network and restored as nearly as possible to a condition that, over the centuries, will come as close as possible to recreating the lost forests.

Grazing on lands selected from the public domain would stop, and the new agency would initiate management to restore the land to excellent condition. To ensure that continued use by livestock on other parts of the public domain does not threaten the reserves and corridors, the new agency would cooperate with other land-management agencies to develop a system that permits grazing at increasing intensity in concentric zones surrounding lands set aside for biodiversity protection.

The new agency would also create a new category of protected lands—endangered ecosystems. Gap analysts would help select these lands for inclusion in the ecosystem/biodiversity network. The new law, in language borrowed from Canada's 1991 proposed endangered species act, would define an endangered ecosystem as one that has been significantly altered across 85 percent or more of its original range or that is in danger of being altered throughout a significant portion of its range. While gap analysts within the new agency would have primary responsibility for identifying endangered ecosystems and designating them as candidates for listing, private citizens also could nominate ecosystems for listing.

Endangered ecosystem management would be a major component of the new agency. As outlined by Constance C. Hunt in the *Endangered Species Update*, published by the University of Michigan School of Natural Resources, endangered ecosystems would be subject to an intensive recovery effort, as are endangered species. The primary goal of endangered ecosystem management would be preservation of listed ecosystems as self-sustaining biological entities. Development in these areas would be banned, as would federal subsidies to projects likely to jeopardize listed ecosystems. The new agency would also be charged with creating recovery plans for the management and improvement of listed ecosystems, and it would make grants to the states for the study and management of endangered ecosystems.

The endangered ecosystems component of the new law would remedy two persistent problems.

First, lack of focus on ecosystem management, particularly the protection of vanishing ecosystems, tends to create endangered species. The northern spotted owl is an example. The owl would not be endangered today if its habitat had not been widely destroyed. Habitat destruction produces endangered species, which leads to expensive recovery plans and intense political, economic, and social conflict. The United States has long been a leader in endangered-species production, and it is time that we shut down the machinery of that production. This can be done through the protection of vanishing ecosystems.

Second, habitat protection in the United States has been conducted indirectly through the protection of endangered species. Once a species is listed as endangered, the Fish and Wildlife Service is supposed to designate where the species' critical habitat lies. This habitat is then supposed to be protected for the benefit of the species. A major failing of this approach is that management does not begin until the species, and often its habitat, are in crisis. This is costly and, in any event, offers no protection to an ecosystem. For example, northern spotted owls are protected by the Endangered Species Act, but their habitat is not. To paraphrase Constance Hunt, the continued existence of the owl in some tracts of forest could be used to justify the cutting of forests elsewhere. The endangered ecosystems component of the new law focuses protection on the ecosystem regardless of the occurrence of endangered species.

But endangered ecosystems are only a part of the broader ecosystem-management objective that would be achieved through the linking of protected lands by corridors. The law cannot focus exclusively on endangered ecosystems because that would leave nonendangered ecosystems subject to destruction until they become endangered. The point of biodiversity and ecosystem protection is to avoid the creation of such biologically and administratively expensive crisis management.

The question of funding remains. Congress would appropriate funds for the administration of the new agency and for the acquisition and management of the new ecosystem/biodiversity network. The law would include an appropriation of $6 million over a six-year period to speed the completion of gap analysis nationwide. Under present funding, gap analysis will not be completed until 2006. Raising the funding from $300,000 yearly to $1 million yearly will cut the process to six years. This will help ensure that more species do not become endangered as critical ecosystems remain unprotected.

Ideally, the new agency should become self-sustaining in the long run by charging user fees. As outlined in the chapter on national forests, economist Randall O'Toole has shown that user fees—such as might be charged for camping, hiking, and hunting—could generate billions of dollars for the Forest Service. The new network will provide visitors with the nation's premiere wildlife and wildlands experiences and should charge accordingly.

In addition, Congress should also, when enacting the law, create a one-time $50 billion appropriation for the new agency. This money would be used for safe, long-term investments paying 8 to 10 percent interest and generating income for years. William Reffalt suggested this idea, grasping it from the air where it has been floating about for some years now. He says that the nation "has had such bad leadership lately that conservationists' brains have atrophied. We're not dreaming and thinking. We're down in the gutter and can't get out." In addition, we have mortgaged our children's future with a record-breaking national debt "so how can our children give the environment its due?" To finance an environmental agenda in the future, he says, we need 50 billion interest-generating dollars. "We need Congress to say, as long as we're mortgaging the future, we may as well put aside $10 billion yearly for the environment."

Although the new agency will require start-up appropriations from Congress, once it is up and rolling it should fund itself from the $50 billion investment capital and from user fees and other income sources.

In short, Congress should enact a National Biodiversity Organic Act that:

1. sets protection of natural biodiversity as a national goal;
2. streamlines federal land management by creating a new biodiversity-protection agency that takes over the wild-

land management responsibilities of existing agencies (with the exception of the Fish and Wildlife Service), reducing their budgets and staff;

3. authorizes the acquisition of existing public lands for creation of a nationwide ecosystem/biodiversity network of wildland reserves connected by corridors;
4. creates an endangered-ecosystem program patterned after the Endangered Species Act, in the hope, ultimately, of bringing expensive crisis management to an end;
5. provides funding to complete nationwide gap analysis within six years after enactment and
6. creates a funding system that makes the new agency self-sustaining.

This proposal would save funds by reducing the federal wildlands bureaucracy, initiating a program designed to reduce further creation of endangered species, and eliminating redundancies among existing federal agencies.

Now that all this has been said, the vultures of common sense descend with an analysis of why this will not happen. First, the present federal agencies will rabidly oppose it because it threatens their land holdings and could reduce their budgets. Even the conservative biodiversity-act proposals already before Congress are opposed by these agencies for similar reasons. Their opposition, however, is not insurmountable. The national parks and the wilderness areas were created over the objections of other land-management agencies.

Second, every industry using public lands in the nation will come out against this proposal. They already threaten to gut the Endangered Species Act and wipe from the books other environmental laws, such as the National Environmental Policy Act and certain restrictions of the Clean Air and Clean Water acts. On the other hand, these laws were enacted over the objections of industry in the first place. Fighting the heavy guns of commerical interests is difficult, but not impossible.

Eventually, it all comes down to people. As Vice-President Albert Gore has said, "When politicians see enough people demanding action on the environment, then the laws will change." In recent years we have seen vocal and adamant public support affect policies concerning land and biodiversity protection. Remember when the Exxon *Valdez* oil tanker spilled 11 million gallons of petroleum in Alaska's Prince William Sound? At that time, the conservation community was fighting a pitched battle in Congress to keep the oil industry from building a colony of grimy oil refineries and swill-dumping wells on the last 100-mile stretch of undeveloped arctic coast. This coast lies in the Arctic National Wildlife Refuge and is vitally important to a variety of animals as well as local Native Americans. Some conservationists thought we had lost the battle. Others thought we still had a chance. All doubt was removed after the spill. People were so outraged by the spill, and by the mindless arrogance displayed by the head of Exxon, that Congress has yet to open the refuge to oil and gas development. The public made the difference. I had dinner recently with an Exxon and a Conoco executive. The Conoco man said, "We had the Arctic Refuge all sown up. We had the votes in Congress in our pocket. And then those guys"— and he pointed at the Exxon man—"dumped all that oil and we lost it."

If we can keep the outrage burning—outrage at the destruction of public forest and public grasslands, outrage at the poisoning of oceans and rivers—then we can continue to pull Congress out of the pockets of the developers. Private commercial interests have plenty of private land upon which to make their fortunes.

So it all comes down to individuals, which brings us again to Aldo Leopold and the land ethic. For when we talk about the support of the public, we are talking about the support of motivated individuals. And what motivates them is a personal ethic. In regard to public wildlands the ethic says, No more.

Although Leopold's demand for ecological ethics may long elude us, it is still crucial to successful conservation. As recently as 1988, E. O. Wilson wrote,

In the end, I suspect it will all come down to a decision of ethics—how we value the natural worlds in which we evolved and now, increasingly, how we regard our status as individuals. . . . The drive toward perpetual expansion—or personal freedom—is basic to the human spirit. But to sustain it we need the most delicate, knowing stewardship of the living world that can be devised. . . . The depth of the conservation ethic will be measured by the extent to which each of the two approaches to nature is used to reshape and reinforce the other.

What this rightly suggests is that we cannot stop at merely passing laws.

An Earth Ethic

Our nation is composed of laws. In the modern age, a nation's laws define its place in the international arena. Long accustomed to thinking in terms of laws and living under them, we find it easy to believe that once we have enacted a law to redress some social, political, or economic ill, we have solved the problem. This presumption seems especially prevalent among the lobbyists and social activists in Washington, D.C.

In so far as we are a nation of laws, the presumption is correct. But it errs in forgetting that we are also a nation of people, and that people are at heart anarchists. They want laws to govern the actions of others. They rarely if ever want laws to govern and moderate their own actions. When a law is passed, those it governs often find ways to evade it.

This is the great weakness of any legislative solution to environmental problems. Laws designed to protect wildlife and wildlands are persistently evaded or ignored by industry, by bureaucrats, and by elected officials. The political appointees who take over the federal agencies after each presidential election often pose obstacles to the diligence of their own staffs. Elected officials also work in behalf of industries that swell election coffers. The preservation of federal mining, grazing, and logging laws—which together result in the loss of roughly a billion dollars in federal revenue yearly—are testimony to this.

The final arbiter of human action is not law but conscience, a sense of right and wrong. A law is only effective in so far as it can be implemented and enforced. As we know from watching the civil rights movement, laws alone will not correct social problems. They will, however, signal that society at large no longer condones the actions that a law forbids. The enactment of a law is a sign that society is evolving, and while society will change slowly after the legislative signal is given, it will nevertheless change. Today's laws build tomorrow's societies.

Enacting a law, then, can be a foundation to the development of an ethic—in this case Leopold's land ethic, which in modern parlance might be better called an Earth ethic. But law alone will not sire this ethic. It will only help produce the shift in individual values that ultimately will give rise to a shift in conscience. To value fully the protection of biodiversity, society will require, in addition to laws, a citizenry that understands the role that nature plays in human life.

This understanding springs from science education.

Education

For thousands of years the development of technology and the bulk of humanity's quest for knowledge have been designed to overcome nature. Only in very recent years—the past quarter-century, really—have we attempted to understand nature better. During the past 25 years, science has learned more about the workings of the natural world than was known in all the centuries that went before. A hundred years ago, scientists could be confident about their knowledge of the natural world, because they knew so little. The less you know, the simpler it all seems. Today, we know so much about the biological systems of the globe that we have begun to realize how little we really do know, a nice paradox and a soundly humbling one. Aldo Leopold made this point some 50 years ago when he wrote, "The ordinary citizen today assumes that science knows what makes the [biological] community tick; the scientist is equally sure that he does not. He knows that the biotic mechanism is so complex that its workings may never be fully understood."

The humility that biologists feel when confronted with the profoundly complex, perhaps unfathomable mysteries of the natural world is a byproduct of knowledge. Perceiving the intricacies of the planet, how the relationships of the natural world affect humanity, is sobering. It makes us much less inclined to rush along with development schemes heedless of their effect on the natural environment. It deflates any notion that humanity stands apart from the natural world.

If knowledge alone were a solution to serious environmental problems, these problems would be neither serious nor, for very long, problems. Our society is, after all, highly educated and awash with the knowledge that education brings. But as a means for solving any serious social problem, education needs to be aimed at the specific problem in question. The United States has produced a plethora of M.B.A.s, but the people who completed these degrees were trained to run businesses. They may still remain scientifically illiterate, with little or no comprehension of the significance of biodiversity to human life, of the intimate natural relationships that support life, and of the dangers that ecological degradation brings to our society. To comprehend the bond between the human animal and biodiversity requires an understanding of the natural sciences, an understanding that assumes an increasingly vital importance as environmental problems, species declines, and habitat destruction grow rampant.

While some conservation groups engage in public education, most emphasize working in the legislative and judicial arenas, passing and enforcing laws. They cannot hope to enact a law requiring better national science education, so with rare exceptions the groups do not emphasize national education policy in their daily work. This needs to change if the environmental community is to offer the nation a complete package for biodiversity protection. A national-conservation-policy law would set the course of management efforts, but science education is needed to ensure that citizens understand the importance of biodiversity protection and support implementation of the environmental laws and regulations. Science education is the foundation of an Earth ethic.

Presently, U.S. students show an alarming lack of scientific understanding. A national test given in 1991 to some 20,000 students in fourth, eighth, and twelfth grade by the National Assessment Governing Board showed that less than half of U.S. high-school seniors possessed in-depth knowledge of scientific subjects or could evaluate scientific experiments. Although all three grades had command of basic scientific facts, they were not equipped to analyze or to apply what they knew. Differences between public and private school students were slight overall.

Shortcomings in science education are not limited to students. Up to 30 percent of eighth-grade teachers interviewed by the assessment board said they were poorly prepared for teaching science and had to work with outmoded equipment. They also complained that schools place a low priority on science.

This bodes ill for the nation. If U.S. students fail to improve their record on science course work, the next generation upon which the conservation community must call for support will be scientifically deficient and poorly equipped for dealing with the crucial environmental issues that face them.

A major component of any effort to protect biodiversity must include the educational system of this nation. This goes beyond the realm of traditional land management and conservation. Rather than simply working within the Department of the Interior and the Department of Agriculture, the conservation community needs to invade other arenas, notably the federal and state departments of education. Conservationists should work particularly with the education departments of California and Texas which, because of their massive purchases of textbooks and other educational equipment, set much of the nation's educational agenda. Many textbooks, computer programs, and other materials are designed specifically for these two states and foisted upon the other 48 by default. Whether this is good or bad for national education is a moot point, but the dominance of these two states definitely reduces the conservationists' problem to a workable size, offering environmentalists a chance to influence the nation by focusing sharply on just these two states.

The conservation community needs to initiate a program that emphasizes natural-science education throughout the nation's school system. This will not only help create an Earth ethic and build a constituency for the environment, but will also prepare the nation's work force for competing in international markets in which environmental technology is a rapidly growing field. Objectives should include a national science curriculum, with instruction beginning in elementary schools and continuing yearly through grade 12. Colleges and universities should be encouraged to require at least an undergraduate course in environmental science for all potential graduates. This will contribute to ending the scientific illiteracy that threatens us both environmentally and economically.

The conservation community, and the nation, need also to face another critical issue if we are to succeed in stemming the collapse of the natural world. This is the question of jobs and how they are affected by environmental protection.

Commerce and Economics

Commerce dominates much of our thought and probably a good 90 percent or more of our politics, both nationally and internationally. This is doubtless as it should be, given that economics underlies virtually all of human life, from cradle to grave, even rushing us more or less rapidly from one to the other depending upon personal and national wealth. Economics determines what we eat, where we live, when and if we will work and play, where we will go, what we will enjoy, and what we will suffer. Economics as a condition and concern of human life is inescapable.

But so is the environment. No living thing can escape it. Winds, rivers, and seas bring to us whatever we put into them, good or ill. The air we breathe and the foods we eat bring into our living tissues the chemicals that we spread upon the Earth. We merge with our environment, we exist with it seamlessly, we are all of us at every moment turning part of the atmosphere and the Earth into ourselves, and turning part of ourselves into atmosphere and Earth. As does economics, ecology determines the quality and quantity of our lives. We can no more disregard our ecological life than we can disregard our economic life. If we lose enough of the species that, together, make our world work—if we destroy the forests, grasslands, and seas that sustain us—we will face an environmental deficit more deadly and more permanent than any economic depression. The loss of biodiversity is to our ecological life what loss of entire industries is to our economic health.

Nevertheless, environmental conditions often are sacrificed to economics because economics is an immediate barometer of human well-being, while ecological threats are more difficult to measure and demonstrate. When the economy falters and jobs vanish, we see the results immediately and are stimulated to correct the problem. The collapse of biodiversity and of ecosystems is a subtle event, first recognized by experts who often fail to convey their concerns persuasively to the public. The damage builds slowly and, at first, is imperceptible. But once the buildup begins it may be impossible to stop within a reasonable amount of time. Global climate change and acid precipitation, which jeopardize biodiversity on a global scale, are examples of ecological problems that gradually intensify to a deadly crescendo that will echo for decades if not centuries even if we move now to solve the ecological degradations that caused them.

To top it off, the benefits of environmental protection, from cleaner air to biodiversity protection, often can be measured only in terms of what does not happen. For example, the reductions in air pollution brought about by the Clean Air Act have doubtless saved thousands of human lives. We can surmise this because certain types of air pollution have been reduced by the act and because certain remaining types of particulate air pollution kill about 60,000 people in the United States every year, according to the Environmental Protection Agency. Were air pollution worse, we can safely predict that more deaths would occur. But how do you show politicians and the public the value of a program that has made something not happen? Opponents of clean-air programs can argue that the programs are costly, illustrating their point with dollars and cents, while clear-air proponents are faced with the difficulty of showing the extent and significance of what did not happen because of cleaner air. Economic rewards always include a material component, making them seem substantial arguments for giving economic concerns precedence over all others.

Because economic concerns make such a strong argument in any debate, conservationists have adopted the approach in recent years of using economic figures to support the need for biodiversity protection and other ecological measures. We rarely hear among us a John Muir, advocating that trees have a right to exist or that those who enjoy an untouched forest have a right to that pleasure. Instead, the dominant voices in conservation today attempt to build sound economic arguments for biodiversity protection, arguing pragmatically that we should end the destruction of forests because it costs hundreds of millions of tax dollars yearly, and so on. These are powerful arguments and should be used because they do show convincingly the folly of federal land management today.

But what happens when the figures do not support the cause of biodiversity? In 1973 C. W. Clark, an applied mathematician at the University of British Columbia, proved in an article for the *Journal of Political Economy* that it would be more economic for the Japanese to kill off every blue whale in the seas and to invest the profits in growth industries than to let the whales recover to population levels that would permit a revival of hunting. Similarly, as Rutger's University biologist David Ehrenfeld pointed out in E. O. Wilson's *Biodiversity*, the pharmaceutical industry believes it can develop new drugs faster through computer modeling than through assessment of the medical potential of various plant species.

This makes economics an unreliable witness in behalf of

biodiversity conservation. Once you accept economics as a sound basis for determining which species and places should be protected, you risk losing every battle in which destruction produces greater profits than does preservation. Moreover, even when dollar value in the long term is on the side of conservation—as in the Pacific Northwest, where the potential long-term profits of tourism are greater than the quicker profits of logging—developers persist in ecological destruction anyway, reaching for today's smaller profit rather than tomorrow's larger one, robbing the purses of future generations by destroying forests and grasslands, wetlands and deserts that, but for our touch, would last for centuries. Because our society is geared to short-term gains, economic arguments for conservation will be always a double-edged sword that is decidedly sharper on the side of environmental negligence.

We need to face the simple truth that many of our industries use methods and technologies that are ecologically threatening and hazardous to our well-being, that some aspects of business can no longer be conducted as usual if we are to apply our best scientific knowledge in pursuit of a healthier and more stable ecological and economic world, and that making the industrial changes needed to put our economy on a safer and sounder environmental track will cause in some cases and in some areas a certain level of economic disruption. Too much of our nation's productivity is based on the false and empty environmental presumptions of a less-scientific era. Dumping industrial wastes into rivers and air, destroying entire ecosystems, and wiping out whole species are artifacts of a time when society little understood what it was doing and what the effects of its actions were. We no longer enjoy the bliss of this ignorance, and all business interests must without fail assume the responsibilities that fresh scientific knowledge has thrust upon them.

Fortunately, survey after survey during the past decade has shown that citizens are willing to pay higher taxes or higher prices for material goods if, in return, they receive a cleaner, healthier, ecologically more stable environment. Many politicians have failed to keep up with the times and have stood as obstacles to growing environmental concern. Politicians who remain dreadfully out of touch with the will of their own nation seal their own fate. Citizens at large support environmental protection even, in many cases, if the financial costs are higher.

Nevertheless, this support erodes quickly among individuals who believe their livelihood is threatened by such measures as endangered-species and biodiversity protection. Their support, however, is critical to the conservation community and will be preserved only if conservationists add to every environmental measure a component for the economic as well as the ecological protection of all citizens. Job loss as a result of environmental protection is clearly a condition that the nation must face. In some cases, a sound environment and current economic bases are mutually incompatible. For example, it may well be that some logging jobs will be lost if forests are to be protected. Or some ranchers may be put out of business by stricter grazing regulations. But no job can long survive if it is dependent on a vanishing ecosystem. The old-time buffalo hunters had to find something else to do when the bison ran out. People who, in our own time, are dependent on vanishing ecosystems will have to do likewise. It is critical to biodiversity protection that we shut down destructive uses before ecosystems are destroyed. People are certainly more adaptable than are ecosystems, and it is cheaper to retrain workers than to recover species endangered by habitat loss, though both people and the environment must be protected. As the Earth Charter, a statement of principles drawn up during the 1991 Earth Summit, put the issue, "Attempts to eradicate poverty should not be a mandate to abuse the environment, and attempts to protect or restore the environment should not ignore basic human needs."

When dealing with developing nations, private conservation groups readily embrace the idea of incorporating local people into the protection process. For example, efforts to protect wildlife at Kenya's Masai Mara National Park were thwarted by local Masai people until the Wildlife Service adopted the policy of sharing park fees with the Masai. The Masai now make about $1 million yearly from the park and have given up the poaching that threatened park wildlife. Similarly, Costa Rica has developed biodiversity-protection plans that incorporate local interests and has hired people living near protected lands to help with wildlife surveys and other activities.

Surely we can incorporate our own citizens into our conservation efforts. Those of us dedicated to protecting biodiversity need to join our demands for wildlands protection with a demand for economic protection of people displaced by environmental regulation. Often, the figures for jobs lost are exaggerated by affected industries, but the loss of even one job is a serious matter to the individual who loses it.

Measures to remedy job losses include employment on protected lands or retraining of displaced workers for other jobs. One critical component for success is increased federal funding for research on environmental technology, which is a potential source of new jobs. Environmental regulation is already creating jobs. When the Clean Air Act requires power plants to install scrubbers on smokestacks to reduce effluents, a wide array of jobs are opened up. Someone has to design the scrubber, someone has to build it, someone has to supply the raw materials, someone has to deliver both the raw materials and the finished product, someone has to install the scrubber. At present, environmental services in the United States account for about 70,000 businesses and a million employees (10 times the number supported by logging in the national forests) with a 1991 income of $130 billion.

In short, the conservation community too often seeks purely legislative solutions to environmental problems. For many groups, working on Capitol Hill is the only work they really do. They need to consider, in addition to a national biodiversity law, two other critical social factors. They need to work with education professionals to establish a national science curriculum that will be applied in all public schools to all students from elementary school through graduation. And they need to find means for making the protection of wildlands remunerative to people living near the lands.

Attacking biodiversity protection from three angles—legislation, education, and economics—suggests a major undertaking and a complicated process of coordination. But as biologists Paul Ehrlich and Edward O. Wilson make clear in their paper, "Biodiversity Studies: Science and Policy," a major undertaking is precisely what declining biodiversity demands. "In many cases, new social and economic systems must be developed in which preservation of biodiversity and its sustainable exploitation go hand in hand," they write. "The social, political, economic, and scientific barriers to achieving the goal are so formidable that nothing less than the kind of commitments so recently invested in the Cold War could possibly suffice to accomplish it. And we are 45 years late in starting."

Epilogue

I fear that he who walks over these fields a century hence will not know the pleasure of knocking off wild apples. Ah, poor man, there are many pleasures which he will not know!

Henry David Thoreau

Hope is important, because it can make the present moment less difficult to bear. If we believe that tomorrow will be better, we can bear a hardship today. But that is the most that hope can do for us—to make some hardship lighter. When I think deeply about the nature of hope, I see something tragic. Since we cling to our hope in the future, we do not focus our energies and capabilities on the present moment.

Thich Nhat Hanh, Peace Is Every Step, *1991*

≋

When I think of the many professional and amateur conservationists around the globe who are striving to snatch from the hungry maw of humankind our last wild places and our beleaguered wild species, I recall an essay by Loren Eiseley, "The Star Thrower," from his book *The Immense Journey*. On a Mexican beach Eiseley encounters a stranger who sorts through starfish beached by the ebbing tide, picks out the living starfish, and throws them back into the sea. At first Eiseley has no sympathy for the stranger, whose task is hopeless at best. "The star thrower is a man," Eiseley writes, "and death is running more fleet than he along every seabeach in the world." And yet, when Eiseley looks back at the stranger after continuing down the beach, he sees that, "in the changing light, the sower appeared magnified, as though casting larger stars upon some greater sea." Eventually Eiseley concludes that this man represents a break with the ancient Darwinian struggle for survival, in which only the strong and self-promoting survive. "For a creature, arisen from that bank and born of its contentions, has stretched out its hand in pity." And the star thrower continues to stretch out his hand in pity, despite the enormousness of his task and its larger futility.

Eiseley joins in the throwing of starfish into the sea "while all about us roared the insatiable waters of death." In the end it does not matter whether he saves only a few starfish or none at all, it matters only that he has tried, that he can reach out in pity and concern. "Somewhere, my thought persisted, there is a hurler of stars, and he walks, because he chooses, always in desolation, but not in defeat."

The struggle to save the world's wildness—its wild places and wild creatures—is an eternal and, one might guess, futile battle. We can save a forest from destruction this year, but next year, or the year after, the chainsaws will return. We have to fight again and again the same battles, struggling always in desolation, yet never in defeat.

The starfish we are trying to save today are the last of the nation's wild places. They are surrounded by an increasingly brutal sea. The latest wave of assault is the Wise Use movement, which has confounded Gifford Pinchot's concept of wise and sustainable use with unbridled gluttony for public lands. The movement's objectives are spelled out in a book called *The Wise Use Agenda*, which includes these goals, preposterous as they may sound:

- cut all decaying and oxygen-using forest growth on national forest land and replace it with yong trees to reverse global warming
- rewrite the Endangered Species Act to remove protection for nonadaptive species such as the California condor
- open all public lands—including national parks and wilderness areas—to mineral and energy production
- expand national-park concessions by turning them over to private firms such as The Walt Disney Company, an expert people-mover
- initiate civil penalties against anyone who challenges economic action or development of federal lands
- recognize private rights to mining claims, water, grazing permits, and timber contracts on public lands
- create a national mining system that will embody all the provisions of the Mining Law of 1872
- forbid any reduction in visitation to the national parks

and so on for another 17 more major goals. They can all be summed up in a single statement uttered by one of the leaders of the movement in 1984 at a Canadian timber-industry seminar: "You must turn the public against environmentalists. . . ."

The Wise Use leadership claims that the movement is a grass-roots effort. The "grassroots" groups supporting Wise-Use organizations include Exxon USA, the National Cattleman's Association, the Motorcycle Industry Council, Chevron USA, Kawasaki, Yamaha, and the American Farm Bureau Federation, which represents 4 million farmers. The advisory board of one Wise Use organization, the Center for the Defense of Free Enterprise, includes former Secretary of Defense Richard Cheney as well as seven U.S. senators and nine U.S. representatives—not bad for grassroots. Another group that has sponsored Wise Use conferences is the American Freedom Coalition, set up by the Reverend Sun Myung Moon and the Unification Church, in alliance with Christian fundamentalist Gary Jarmin, to further the Reverend's political dream: a Moon-based third U.S. political party. It brings to mind once again John Muir's words, "Complaints are made in the name of poor settlers and miners, while the wealthy corporations are kept carefully hidden in the background."

When you examine the history of the conservation movement, beginning with Muir, you notice that although we fight the same battles again and again against the same foes, each time we begin with less wilderness than we had before. Yet still it is the fashion among conservation groups to shed favorable light upon environmental accomplishments, to paint as bright a picture as possible, waving the banner of hope as an inspiration. It is hard, year after year, to stand on the midnight beach and pitch living starfish back into a life-vomiting sea. Arrayed against the conservation community are the most powerful business interests in the world. Some corporate executive officers draw yearly salaries that exceed the entire budgets of the largest conservation groups. Conservationists are dwarfed by their opponents. No wonder they grasp at hope to sustain them.

But hope is an indulgence. As Thich Nhat Hanh has written, hope leads to diversion from action. We do not need hope to fight an inexorable sea of destruction. We need resolve, a cool resolve that frees us from thoughts of winning or losing, strengthening us instead with thoughts only of persisting, every voice raised,

every action taken. We need resolve to ensure no further compromise on the need to protect remaining wildlands, for no compromises remain to be had. We need resolve to tell the private
claimants of public lands that if ever the last ancient tree should
fall or the last wild prairie be plowed, we nevertheless will be
there fighting to ends bitter or sweet. We need resolve to stand
eternally on that sea-hissing shore, returning to the waves the
last living starfish even as the sun sets upon humanity for the
final time.

> When the desires of men are curbed,
> there will be peace,
> And the world will settle down
> of its own accord.
> *Tao Teh Ching*

BIBLIOGRAPHY

Albright, Horace M., and Robert Cahn. 1985. *The Birth of the National Park Service: The Founding Years, 1913–33*. Howe Brothers. Salt Lake City.

Anonymous. 1991. "Land Protection Plan, East Everglades Addition, Everglades National Park." National Park Service, Department of the Interior. Washington, D.C.

Anonymous. 1991. "Save Our Everglades: A Status Report by the Office of Governor Lawton Chiles." State of Florida.

Barton, Katherine. 1985. "Wildlife and the Bureau of Land Management." In *The Audubon Wildlife Report 1985*, Roger L. Di Silvestro, ed. National Audubon Society. New York.

———. 1987. "Bureau of Land Management." In *The Audubon Wildlife Report 1987*, Roger L. Di Silvestro, ed. Academic Press. Orlando, Fl.

Barton, Katherine, and Whit Fosburgh. 1986. "The U.S. Forest Service." In *The Audubon Wildlife Report 1986*, Roger L. Di Silvestro, ed. National Audubon Society. New York.

Bean, Michael J. 1983. *The Evolution of National Wildlife Law*. Praeger Publishers. New York.

Brackenridge, Hugh Henry. 1964. "The animals, vulgarly called Indians." In *The Indian and the White Man*, Wilcomb E. Washburn, ed. Doubleday. Garden City, N.Y.

Brower, David. 1990. *For Earth's Sake: The Life and Times of David Brower*. Peregrine Smith Books. Salt Lake City.

Bumpers, Dale. 1991. "Mining reform will stop 'giveaway' of federal land and create over $200 million in royalties." *Roll Call*. Nov. 18.

Byrnes, Patricia. 1992. "The counterfeit crusade." *Wilderness*. Summer:29–31.

Cahn, Robert, and Patricia Cahn. 1992. "Parallel parks." *National Parks*. Jan./Feb.:24.

Carstensen, Vernon, ed. 1968. *The Public Lands: Studies in the History of the Public Domain*. The University of Wisconsin Press. Madison.

Catlin, George. 1989. *North American Indians*. Penguin Books. New York.

Chandler, William J. 1985. "The U.S. Fish and Wildlife Service." In *The Audubon Wildlife Report 1985*, Roger L. Di Silvestro, ed. National Audubon Society. New York.

Chittenden, Hiram Martin. 1915. *The Yellowstone National Park*. Stewart & Kidd. Cincinnati.

Clepper, Henry. 1971. *Leaders of American Conservation*. The Ronald Press. New York.

Congress. 1990. "Review of the Management of the National Wildlife Refuge System." Joint Hearing before the Environment, Energy, and Natural Resources Subcommittee of the Committee on Government Operations and the Subcommittee on Fisheries and Wildlife Conservation and the Environment of the Committee on Merchant Marine and Fisheries, House of Representatives. U.S. Government Printing Office. Washington, D.C.

Cordell, H. Ken, and Patrick C. Reed. 1990. "Untrammeled by man: Preserving diversity through wilderness." In *Preparing to Manage Wilderness in the 21st Century*. Patrick C. Reed, ed. Southeastern Forest Experiment Station. Asheville, N.C.

Defenders of Wildlife. 1992. "Putting Wildlife First: Recomendations for Reforming Our Troubled Refuge System." Defenders of Wildlife. Washington, D.C.

Di Silvestro, Roger L. 1989. *The Endangered Kingdom: The Struggle to Save America's Wildlife*. John Wiley and Sons. New York.

———. 1990. *Audubon Perspectives: Fight for Survival*. John Wiley and Sons. New York.

———. 1992. *Audubon Perspectives: The Rebirth of Nature*. John Wiley and Sons. New York.

Douglas, Marjory Stoneman. 1975. *The Everglades: River of Grass*. Mockingbird Books. Atlanta.

Ehrenfeld, David. 1990. "Why put a value on biodiversity?" In *Biodiversity*, E. O. Wilson, ed. National Academy Press. Washington, D.C.

Ehrlich, Paul. 1990. "The loss of diversity: Causes and consequences." In *Biodiversity*, E. O. Wilson, ed. National Academy Press. Washington, D.C.

Ehrlich, Paul, and Edward O. Wilson. 1991. "Biodiversity studies: Science and policy. *Science*. 253:758.

Eldredge, Niles. 1991. *The Miner's Canary: Unraveling the Mysteries of Extinction*. Prentice Hall Press. New York.

Elfring, Chris. 1985. "Wildlife and the National Park Service." In *The Audubon Wildlife Report 1985*, Roger L. Di Silvestro, ed. National Audubon Society. New York.

Farnsworth, Norman R. 1990. "Screening plants for new medicines." In *Biodiversity,* E. O. Wilson, ed. National Academy Press. Washington, D.C.

Flader, Susan L., and J. Baird Callicott, eds. 1991. *The River of the Mother of God and Other Essays by Aldo Leopold.* The University of Wisconsin Press. Madison.

Fosburgh, Whit. 1985. "Wildlife and the U.S. Forest Service." In *The Audubon Wildlife Report 1985,* Roger L. Di Silvestro, ed. National Audubon Society. New York.

Fox, Stephen. 1981. *The American Conservation Movement: John Muir and His Legacy.* The University of Wisconsin Press. Madison.

Franklin, Jerry F. 1990. "Structural and functional diversity in temperate forests." In *Biodiversity,* E. O. Wilson, ed. National Academy Press. Washington, D.C.

Freud, Sigmund. 1961. *The Future of an Illusion.* W. W. Norton. New York.
————. 1961. *Civilization and Its Discontents.* W. W. Norton. New York.

Gilliam, Ann, ed. 1979. *Voices for the Earth: A Treasury of the Sierra Club Bulletin, 1893–1977.* Sierra Club Books. San Francisco.

Graham, Bob. 1991. "Rescuing our refuges." *Defenders.* Nov./Dec.:10.

Harris, Larry D. 1988. "Landscape linkages: The dispersal corridor approach to wildlife conservation." *Transactions of the North American Wildlife and Natural Resources Conference.* 53.

Harris, Larry D., and Peter B. Gallager. 1989. "New initiatives for wildlife conservation: The need for movement corridors." In *In Defense of Wildlife: Preserving Communities and Corridors,* Gay Mackintosh, ed. Defenders of Wildlife. Washington, D.C.

Hudson, Wendy E., ed. 1991. *Landscape Linkages and Biodiversity.* Defenders of Wildlife. Washington, D.C.

Hunt, Constance E. 1989. "Creating an endangered ecosystems act." *Endangered Species Update.* 6:1.

Kahaner, Larry. 1988. "Something in the Air." *Wilderness.* Winter:19.

Kaufman, Les, and Kenneth Mallory, eds. 1987. *The Last Extinction.* The MIT Press. Cambridge, Mass.

Knize, Perri. 1991. "The mismanagement of the national forests." *Atlantic Monthly.* Oct.

Langford, Nathaniel Pitt. 1972. *The Discovery of Yellowstone Park.* University of Nebraska Press. Lincoln.

Leopold, Aldo. 1989. *A Sand County Almanac.* Ballantine Books. New York.
————. 1991. *The River of the Mother of God and Other Essays by Aldo Leopold.* Susan L. Flader and J. Baird Callicott, eds. The University of Wisconsin Press. Madison.

Lillard, Richard G. 1947. *The Great Forest.* Alfred A. Knopf. New York.

Little, Charles E. 1987. "The challenge of Greater Yellowstone: A report on the 'crown jewel' of the nation's ecosystems." *Wilderness.* Winter:18.

Maclean, Norman. 1976. *A River Runs Through It and Other Stories.* The University of Chicago Press. Chicago.

Marine Sanctuaries Panel. 1991. "National Marine Sanctuaries: Challenge and Opportunity." National Oceanic and Atmospheric Administration, Department of Commerce. U.S. Government Printing Office. Washington, D.C.

Meine, Curt. 1988. *Aldo Leopold: His Life and Work.* The University of Wisconsin Press. Madison.

Mitchell, John G. 1985. "In wildness was the preservation of a smile: An evocation of Robert Marshall." *Wilderness.* Summer:10.

Murphy, Dennis D. 1990. "Challenges to biological diversity in urban areas." In *Biodiversity,* E. O. Wilson, ed. National Academy Press. Washington, D.C.

Nash, Roderick. 1982. *Wilderness and the American Mind.* Yale University Press. New Haven, Conn.

National Audubon Society, The Wilderness Society, Defenders of Wildlife, and the National Wildlife Refuge Association. 1991. "Harmful Activities in the National Wildlife Refuge System: A Sampling of Problems." Audubon et al. Washington, D.C.

National Parks and Conservation Association. 1991. "A Race Against Time: Five Threats Endangering America's National Parks and the Solutions to Avert Them." National Parks and Conservation Association. Washington, D.C.

———. 1992. "Parks in Perils: The Race Against Time Continues." National Parks and Conservation Association. Washington, D.C.

Nations, James D. 1990. "Deep ecology meets the developing world." In *Biodiversity,* E. O. Wilson, ed. National Academy Press. Washington, D.C.

Newmark, William D. 1987. "A land-bridge island perspective on mammalian extinctions in western North American parks." *Nature.* 325:430.

Norton, Bryan. 1990. "Commodity, amenity, and morality: The limits of quantification in valuing biodiversity." In *Biodiversity,* E. O. Wilson, ed. National Academy Press. Washington, D.C.

Noss, Reed. 1983. "A regional landscape approach to maintain diversity." *BioScience.* 33:700.

———. 1987. "Protecting natural areas in fragmented landscapes." *Natural Areas Journal.* 7:2

———. 1990. "What can wilderness do for biodiversity?" In *Preparing to Manage Wilderness in the 21st Century.* Patrick C. Reed, ed. Southeastern Forest Experiment Station. Asheville, N.C.

Noss, Reed, and Larry D. Harris. 1986. "Nodes, networks, and MUMs: Preserving diversity at all scales." *Environmental Management.* 10:299.

Ogden, John C. 1985. "The Wood Stork." In *The Audubon Wildlife Report 1985,* Roger L. Di Silvestro, ed. National Audubon Society. New York.

O'Toole, Randal. 1988. *Reforming the Forest Service.* Island Press. Washington, D.C.

Perlin, John. 1989. *A Forest Journey: From Mesopotamia to North America.* W. W. Norton. New York.

Randall, Alan. 1990. "What mainstream economists have to say about the value of biodiversity." In *Biodiversity,* E. O. Wilson, ed. National Academy Press. Washington, D.C.

Risser, Paul G. 1990. "Diversity in and among grasslands." In *Biodiversity,* E. O. Wilson, ed. National Academy Press. Washington, D.C.

Robblee, Michael B., and W. Jill Di Domenico. 1991. "Seagrass die-off threatens ecology of Florida Bay." *Park Science.* Fall.

Satchell, Michael. 1992. "The rape of the oceans." *U.S. News and World Report.* June 22:64.

Scott, J. Michael, Blair Csuti, James D. Jacobi, and John E. Estes. 1987. "Species richness." *BioScience.* 37:782.

Soule, Michael E. 1991. "Land use planning and wildlife maintenance: Guidelines for conserving wildlife in an urban landscape." *Journal of the American Planning Association.* 57:313.

Stegner, Wallace. 1989. "Our common domain." *Sierra.* Sept./Oct:42.

Tarnas, David A. 1988. "The U.S. National Marine Sanctuary Program: An analysis of the program's implementation and current issues." *Coastal Management* 16:275.

Teale, Edwin Way, ed. 1988. *The Thoughts of Thoreau.* Dodd, Mead. New York.

Tobin, Richard. 1990. *The Expendable Future: U.S. Politics and the Protection of Biodiversity.* Duke University Press. Durham, N.C.

Turner, Tom. 1992. "There hasn't been any mining going on around here in years." *Wilderness.* Summer:26–29.

Twain, Mark. 1979. *Roughing It.* In *The Unabridged Mark Twain.* Running Press. Philadelphia.

U.S. Fish and Wildlife Service. 1990. "Management Actions on Report Recommendations, 1968–1987: A Response to Congress." Department of the Interior. Washington, D.C.

U.S. General Accounting Office. 1989. "National Wildlife Refuges: Continuing Problems with Incompatible Uses Call for Bold Action." General Accounting Office. Washington, D.C.

———. 1991. "Rangeland Management: BLM's Hot Desert Grazing Program Merits Reconsideration." General Accounting Office. Washington, D.C.

Waak, Pat, and Kenneth Strom. 1992. *Sharing the Earth: Cross-Cultural Experiences in Population, Wildlife and the Environment.* National Audubon Society. New York.

Watkins, T. H. 1992. "Law and liquidation." *Wilderness.* Summer:10–13.

———. 1992. "Deep enough." *Wilderness.* Summer:31–33.

Whitfield, Estus. 1988. "Restoring the Everglades." In *The Audubon Wildlife Report 1988/1989,* William J. Chandler, ed. Academic Press. San Diego.

Wilson, E. O. 1990. "The current state of biological diversity." In *Biodiversity,* E. O. Wilson, ed. National Academy Press. Washington, D.C.

Wolf, Edward C. 1987. "On the brink of extinction: Conserving the diversity of life." Worldwatch Institute. Washington, D.C.

Wuerthner, George. 1992. "Hard rock & heap leach." *Wilderness.* Summer:14–21.

Zaslowsky, Dyan, and The Wilderness Society. 1986. *These American Lands: Parks, Wilderness, and the Public Lands.* Henry Holt. New York.

INDEX

Native Americans (*continued*)
Catlin's portrayal of, 49
in the Everglades, 7–8
territorial claims of, 38
and the Yellowstone region, 40–41
Nature Conservancy, The, 210
New Mexico State Game Commission, 115
Newmark, William, 20, 201–2, 204
Nitrates, concentration in the Everglades, 13
Noble, John W., 66, 67
Noranda Minerals, 126
Northeast Shark River Slough, 15
Northern spotted owl, 81, 84–92, 230–31
Northwest Ordinance (1785), 104
Norton, Bryan, 22
Noss, Reed, 194, 196–97, 199–200, 202, 203–4, 205, 217

Ocean Dumping Bill. *See* Marine Protection, Research and Sanctuaries Act
Okeechobee, Lake, 4, 6, 7, 8, 9, 12, 13, 15
Okeechobee Flood Control District, 9
Okeefenokee, 56
Old Faithful, 44
Olmstead, Frederick Law, Jr., 154
Olympic National Park, 81, 126, 158
O'Sullivan, John Louis, 38–39
O'Toole, Randall, 75, 77, 98, 100–101, 232

Pacific Northwest, 56, 79–92, 199, 242
Panther, Florida, and mercury poisoning, 13
Parks, national, 151–68
Pelican Island, 131
Phillips, William Hallett, 66

Phosphate, concentration in the Everglades, 12–13
Pinchot, Gifford, 51, 68–69, 70, 71, 72, 73–74, 154, 249
Plants
in agriculture, 29–30
as food source, 29
as foundation of ecosystems, 206–7
and the pharmaceutical industry, 29
Pomeroy, Samuel C., 47
Public lands
dominant-use, 59–60
harmful use and, 142–46
multiple-use, 59
protection of, 3–21, 56–61
secondary use and, 141–46
state protection of, 18
Punk tree, 18

Quammen, David, 205

Rahall, Nick Joe, 127
Railroads
importance of scenery to, 39, 43
and park visitation, 156
RAMSAR convention, 6
Range lands, 103–28
Reagan, Ronald, 120
Reagan administration, 85, 111, 163, 185
Recreation, and public lands, 100–101
Red-cockaded woodpecker, 94
Reffalt, William, 147, 148–49, 227, 232
Refuge Manual, 133–36, 141, 146, 147, 148
Riparian zones, 115–17
River Runs Through It, A, 124
Road hazards, 200–201
Robblee, Michael, 16–17
Robertson, F. Dale, 96
Robinson, Robert, 129
Rocky Mountain Fur Company, 41